'Since th ⋯⋯ ⋯⋯ ⋯⋯0 was published in 2005 I ⋯⋯ have dra⋯ ⋯⋯ ⋯e history and British social history-f⋯ ⋯⋯ ⋯th the key historiography and core para⋯ ⋯⋯ ⋯nd accessible form. For postgraduates and academic⋯ ⋯⋯ ⋯⋯ent overview of the field. This very welcome second e⋯ ⋯⋯ This b⋯ ⋯th the inclusion of a "modern parallels" section in each chapter, bringing the field topically up-to-date and ensuring the appeal of the book to a broad audience.'

Heather Shore, Reader in History,
Leeds Beckett University, UK

'This is a very timely book. It breaks the boundaries between criminology, crime history and social history and shows just how vital it is for us to connect past and present debates.'

Pamela Cox, Professor, Department of Sociology,
University of Essex, UK

'This revised and updated edition is a readable and comprehensive overview of key themes in the history of crime and criminal justice since 1750. New case studies of "modern parallels" provide historical analysis of contemporary issues in crime and justice, offering crucial insight and understanding for history and criminology readers alike.'

Helen Johnston, Senior Lecturer in Criminology,
University of Hull, UK

Crime and Justice Since 1750

This book provides a comprehensive introductory text for students taking courses in crime and criminal justice history. It covers all of the key historical topics central to an understanding of the current criminal justice system, including the development of the police, the courts and the mechanisms of punishment (from the gallows to the prison). The role of the victim in the criminal justice system, changing perceptions of criminals, long-term trends in violent crime and the rise of the surveillance society also receive detailed analysis. In addressing each of these issues and developments, the authors draw on the latest research in this rapidly expanding field to explore a range of historiographical and criminological debates.

This new edition continues its exploration of criminal justice history right through to the present day and discusses recent events in the criminal justice world. Each chapter now ends with a 'Modern parallels' section – a detailed case study providing historical analysis pertinent to a specific contemporary issue in the field of criminal justice and drawing parallels between historical context and modern phenomenon. Each chapter also includes a 'Key questions' section, which guides the reader towards appropriate sources for further study.

The authors draw on their in-depth knowledge and provide an accessible and lively guide for those approaching the subject for the first time, or those wishing to deepen their knowledge. This makes the book essential reading for those teaching or studying modules on criminal justice, policing and youth justice.

Barry Godfrey is Professor of Social Justice at the University of Liverpool. He has over 20 years' experience of researching comparative criminology, with particular specialisms in longitudinal studies of crime, comparative international studies of offending and sentencing, and desistance studies. His current research focuses on the long-term impact of youth justice interventions in the period 1850–1945; and he leads the Digital Panopticon project with colleagues in Sheffield, Oxford, Sussex and Tasmania.

Paul Lawrence is Senior Lecturer in History at the Open University. His research is focused on the British police since 1750, particularly their interactions with the poor and socially excluded, police use of violence and the self-image of police officers. His current research focuses on the development of the notion of preventive policing and the evolution and legacy of the Vagrancy Act of 1824. He is currently director of the International Centre for the Study of Crime, Justice and Policing at the Open University.

Crime and Justice Since 1750

Second edition

Barry Godfrey and
Paul Lawrence

Routledge
Taylor & Francis Group

LONDON AND NEW YORK

First published 2015
by Routledge
2 Park Square, Milton Park, Abingdon, Oxon OX14 4RN

and by Routledge
711 Third Avenue, New York, NY 10017

Routledge is an imprint of the Taylor & Francis Group, an informa business

British Library Cataloguing-in-Publication Data
A catalogue record for this book is available from the British Library

Library of Congress Cataloging-in-Publication Data
Godfrey, Barry S.
  Crime and justice since 1750/Barry Godfrey, Paul Lawrence. – Second
  edition.
  pages cm
  1. Crime – Great Britain – History. 2. Police – Great Britain – History.
  3. Criminal justice, Administration of – Great Britain – History.
  I. Lawrence, Paul (Paul Morgan) II. Lawrence, Paul. III. Title.
  HV6944.G63 2014
  364.641 – dc23
  2014021194

ISBN: 978-0-415-70855-5 (hbk)
ISBN: 978-0-415-70856-2 (pbk)
ISBN: 978-1-315-88598-8 (ebk)

Typeset in Times New Roman and Gill Sans
by Florence Production Ltd, Stoodleigh, Devon, UK

Contents

Preface to second edition   xi

1 Introduction   1

  The structure of the book 3
  Does crime history have a history? 7

PART I
Institutions and processes   9

  2 The development of policing   11

  Introduction 11
  The Old Police 12
  The transition to the New Police 16
  A golden age of policing? 23
  Modern parallels 27
  Conclusion 29
  Key questions 30

  3 The role of the 'victim' since 1750   32

  Introduction 32
  'Victims' and the prosecution of crime 33
  Retribution, self-defence and other extra-judicial
  *   action 40*
  Victims and 'private' initiatives 45
  Modern parallels 49
  Conclusion 50
  Key questions 51

4   The law and the courts   52

Introduction 52
An overview of the court system from 1750 53
Historians, law and the courts between 1750 and 1850 57
Historians, law and the courts since 1850 62
Modern parallels 67
Conclusion 69
Key questions 69

5   Punishment since 1750   71

Introduction 71
Changing patterns of punishment since 1750 72
Historians, sociologists and the rise of the prison 78
Debates over punishment and welfare since 1850 82
Modern parallels 88
Conclusion 90
Key questions 90

PART 2
Crime and criminals   93

6   Violence, war and terrorism   95

Introduction 95
Measuring levels of violence 95
Explaining violence and violent crime 102
Terrorism and war 108
Modern parallels 111
Conclusion 112
Key questions 113

7   Criminal others   114

Introduction 114
Poverty, crime and the 'criminal class' 114
Women and crime 119
Ethnicity and criminality 125
Modern parallels 128
Conclusion 130
Key questions 132

8   Youth crime and gangs since 1750   134

Introduction 134
Inventing or discovering juvenile delinquency? 134
Later nineteenth-century 'reform' 137
Twentieth-century care and control 139
Modern parallels 144
Conclusion 146
Key questions 147

9   Control and surveillance since 1750   150

Introduction 150
Workplace theft, 1750–1950 150
Did the factory eradicate workplace theft? 156
Watching the suspicious 158
Modern parallels 162
Conclusion 164
Key questions 165

10   Conclusion   167

Glossary   169
Bibliography   174
Index   191

Preface to the second edition

Since the first edition was published 10 years ago, the world has stayed the same in many respects, but in other ways it has changed fundamentally. The global economy crashed in 2008; Western governments engaged in conflicts in the Middle East and the Baltic; the speed of communication shifted to hyper-speed with mobile phone technology, Twitter and other forms of social media, for the first time allowing us to truly state that we live in a 'digital age'. Together these developments altered the way crime historians, historians generally and social scientists went about their work. There has been a renewed focus on austerity and the hardship faced by many in the UK. Comparisons have necessarily been drawn with the Great Depression of the 1930s, but also the 1880s and the 1980s as well. The wars in Iraq and Afghanistan and the contests between nationalism and imperialism in Ukraine have prompted criminologists to consider war crime (and soldiers as victims) to a much greater degree; and the centenary of the outbreak of the First World War in 2014 generated another wave of interest in the cataclysmic events of the early twentieth century.

Terrorism and crime, which have always been associated with particular (but changing) social, ethnic and political groupings, are all now bound up with the concept of 'risk'. In our second edition, we try to find perspective on who fell under suspicion of being deviants, criminals, or terrorists, and why. To that end we have extended the period we review. The 2005 edition ended in 1950, while this edition seeks to show how historical analysis can illuminate contemporary concerns and dilemmas. As such, a range of post-1950 points of comparison have been included. We have got older. History has moved on. Events that formed part of our childhood are now studied by historians and our book reflects the fact that a longer perspective is needed. Issues that persist in today's society have their roots in the eighteenth or nineteenth centuries.

In the first edition we predicted that, as the focus of history moves ever forwards, studies of crime in the twentieth century would increase in number. We think we have been proved right to some extent (Emsley 2011; Farrall and Hay 2010; Williams, C. A. 2014), but there is still substantial potential for growth in this area.

We also predicted that research studies published in the early to mid-twentieth century would themselves become 'historical' – used as source material by criminal justice historians. The interviews with young offenders growing up in the 1950s and 1960s by Fyvel (1961), for example, have now become historically significant material. Those interviews carried out with those young men in the 1950s, or Cyril Burt's carried out in the 1920s, if handled carefully, provide the means to successfully carry out secondary analysis. Similarly, George Orwell's journey down *The Road to Wigan Pier* (1937), Richard Hoggart's (1955) study of working-class life in Leeds in the 1950s, or Stan Cohen's (2002) study of youth gangs provide a study of criminality or leisure in a particular period, but can also now help to illuminate prevailing theories of social life when the books were originally published.

In 2005 our view was that early twentieth-century research studies were as much primary sources for historians, as milestones in the development of sociology or criminology. We thought that they could make another substantial contribution to our understanding of 'crime', in both the past and the present. We still hold that view, although there has been a slow uptake. It may be that a third edition might be the appropriate time to reassess whether, and to what effect, that process has happened.

Barry Godfrey and Paul Lawrence
June 2014

Chapter 1

Introduction

> In the course of their work, both detectives and sociologists must gather and analyse information. For detectives, the object is to identify and locate criminals and to collect evidence to ensure that the identification is correct. Sociologists, on the other hand, develop theories and methods to help understand social behaviour.
>
> (Sanders 1974: 1)

Historians, like the sociologists described in the quote above, also seek to understand human behaviour, but place greater emphasis on uncovering how and why things happened in the past, and then applying that knowledge to explain how and why things are 'as they are' in the present. As detectives of the past, our concern in this book is to examine, analyse and critically appraise the history of crime. Like us you are interested in modern history, criminology or sociology, and you will probably be questioning which areas of knowledge are important to you and your work and which are not. Disciplinary boundaries may be important. For example, the 'science' of criminology, which developed from the late nineteenth century, has done much to increase attention on crime and criminality and forms part of some social science courses. Criminology itself has a history that stretches back to the late nineteenth century (see Garland 2002a: 7–50). As the 'science' became more sophisticated and developed more nuanced and less crude theories to explain crime, some authors began to chart its progress (and still do; see Godfrey *et al.* 2007b). However, the history of criminology is a different thing from a history of crime and the focus of history modules and criminology modules may also differ, so in this book we concentrate on the history of crime rather than the history of criminology. Nevertheless, the fact that criminologists also study the history of crime, and that historians are becoming more familiar with social science methodologies and criminological theories, means that students of both disciplines should both be interested in the subjects included in this volume.

Our primary task, then, is to explain why historical events in the past 250 years continue to affect crime and criminal justice in the present (and will do for many years to come). The criminal justice system that we experience today has many acknowledged faults. We have a prison system that does not reform inmates (the reconviction rate is considerable, especially for those offenders who serve short sentences and end up in prison time and time again). Senior officers have recently described police forces as 'institutionally racist'. Police forces are struggling to accommodate all of the tasks demanded of them in the face of severe financial cutbacks. If we were designing a criminal justice system to meet the needs of today's society, would it look like the one we actually have? Almost certainly it would not, because the institutions of criminal justice – the police, prisons and the courts – have all been shaped and influenced by events and ideas over a long period of time. For example, a preventative, publicly funded police force in distinctive uniform did not come out of nowhere in 1829. It emerged from models of policing that were much older; property recovery associations and local watchmen of the eighteenth century, for example. We can only fully understand why the police force works the way it does (prioritizing the maintenance of public order, being organized in counties rather than being 'The British Police Force', being largely unarmed, etc.) by looking at the changes made over 200 years of history.

In addition to institutional changes, historical research can also reveal attitudinal changes towards crime and risk in contemporary society. For example, youth crime appears to be a persistent problem for modern society. Media debates about joy riding and the drug/rave culture have recently given way to controversies over Anti-Social Behaviour Orders (ASBOs) and their effectiveness (or otherwise) against youth 'yob culture'. However, when did juvenile delinquency become a pressing problem, what particular sets of anxieties or events made it so, and are those factors still present today? Was delinquency always waiting to be discovered, or was it 'invented' – can crime be 'manufactured' in this way? If so, what are the conditions that allow us to manufacture crime and do fears about particular types of offenders reflect rising crime or do they feed a system that creates rises in crime?

Do we live in a safer society now than our parents and grandparents did? Statistics tell us that violence fell to its lowest prosecuted level about a century ago and that the rates of violence are now much higher (they peaked around the 1990s and are currently declining). Why is this? Are we safer now? Do we care more about violence now? Are we more worried about violence than we ever were? We are not going to find the answers to such questions by just looking at the situation as it stands today. We need to find meaningful comparisons with the recent and far distant past. We also need to question the assumptions that people readily make about the past – that it was a 'golden age' when police officers clipped unruly teenagers around the ear and people did not need to lock their doors. Was that really true and, if so, how do we know? Why do we imprison women and children in separate prisons to men? Why are men and women sentenced in different ways? What is it about the persistence of eighteenth- and nineteenth-century constructions of femininity that means that we still feel their impact today? These kinds of questions remain relevant to modern criminology and social policy, and they remain pertinent to anyone wanting to understand the social world.

The structure of the book

This book has been written for historians, sociologists and criminologists studying crime and criminal justice at all levels, including A Level students, undergraduates and postgraduates. It intends to give a broad historical overview of crime, policing and punishment within the context of historical processes such as urbanization and industrialization, and it will present different perspectives on a number of 'issues' and debates in current criminological and historical research. Each chapter concludes with a case study ('Modern parallels'), which discusses continuities and discontinuities and draws parallels between the most recent events and their historical contexts. The book itself is divided into two main parts. The first part describes changes to the criminal justice system since 1750. It explores the development of the main institutions and charts procedural and legal changes – from the means of detection, through the changing prosecution and court formats, onto the punishment of offenders. The second part describes how conceptions of crime and criminals altered over time, specifically in relation to the urban poor, female and juvenile offenders and ethnic groups such as Irish, Jewish and West-Indian immigrants. It also discusses more wide-ranging subjects such as the amount of violence and surveillance in society. The two thematic parts are, of course, closely related. Each chapter poses key questions and we suggest some of the main texts you may need to answer the questions, but you should also consult the bibliography at the end of the book. Additionally, there is a glossary of terms (with brief explanations of legal and historical terms used in this book) designed to make a difficult and complex subject easier to navigate. Each glossary term is highlighted in bold on first mention in the text.

Following this introduction, Chapter 2 describes the development of policing in England since 1750. During this period there were three phases of development. Initially, from 1750 up to about 1850, there was an amateur or semi-professional parish system organized by local authorities, a system that varied in quality. Then, following the setting up of the Metropolitan Police in 1829, a more consistently professional system of uniformed New Police was developed. It took almost 30 years of experimentation to consolidate this new style of policing and there have been numerous debates about its purpose among historians. Some argue that it was a rational response to rising crime in rapidly growing cities, while others claim that it was in fact a tool via which the middle classes ensured the sanctity of their newly earned property and point to its 'social control' function. By 1870, however, the new system was firmly established, leading eventually to what has often popularly been conceived of as a 'golden age' of policing, between about 1890 and 1950. Yet police forces were also challenged in the decades following the Second World War by political and industrial disturbances on the streets and by battles with their Home Office masters over their own autonomy. Did this period mark the end of the 'golden age', even if it had ever existed? How should we explain the problems with modern policing (the controversial policing tactics employed during G-20 protests, the 'kettling' of anti-war and anti-austerity demonstrators and so on) in the light of the golden age?

After Chapter 2 has considered these issues, the following chapter examines another role that the police played in the nineteenth and twentieth centuries – representing the victims of crime in the courtroom. Chapter 3 starts by examining the part that victims themselves played in choosing either informal reactions to victimhood – demanding reparation from offenders, treating them to a form of 'rough justice' – or the formal route of taking them to the courts for judgement. The chapter then explores how the police then took over the prosecution of offenders first on behalf of victims of crime and later on behalf of a notional community of the law-abiding. Police control over which and how many offenders were prosecuted in court gave them enormous influence over crime rates and, ultimately, as the case study in the 'Modern parallels' section shows, this led to crises in policing, and to declining public confidence in criminal statistics in the twenty-first century.

The following chapter on the court system is also concerned with legitimacy, and also with accessibility and efficiency. The major question in Chapter 4 is whether the courts acted as unbiased arbiters of justice or whether they primarily served the interests of a small, privileged elite. If the latter, how long did that situation persist? Marxist assertions that the courts simply dressed up raw power in legal language and mystique in order to legitimize class relations have given way to more nuanced explanations as to why many began to view the court as independent arbiters of justice. This first section of this chapter provides a broad overview of some of the main changes that occurred in the administration of justice since 1750. The chapter goes on to examine whether the image of the courts as primarily the preserve of a privileged elite changed significantly during the nineteenth century. The concluding part of the chapter explores what happened to the public performance of justice in the courtroom in the twentieth and twenty-first centuries.

As with Chapter 4, the following chapter on punishment explores the rapidity and extent of change since 1750. In the late eighteenth century, execution or transportation (initially to the American and then to Australian colonies) were the norm for serious (and even minor) offences. Prisons were used sparingly and then only to detain offenders before and after trial or to imprison debtors who could not pay their fines. By 1850, however, prison was used almost exclusively for all serious criminal cases. While the death penalty was not finally abolished until 1969, public executions had ended in the 1860s, along with transportation, and imprisonment had long been the primary punishment inflicted by the courts. For much of the late nineteenth and twentieth centuries, the prison population never exceeded 20,000. However, in the first decade of the twenty-first century, England and Wales would have their highest ever prison population – over 80,000 people. Historians, criminologists and social commentators have all debated these dramatic changes. They question whether the rise of the prison indicates a growth of 'humanitarianism', or just a switch to a different (but similarly severe) method of discipline. Was there a relationship between changing modes of punishment and the rise of industrial society, and, later, the emergence of the welfare state? When precisely did the 'rise of the prison' occur? Chapter 5 provides a basis for answering these questions by first outlining the extent of the changes in managing offenders before exploring why these changes took place. It concludes by examining the role that early release schemes (ticket of leave or licensing) played in making the prison system financially viable, even if the scheme itself has not always been popular with the general public or the media.

Some of the most important and interesting questions that we can ask about ourselves involve 'violence'. How violent are we as a society and how do we compare with other countries? Is violent crime rising or falling? Is aggression against others innate – a biological imperative – or an effective and convenient means of communicating power and authority over others? Who can use legitimate violence and does violence have 'rules', as some suggest? Does the experience of war make society more violent in the aftermath? Is terrorist violence qualitatively different from other types of violent crime?

Chapter 6 examines how we might go about answering these questions. The media and older generations of society constantly tell us that violent crime and public disorder are now much higher than they were at some (usually undefined) point in the past. We are also familiar with historical reconstructions of Victorian streets where murderers lurk around every murky, fog-laden London street corner. Neither myths of a putative 'golden age' in the 'peaceable kingdom' nor media depictions (past and present) of ever-escalating social violence seem entirely convincing or particularly analytical. This chapter will take a more rigorous approach. The first part of the chapter consists of a consideration of changing rates of violent crime since 1750, including the statistical measures taken from 1857 onward. It goes on to question the reliability of those statistics and offer suggestions as to why the statistics should be treated critically. After discussing whether levels of violence in society have changed, it will discusses whether the 'meaning' of violence has also changed. After this review of a number of the different theoretical and empirical explanations for changing levels of violent crime, the final part of the chapter offers some historical perspectives on two very specific aspects of violence, both closely related to any consideration of the criminal justice system – war and terrorism.

One constant in discussions of criminality over time has been the view that crime is usually committed by 'others'. Chapter 7 discusses why and in which ways conceptions of criminality (who was responsible for crime, and what sort of crime) changed over time. In the eighteenth century, criminality was thought to indicate a deficiency in morality. Criminals were seen as simply too greedy or lazy to control their most base desires, as individuals who *chose* to steal rather than earning money through honest work. Those who did not work, or who worked in low-earning occupations, were associated with crime, but the role of poverty in engendering crime often went unacknowledged. By the turn of the twentieth century, however, this view of crime as a 'choice' taken by rational individuals had declined. Instead, early criminologists, psychologists and social commentators had shifted towards the view that crime was often the product of either inbuilt hereditary deficiencies, or the exhausting and degrading urban environment in which much of the population now lived. This change in turn altered the dominant perceptions of criminals themselves and this chapter initially considers the different ways in which criminals and criminality were conceptualized and represented. Specific (often marginal) groups within society have often been particularly associated with criminal behaviour. So this chapter considers how and why women and particular ethnic communities have been singled out as problematic since 1750. Although complex, it is important to consider these developments, as the views that prevail in society regarding the essential nature of criminality have a strong influence on the ways in which laws are written and policing is organized.

Chapter 8 examines another kind of criminal 'other', the juvenile delinquent. In addition to considering the 'reality' of juvenile offending, this chapter discusses how conceptions of 'ideal childhood', changes in legislation, and the processes of industrialization and urbanization 'created' the problem of juvenile delinquency. It then explores how offending children were punished and which factors decided whether children ended up incarcerated, or in care institutions. Of course the distinctions between juvenile institutions of care and control were blurred for children who had committed offences, were 'beyond parental control' or who were simply alone and vulnerable. The chapter also discusses the differential treatment received by girls and boys and concludes with an examination of the longer history of gangs. Gang-related violence is a major focus of popular concern about young people in the UK, as is reflected in the intense media focus on the issue, and hence this chapter explores changes in attitudes towards youths and youth delinquency since 1750.

Chapter 9 begins by trying to identify the roots of the widespread state surveillance we have now become accustomed to. The introduction of the factory system in the 1840s has been seen as a key weapon in the employers' fight to control workers in their employ, and the system relied not only on a private form of policing, but also on increased surveillance over employees. While these techniques were used to control those inside institutions (factories), other forms of control were introduced from the 1860s over those leaving institutions (prisons). Ex-convicts and habitual offenders were subject to regulations designed to watch over them and to prevent re-offending. In some ways these forms of control paved a way for the general surveillance of all citizens. However, in the late twentieth century, there was a massive increase in the use of CCTV and the intrusive electronic monitoring of communications and email. This surveillance was not just over those who repeatedly broke the law, or those suspected of being a danger to the public (terrorists, paedophiles, violent offenders), but also over protestors, activists and just 'normal' people. The concluding part of the chapter therefore discusses whether the impulse of the state to control citizens has created a 'Big Brother' society?

Does crime history have a history?

Crime history itself has created a history – a 'historiography'. Since the subject began to develop out of the general upsurge in popularity of social history generally – mainly through the work of Leon Radzinowicz (1948–86), Doug Hay *et al.* (1975) and Edward Thompson (1975) – it has now grown to be a substantial sub-discipline in its own right. Whether the subject is properly situated within 'history' or 'criminology' is an interesting question, and you will find crime history articles in both historical and criminological journals. A growing number of authors have attempted to review the field and construct a narrative of crime and its control from the mid-eighteenth to the mid-twentieth centuries (Philips 1983; Innes and Styles 1986; Sharpe 1999; Godfrey *et al.* 2007b; Emsley 2010a; Taylor 2010; Lawrence 2012; Godfrey 2014). Where once one would struggle to find a course containing a history of crime element, it is now extremely common for criminal justice and criminology courses to include modules on crime history or the history of deviance, as well as on the foundations of criminology itself. History degree courses too, even when not specifically addressing the issue of crime, usually include modules on large-scale disorders (industrial disputes and labour relations, food riots and the economy, political movements, which were heavily policed, etc.). The extraordinary growth in interest in lawbreakers and the policing of society has been matched with a growing body of academic literature. However, the wealth and diversity of literature can be bewildering, and we have therefore structured this book in order to guide us through the complex literature to reveal the key aspects of crime history.

For every book that can be read on aspects of crime history – juvenile delinquency, violent crime, policing and so on – there are tens, maybe hundreds that will be missed. This book is therefore our attempt to provide a guide, both to the main facts, problems and discussions associated with the history of crime and also a guide to the key literature that others have contributed. This should not prevent students from searching out literature (in libraries, or more likely, online), which will also enlighten and entertain, but our book is a good starting point for those interested in the history of crime and criminal justice since 1750.

Part I

Institutions and processes

Chapter 2

The development of policing

Introduction

The development of policing in England and Wales from 1750 can be roughly divided into three phases. Initially, from 1750 up to about 1850, what has become known as the Old Police was in operation. This was a system of amateur or semi-professional parish **constables** and night watchmen. While reputedly ineffective at enforcing legislation, this system actually worked remarkably well in many places. Although there were debates over the necessity for police reform from 1750 onwards, it was not until the advent of the Metropolitan Police in 1829 that a more consistently professional system – the so-called New Police – began to be developed. The New Police forces, which were implemented across England over the latter half of the nineteenth century, featured salaried, uniformed officers, a hierarchy of ranks and a pattern of operation based on patrol and prevention. It took almost 30 years of experimentation to consolidate this new style of policing and there have been numerous debates about its purpose among historians. Some argue that it was a rational response to rising crime in rapidly growing cities, while others claim that it was in fact a tool via which the middle classes ensured the sanctity of their newly earned property, and point to its 'social control' function.

By 1870, however, the new system was firmly established. Following a period of social turbulence in the 1880s, what has often popularly been conceived of as a 'golden age' of policing began, which lasted from about 1890 to around 1950. Yet police forces went through many further changes during this period, too, and arguments with the Home Office over centralization, often violent clashes with demonstrators and pickets, and disputes over pay were at least as typical as the amiable approach of *Dixon of Dock Green* (a long-running TV series depicting a kind, fatherly and friendly policeman who was supported by all the law-abiding people on his beat).

Throughout the history of policing, therefore, there has been a marked divergence between the image and reality of policing – between what the police have been asked to do and the extent to which they have actually done this. This divergence in enforcement, and the nature of police discretion, is a key theme in current research into the history of policing. This chapter gives an account of the historical development of the English police, starting at a point (1750) where almost all its modern features had yet to appear, and will thus help you to think critically about the nature of enforcement. It will also introduce you to a specific academic debate over the development of the New Police during the nineteenth century, and will debate whether any golden age of policing ever really existed.

The Old Police

The Old Police system, which operated in many parts of Britain until the middle of the nineteenth century, consisted of three elements: the rural and urban 'amateur parish constables', the (mainly urban) semi-professional or professional 'acting constables' and the urban '**watch** forces'. This loose 'system' of policing had evolved gradually over a considerable period of time and was only gradually dismantled (under protest in some cases) during the nineteenth century. The Old Police system varied considerably from area to area, however, and the different components (parish constables, acting constables and night watches) operated in very different ways. Hence, it is perhaps easiest to consider each element in turn.

The parish constable's authority derived from a large number of laws, some dating from the Middle Ages and many more from the seventeenth and eighteenth centuries. In theory he was an amateur – a free-born Englishman of the 'middling sort' carrying out a number of essential public duties. He was an expression of an ideology of government which saw a small, cheap national state as desirable and assigned essential administrative tasks whenever possible to local government. Local control of policing (and other elements of social administration) was a strong feature of English regional government, and opposition to reform of the police was often couched in these terms. For example, the **Select Committee** on the Police of 1822 (investigating the possibility of police reform) concluded that:

> It is difficult to reconcile an effective system of police, with that perfect freedom of action and exemption from interference, which are the great privileges and blessings of society in this country; and your Committee think that the forfeiture or curtailment of such advantages would be too great a sacrifice for improvements in police, of facilities in detection of crime, however desirable in themselves if abstractly considered.

Such sentiments clearly indicate a desire for minimal central interference in local affairs. The constable was under a form of supervision by the **Justices of the Peace**, who were in this period not merely the basic judicial authority, but also the main institution of local government when they met periodically in **quarter sessions**. This relationship was often a tense one and thus has left a succession of orders and exhortations from **magistrate**s for the parish constables to be more vigilant.

Parish constables were usually simply householders, picked every year to serve. In some cases the constable was selected by the vestry, the body elected by all the property-owners who ran the affairs of the parish. In others he was picked at the local baronial **court leet**, an annual assembly of the ratepayers. If he refused to serve, or to find a substitute willing to take his place, he could be prosecuted and fined. He had a responsibility, through his powers of arrest and entry, to assist in the working of the criminal law, but his job also involved administrative tasks such as preparing the militia lists, fixing the rates for billeting soldiers and moving paupers through the parish.

When it came to coercion, the parish constable had a variety of powers, but most of these depended on the specific offence that he was dealing with. For example, in the case of **vagrants** he was empowered to arrest them and convey them to a magistrate. If a witness could be found who was prepared to go to a magistrate and swear that the constable had failed to apprehend a vagrant, he was subject to a fine of ten shillings for dereliction of his duty. In **felony** cases he had wider powers. He could enter houses to search for suspects, stop, search and arrest if he thought that a serious crime had been committed. 'Felony' in the late eighteenth century consisted of the crimes of theft, robbery and burglary, murder and attempted murder, rape and other offences involving the stealing of property or serious violence. Assault was not a felony but fell into the category of **misdemeanour**. The constable could only arrest for an assault if he saw it committed: otherwise his role was to advise the victim or their friends to get a **warrant** against the perpetrator from the justices. He did have power to intervene if he thought there was likely to be a breach of the peace.

Constables were obliged to **serve** all kinds of justices' warrants, for non-payment of rates or failure to perform legally mandated duties, as well as for criminal offences. In most cases their power was derivative: the initiative lay with the private citizen. The constable mainly acted when called upon: he would chase up cases of theft, arrest suspects or receive them into custody, take them before the magistrates and collect evidence for the prosecution, but it was up to the victim to ask him to do so and to promise to reimburse his expenses. The role of the victim in the criminal justice system is the focus of the following chapter.

In the main, the system seems to have worked adequately (Morgan and Rushton 1998: 29). However, the rural constable, alone in his community and knowing that he would need to live and trade there as a private citizen after his term of office was over, could find it difficult to enforce legislation dealing with 'victimless crimes'. He certainly tended to turn a blind eye to laws against drunkenness and swearing. Some constables even connived in 'social crimes' – such as the rural constable in Devon who recorded in his diary how he took part in smuggling trips during his year in office (Sayers 1997: 24–6). But the pattern of authority and work revealed by this man – Michael Evans – is complex. On one single day in 1836, he bought a bottle of smuggled brandy, took part in an unpopular eviction and suffered community disapproval for it, and helped to investigate a theft. He also applied himself to his day-job as a tailor. So here we have a man who was quite capable of conniving at some illegal activity that had community support, but was in other contexts quite willing to uphold the letter of the law even if it led to his unpopularity. It is difficult, therefore, to label this one man – let alone the whole institution – as 'efficient' or 'inefficient'.

Not all constables were 'amateur', however. Let us now consider the semi-professional or professional 'acting constables'. Often, the job of constable was taken year after year by the same man, who used the income from fees to supplement his trade at another occupation. In this way, as John Beattie has shown (2001: 151), he would be in a position to gain expertise as a constable over the years. In many towns there was too much business for the average householder to perform the duties adequately – especially if he did not want to neglect his day job while he was occupied with it. But business also meant rewards and expenses: enough income to maintain a number of constables. The rewards of thief-taking could be large: there were statutory rewards of up to £100 given out for the conviction of robbers in London. So if the same man volunteered as substitute every time, the post of constable could become full-time. Some of these men were the subject of accusations that they operated rackets for their own benefit, notably allowing young thieves to get away with crime until they were old and reckless enough to commit a **capital crime**, in which case the thief-taker would arrest them, prosecute them and earn a large reward when they were executed. One such thief-taker, the notorious Jonathan Wild, while highly successful at recovering stolen property also became a major receiver (one who accepts goods knowing them to be stolen) and was eventually executed for this in 1725.

These men were called 'acting constables' to distinguish them from the 'constable', which became an honorary post for a member of the middle classes. Often they were attended by assistant constables. Acting constables were men of some standing who had to be literate and trustworthy. Their assistants could only succeed them if they were literate; if not, they had to stay as 'runner' to another man once their masters retired.

In the early nineteenth century, the acting constables of the large towns in England were powerful men. They could and did travel round the country in search of stolen property. Joseph Nadin, who acted in Manchester during the early years of the nineteenth century and was in charge at the Peterloo Massacre of 1818, was reputed to be one of the most powerful men in the town. It is hard to estimate exactly how much they earned, but it is likely that their income put them in the class of respectable tradesmen. When Sheffield created a New Police force in 1843, the town took on its two acting constables as officers to serve warrants for the magistrates. Their salary replaced their fee income: it was £150 a year, over three times what a policeman got, and only £100 less than the head of Sheffield's New Police.

Aside from the two types of constable discussed above, the final element of the Old Police system was the **night watch**. Watch forces were an exclusively urban phenomenon. They were financed by a tax on the wealthy inhabitants of a particular limited area, and generally they were controlled by a committee elected from these ratepayers or from a subsection of them. Their job was to patrol the streets of their area, from a fixed box, often taking turns to stand still while their counterpart walked the rounds. They had more limited powers of arrest than constables, restricted to apprehending suspicious 'night walkers'. Many called the hour of the night to announce their arrival; in some places they alternated calling – thus acting as a deterrent – with walking their beats silently so as not to warn malefactors of their approach. Especially before the arrival of gas light in the early years of the nineteenth century, English towns generally had an informal curfew even when the old seventeenth-century curfew laws were no longer enforced. Chester, for example, bolted the doors to the city walls every night at nine o'clock up until 1914. If a watchman encountered anyone on the streets after dark, the onus was on the stranger to prove his business or he would be searched as a matter of course for stolen property.

Watchmen were potentially the weak link in the chain of the Old Police. It was hard to make a decent living on their wages, and correspondingly difficult to attract able-bodied men. On the other hand, it provided steady employment in an age where most jobs of work were highly susceptible to fluctuations in the economy. Night watches were no pushover. There are documented cases of the City of London's watch getting involved in fights with would-be burglars, robbers and thieves on the streets. In Sheffield during the 1820s, the approach of the watch often scared off miscreants, and they were regularly willing to risk injuries to make arrests, as the following extract demonstrates:

A person by the name of Monk was stopped by two men in Garden Street on Saturday night last, who took his neckcloth off, and attempted to cut his throat; but on hearing the approach of the watchmen, they decamped, after robbing him of a few shillings, and otherwise ill-using him.

(*Sheffield and Rotherham Independent*, 14 October 1820)

By the end of the eighteenth century, many watch forces had become highly sophisticated. Elaine Reynolds (1998: 63, 120) has shown that the Marylebone Watch, in northern Westminster (London), introduced a three-tier command structure in 1775, a uniform and a system of beats. It served as a starting point for the plan for Peel's Metropolitan Police. The beginning of our period saw the creation of a variety of small forces of constables in London. These followed the model of the professional 'thief-taking' constable, but they were created by laws that put them under the direct control of stipendiary magistrates – full-time paid magistrates, appointed by the government. The pioneers were the **Bow Street Runners**, created in the 1750s on the initiative of the novelist and magistrate Henry Fielding. These men followed the money: they were often sent outside London on errands for the rich – up to and including the monarch – who needed police services to be performed for whatever reason. After Henry's death, his half-brother John (also a magistrate) moulded these men into a well-known and established group of officers with considerable expertise in investigating crimes and presenting evidence in court. In some ways the Runners in London might be considered 'the first detectives', although the term itself wasn't coined until the nineteenth century

(Beattie 2012: 2). Building on this innovation, the 1792 Middlesex Justices Act created a group of police offices on the Bow Street model, covering much of London's suburbs. Each office was staffed by three stipendiary (salaried) magistrates, with six constables attached to each office.

In summary, it is important to realize that the Old Police were by no means a uniform institution. Parish constables in highly populated areas had a chance to make a good living at their job, once fees and rewards were taken into account. On the other hand, they did not have a guaranteed steady income. This may have led to a rather 'entrepreneurial' approach to crime-fighting. The night watch did receive a wage, but it was rather a poor one. Hence, they may well have been less willing to act on their own initiative and more willing simply to do the minimum required of them. Overall, the Old Police appear to have been reasonably good at catching criminals (particularly in London) and reasonably good at patrolling the streets at night. However, they were not very effective at dealing with public disorder and were very bad at imposing legislation that did not have public support (such as anti-smuggling laws). In such instances, a 'live and let live' approach was very much the order of the day. It should also be noted that this survey has only considered the constituent parts of what might be called the 'official' police system. There were, of course, other private police agencies, usually concerned with the regulation of trade and industry. Some of these, such as the Worsted Inspectorate, are discussed in Chapter 9.

The transition to the New Police

As we have seen, the Old Police were probably quite good at enforcing some types of legislation, and less good at implementing other types. However, from the 1750s onwards, there was increasing debate about the efficiency of existing systems of policing. Many people condemned the Old Police as inadequate and a range of proposals for reform were advanced. Some, such as Henry Fielding, believed that a more effective *detective* force was crucial, while others, such as the magistrate and police commentator Patrick Colquhoun, believed that a new form of *preventive* police was preferable (Neocleous 2000). In his widely read *Treatise on the Police of the Metropolis*, Colquhoun (1800: 107) argued that night watches were 'without energy, disjointed, and governed by almost as many Acts of Parliament, as there are Parishes, Hamlets, Liberties and Precincts'. He believed that:

> Watchmen and Patroles, instead of being, as now, comparatively of little use, from their *age, infirmity, inability, inattention*, or *corrupt practices*, might almost at the present expense, by a proper selection, and a more correct mode of discipline, by means of a general superintendence over the whole to regulate their conduct, and keep them to their duty, be rendered of great utility in preventing Crimes, and in detecting Offenders.

Initially centred primarily on London (by far England's largest city and hence the inevitable crucible of reform), criticism intensified during the early part of the nineteenth century and eventually led to a variety of Royal Commissions and Acts of Parliament, which established the New Police – a shorthand term used by historians to signify a markedly different approach to the control of crime and the regulation of society. The New Police were greater in number than the Old Police, were uniformed and were supposedly both more efficient and more professional than their eighteenth-century counterparts. Essentially, they evolved into the police we know today, although 'old' and 'new' forces overlapped for a period in London and other jurisdictions (Lawrence 2011: xiv). But the various New Police forces were often very dissimilar from one another. Initially, the development of new forms of policing was marked by contesting visions of appropriate duties and by a tussle between local and national authorities as to who should control these new forces. Subsequently, the relative effectiveness of the New Police has been the subject of very different interpretations by historians.

The first step in the construction of the New Police was the establishment of the Metropolitan Police in 1829. Sir Robert Peel had become Home Secretary in 1822 and, partly reacting to concerns over radical demonstrations, argued the need for a new 'vigorous system of police'(Gash 1961: 310). At this stage many, even within the establishment, were concerned that this would lead to the development of a centralized 'state' police (such as was perceived to exist on the Continent). However, Peel handled the political dangers of this sensitive topic very skilfully. As David Philips (1980: 186) has noted, Peel took care 'to conceal the fact that he had already made up his mind about the form the reform should take'. He made shrewd use of crime statistics, newly available for the first time, which appeared to show a tide of rising criminality. Taking the 7-year periods 1811 to 1818 and 1821 to 1828, he had figures to show a population increase of 19 per cent in London and Middlesex, but an increase in crime of 55 per cent. Although the validity of these statistics was probably minimal, in 1829 the Metropolitan Police Improvement Bill was passed and 3,000 uniformed constables replaced the various local watch forces and took to their beats. Initially there was a period of confusion, as the new and the old forces worked in parallel. Then, the Metropolitan Police Bill of 1839 transformed the Old Police offices into **police courts** and offered the remaining Bow Street patrolmen the opportunity of transferring into the Metropolitan Police. However, throughout the 1830s there had been vociferous criticism of Peel's new force, and this by no means abated in 1839. Many commentators felt the uniforms of the New Police betrayed their essentially 'military' character, associating them with the gendarmeries of the Continent, who were seen to serve political ends. Others griped at the cost of the new system, which was more expensive than the old but that still had to be paid for out of the rates.

Moreover, a new kind of permanent police force in the provinces was to prove much harder to accomplish, due largely to a marked aversion to central government interference on the part of regional authorities. Many towns had been reforming their police piecemeal before the Act of 1835 that obliged them to set up a police force. There was still concern over a perceived rise in crime in the countryside, as is perhaps evidenced by the increase in private prosecution societies (Philips 1989: 113–70). The **Luddite disturbances** of 1811–12 also acted to fuel fears of rural unrest. As Philips (1980: 180) notes, such events 'caused men of property to think more favourably of a strong police force, which might protect their persons and property from such attacks', and some counties thus began their own initiatives, usually based on an extension of the old system of policing.

Then, in 1836, the Home Secretary Lord Russell agreed to Sir Edwin Chadwick's requests for a Royal Commission to investigate rural policing. Chadwick, a disciple of **Jeremy Bentham**, was always keen to extend the influence of central government. He unhesitatingly asked leading questions and distorted the evidence presented to the Commission (Storch and Philips 1999: 111–35). Drawn from anecdotal materials, and ignoring the detailed evidence presented concerning policing experiments in various parts of the country, the Commission's report was damning about the quality of policing in rural England. However, due to the delicate nature of the central/regional power balance, the Rural Constabulary Act of 1839 omitted most of the Commission's more contentious centralizing recommendations. It left the decision to establish a rural police and the control of that police in the hands of the county magistrates, although that year the government did take control out of the hands of local authorities in three large industrial cities: Birmingham, Bolton and Manchester. Thus, as Emsley (1996: 43) notes, 'as the 1840s dawned there was still no single model of policing dominant in England'.

In fact, wrangling continued even as late as the 1850s, when not only was there still a variety of different models, there were still local authorities who had yet to set up any new provision at all (Hart 1955). Thus, in the mid-1850s, more legislation was drawn up with the aim of ending the consolidation of traditional systems of policing. Home Secretary Lord Palmerston was the driving force behind the 1853 Select Committee appointed to consider the issue. Again, as in 1839, the Committee was far from open-minded. It recommended a more centralized system, with closer contact between Chief Constables and the Home Office, and some amalgamations of the small towns. Resistance to this was again strong, and hence the new bill introduced by Grey in 1856 was designed 'to provide an efficient police force, for both counties and boroughs, *as is possible under the existing system of local management*' (Hansard 1856). Local control was retained, but the establishment of a force was made mandatory and a degree of central influence was secured by the appointment of three Inspectors who would authorize a quarter of the authority's police costs to be met from central funds if they were satisfied with the force's efficiency.

Even after 1856, policing in England was subject to change and development. Certainly, as Carolyn Steedman (1984) has shown, it would be wrong to interpret the evolution of the New Police as merely the gradual export of an urban-metropolitan model to the provinces. However, by the late 1850s the main contours of the new system were in place. Yet to know this is only half the story – many more important questions remain. Why had this new system been deemed necessary at this particular time? What role did the New Police serve? These are questions to which different historians have provided very different answers.

Initially, twentieth-century historians considering issues of crime and policing accepted fairly uncritically the ideas in vogue at the beginning of the nineteenth century. They accepted that crime *had* been rising at an alarming level, that the old system of police *had* been unable to cope and that the more efficient New Police *had* eventually reversed this situation. Many of these early accounts of the New Police were written by ex-officers and they produced an uncritical, linear account in which the development of the New Police was viewed as 'progressive' (because it was seen to lead to our contemporary system, which they believed to be excellent), and in which those who opposed it were by implication 'regressive', myopic and foolish. This interpretation has subsequently been labelled the 'Whig' view of policing (drawing on Herbert Butterfield's 1931 notion of history written with an in-built assumption of 'progress'). Charles Reith (1943: 3), for example, claimed that:

> In the eighteenth century orderliness in London was almost non-existent, and its endurance in other areas was unreliable. This period and that of the early decades of the nineteenth century are notorious for the absence of public order. [. . .] It is an unquestionable historical fact that the appearance of public orderliness in Britain, and of individual willingness to co-operate in securing and maintaining it, coincides with the successful establishment of the police institution which was inaugurated experimentally in London, in 1839, and was copied throughout the entire area of the country, and of the empire, in the short space of thirty years.

Similarly, T. A. Critchley (1967: 22) argued that the early nineteenth century was a period in which there had been a 'danger of a total relapse into barbarity' (due to the corruption of the old constables and the social and economic upheaval of the eighteenth century), which was only averted by the far-sightedness of police reformers such as Henry Fielding, Patrick Colquhoun and Sir Robert Peel.

However, there are many problems with this interpretation of events. First, there is no real way of measuring whether crime and disorder were actually rising in England immediately prior to the creation of the Metropolitan Police. Certainly, there was a widespread *fear* of crime, but this is rather different from proving that crime was actually on the increase. Second, these 'Whig' historians fell into the trap of accepting the distorted reports of the nineteenth-century Royal Commissions. For example, one of the questions asked by the 1839 Commission was 'To what causes do you ascribe the failure to bring offenders to justice; and have such failures been ascribable in any cases to the inefficiency of the constables?' (Storch and Phillips 1999: 117). This is clearly a leading question, as it assumed, in advance of any evidence that there had been such a failure.

During the 1970s, an alternative interpretation of the New Police, inspired by Marxist theory, was formulated. This has subsequently been termed the 'revisionist view' of policing. Put simply, the revisionists argued that the way in which societies develop is not determined by consensus (by what is best for everyone) but by class conflict. In other words, those with power in society arrange things to suit themselves. Thus, according to the revisionists, the New Police were established essentially for purposes of control and surveillance in a society experiencing the upheavals of massive economic change and the need for a more compliant workforce.

Robert Storch (1976: 481), for example, argued that the New Police did far more than prevent and fight crime, claiming that:

> The police had a broader mission in the nineteenth century, however, to act as an all-purpose lever of urban discipline. The imposition of the police brought the arm of municipal and state authority directly to bear upon key institutions of daily life in working-class neighbourhoods, touching off a running battle with local custom and popular culture which lasted at least until the end of the century [. . .] the monitoring and control of the streets, pubs, racecourses, wakes, and popular fêtes was a daily function of the New Police [. . .] In the northern industrial towns of England these police functions must be viewed as a direct complement to the attempts of urban middle-class elites – by means of educational, temperance, and recreational reform – to mould a labouring class amenable to new disciplines of both work and leisure [. . .] In this respect the policeman was perhaps every bit as important a 'domestic missionary' as the earnest and often sympathetic men high-minded Unitarians dispatched into darkest Leeds or Manchester in the 1830s and 1840s.

It is certainly true that a whole host of non-criminal activities was brought under police control during the nineteenth century, from street-trading to fairs, from common lodging houses to licensing legislation. Revisionist historians argued that the police thus did far more than catch criminals and that these extra activities were part of a drive to mould the behaviour of the working classes, to render them malleable and docile. On the other hand, older, eighteenth-century conceptions of the term 'police' did include a broad range of social regulatory activities, so perhaps the work of the New Police in this regard was not entirely novel (Dodsworth 2014).

In some ways this revisionist view is more convincing than the Whig interpretation outlined above, but it still suffers from numerous problems. First, if the police were established to control the new working class, why were they first established in London, since this was not an industrial centre in the new sense, like Manchester or Oldham? Moreover, the revisionists, like the Whig historians before them, underplayed the extent of resistance to the development of the New Police. If they were there for the benefit of the propertied classes, why were there so many complaints from county magistrates and ratepayers about the cost of the new system? Finally, it can be argued that this interpretation omits any notion of police discretion. Recent research on the origins of police officers shows that many of them in fact had working-class backgrounds, and hence had a degree of sympathy and tolerance for those living in the poor areas they policed (Emsley and Clapson 1994; Lawrence 2000).

Thus any interpretation of the New Police that attempts to provide a single coherent explanation for this development is bound to prove unconvincing. Current historical research tends to emphasize the contingent and multifaceted nature of the New Police, building on some elements from both 'Whig' and 'revisionist' histories. On the one hand, it is not hard to argue that the massive explosion of industrial capitalism during the nineteenth century would eventually have required a more structured and regulated police force than previously existed. Moreover, some historians contend that crime statistics (when viewed critically) do show an overall rise and then a decline over the course of the nineteenth century, seeming perhaps to indicate the success of the New Police in preventing and control-ling crime. On the other hand, it is also certainly true that the New Police were initially resented by the working classes and that violence both against, and on the part of, the police was often a feature of policing during the mid-nineteenth century.

During recent years, more historians have looked at the first few years of the New Police forces, and the last few years of the Old Police systems that it replaced. They have reached conclusions that are very different from the accepted view that was advanced by most traditional writers on the early years of the New Police. By looking at accounts, report books and other surviving records from Old Police forces, they have come to the conclusion that most of them were reasonably efficient and popular. Many have recently advanced the idea that the new system of policing developed in the nineteenth century was not actually such a break with the past as had previously been thought and that the much-vaunted 'professionalism' of the New Police existed more in their image than as reality. Elaine Reynolds (1998: 164), among others, notes that:

When we combine our better understanding of the elements, process, personnel, and motivations that were involved in police reform in London during the whole period from 1735 to 1829, it becomes clear that Robert Peel's reform in 1829 was not revolutionary. It rationalized and extended but did not alter existing practices. Centralization, by 1829, seemed logical and worth attempting [. . .] The New Police took on the functions of the old and did them in much the same fashion, drawing on the experience and expertise of the parish watch system. Many of the people who staffed the New Police had staffed the parochial police. The continuity, then, between the 'Charlies' of the night watch and the 'bobbies' of the Metropolitan Police may help to explain the relatively rapid acceptance of the new force.

That said, and especially outside of London, the notion of preventive policing was in some ways novel. Although it rapidly became apparent that plain-clothes detective forces were still required, with the first being set up in London in 1842 (Shpayer-Makov 2011: 2), the New Police constables were subjected to innovative methods to control from the outset. Time discipline and regular salaries took precedence over the former system of fines and rewards, although the latter took some time to die away completely (Williams, C. A. 2014). In addition, recent research has also increasingly focused on the ways in which the New Police did not develop a monopoly (as has often been assumed) on the protection of life and property. In fact, just as the Old Police were part of a patchwork of private security arrangements that included game keepers, private guards on mail coaches and toll-gate keepers to name but a few, so the New Police were also available for private hire initially and worked alongside a range of other private forces (Churchill 2014).

Ongoing research into the outlying areas of Britain also reveals both similarities and differences with England. Wales had the same legal system as England during the nineteenth and early twentieth century, hence policing developments there followed similar patterns. Initial resistance to reform on the grounds of cost and the erosion of local control was followed by gradual acceptance. Scotland, however, had its own legal system. What is evident is the significance of the English model, but also the ways in which it was tailored to local conditions (Barrie 2008). Scottish police forces, as was the case in England and Wales, customarily adopted a pragmatic approach to the many demands placed upon them. More significantly, as in the English case, some elements of working-class culture, such as heavy drinking, remained more resistant to the New Police than both police commissions and town councils would have liked.

Ireland, despite having the same legal framework as England between 1801 and 1922, had particular social, economic and political circumstances, which made issues of law and order (particularly public order policing) especially significant. As in England an Old Police existed in Ireland at the turn of the nineteenth century. Parochial constables had no uniform or training, and were usually only policemen in their spare time, but were tolerably effective in some areas (Malcolm 2006). The duties of the Irish police forces were in many ways similar to those of the new constabularies in England but they were paramilitary in nature. Armed from the start and divorced from local civil control, the police in Ireland had a much more prominent role in the maintenance of public order than forces in mainland Britain.

Although debate remains as to the precise extent and nature of police reform, it is undeniable that by the final quarter of the nineteenth century, 'both the idea and experience of policing had undergone a dramatic transformation from what had been (and had been accepted as) the norm in the 1820s' (Storch and Philips 1999). What has subsequently been popularly perceived as a 'golden age' of policing had begun.

A golden age of policing?

In 1900 the Radical Independent MP John Burns said: 'I believe that the Metropolitan Police, after the City [of London] police, are the best police force in the world' (Emsley 1993: 124). This view persisted in many quarters of British society – not least in the self-image of the police themselves – until at least the 1950s. The works of the rather uncritical historians, like Critchley, discussed above, meant the idea still has currency today. The idea of a 'golden age' of policing, when the public fully supported a professional and efficient police service that did its best to enforce legislation fairly and equally, is seductive. Television programmes such as *Heartbeat* (in fact set in the 1960s but in a provincial part of England that suggested earlier times) demonstrate that this notion remained prevalent well into the twenty-first century. Despite this comfortable image, however, the police underwent a range of significant changes during the twentieth century. For example, police corruption had a profound impact on the organization of police forces in England and Wales. The two world wars produced challenges leading to significant changes such as the introduction of female police officers. Public order issues surrounding the policing of political demonstrations and strikes called police impartiality into question. Despite the persistence of views of a golden age, tensions and confrontations (both internal and external) that marked the police service in this period are at least as typical as the image of a friendly bobby on the beat.

With the notable exception of the Metropolitan Police, jurisdiction over police affairs remained largely a local matter and was jealously guarded. The period 1870–1950 was characterized by an increased centralization of government, but in the matter of policing, the municipalities were able to resist this process – at least until the 1964 Police Act, which finally subsumed city forces into county ones. Centralization had been a desire of the Home Office since the very beginning of the police and the debate had re-emerged at regular intervals throughout the nineteenth century. But it was largely through the police that the boroughs were able to exercise genuine control over the public spaces and even on occasions the private affairs of those living, trading or working in the area. The police were an effective means of controlling the free flow of the highway, either facilitating or hampering trade as desired and many police powers and practices reflected the exigencies and concerns of local trade and commerce. Morality was also regulated through the police by enforcing laws that restricted or banned gambling, drinking or keeping brothels. A less tangible reason for the retention of local control was its symbolic significance and police uniforms often bore unique insignia to reflect the identity of the borough to which they belonged. The true autonomy of the boroughs, however, was compromised by financial considerations. The Police (Expenses) Act of 1874 allowed for half the cost of police wages to be met by the exchequer, but this was conditional on boroughs keeping a force of an approved strength. Although much lower than desired most seem to have been able to accommodate this. Boroughs wishing to avoid this indirect control could do so only by increasing the rates and raising money locally.

The most serious threat to local control came in 1914. The First World War brought wide-ranging centralization of British society as the government took control of raw materials, the means of production and human resources. It signalled a shift in relations between central and local government that would see the ascendancy of the former. The police were not immune from this process and local borough watch committees could be dispensed with and their forces amalgamated with county forces – all for the sake of increased efficiency. Many of the incursions of central government were retained after 1918, but formal control of the police was returned to its pre-war status. However, the precedent had been established and served to clarify Home Office planning. Moreover, tussles over who should control police forces were not the only challenges produced by the war.

The war itself had resulted in extra responsibilities for the police. First, national security issues such as the threat of espionage, the monitoring and arrest of aliens, the 'threat' of pacifist agitation or conscientious objectors and implementing the requirements of the Defence of the Realm Act (DORA), all redefined the police role as national rather than local. For example, Special Branch (originally set up to counter Irish **Fenian** activities and later involved in monitoring suffragettes) was requested by the War Office to monitor the personal advertisements in *The Times* newspaper because it was widely believed that spies were using these to pass cryptic messages about troop and ship movements. For the majority, though, there was probably little change in routine. Police were required to act in support of the armed forces by visiting the home addresses of deserters and pass them to the military authorities for trial. A number of men who had successfully deserted the front and made it home were transported back to France or Belgium to be executed by their army comrades.

The war also brought about the 'dilution' of the workforce, which was topped up by untrained, or at least less trained, staff to cover for those who had enlisted. For the police, this meant replacing male officers with women and making greater use of the part-time Special Constabulary. In this respect the police were little different to most other workers who tended to resent the arrival among them of relatively untrained personnel. **Special constables** were initially issued with armbands to wear on their civilian clothing to denote their status. But this resulted in an unfortunate incident in London's East End when, during the anti-German riots that followed the sinking of the *Lusitania* in 1915, a number of 'specials' found themselves on the receiving end of regular officers' truncheons. Henceforth they were issued with proper uniforms so that they could be more readily identified in a crowd.

The war developed a huge, parallel system of dealing justice to the millions of men under arms (Emsley 2013). However, once fears of a German invasion had died down, the most serious threat to national security on the mainland was thought to be the rise of Bolshevism. The monitoring of suspected Bolshevik agents was carried out by a select few police officers. Industrial unrest was often blamed on communist agitators, whose role was usually exaggerated by the government, but the policing of these disputes could also have a damaging effect on the relationship between police and workers. Arguably though, the most important development of the war for the police was the increased membership of its own union, which had been formed prior to the First World War. This contributed to the police strikes in 1918 and 1919. On 31 August 1918, 12,000 police officers went on strike over the non-recognition of the newly formed Police and Prison Officers Union, as well as demands for a £1 a week pay rise, a 12 per cent war bonus and to protest at the dismissal of a union official. The dispute was only resolved when the Prime Minister, Lloyd-George, intervened.

Lingering discontent over pay and conditions and union recognition were the main causes of the strikes by police in London and Liverpool in 1919 (Klein 2010; Godfrey 2014). These resulted in the setting up of the Desborough Committee. Under the 1919 Police Act police trade unions were prohibited and the Police Federation set up to safeguard members' interests. Significantly, the Home Secretary was given powers to make police pay and conditions the same across the country. The Act simultaneously removed the police from the sphere of labour relations and dealt a blow to local control of the police when responsibility for pay and conditions was centralized. During the 1920s the Home Office also began to intervene in the appointment of Chief Constables.

It is difficult to measure how this affected policing itself or the impartiality of 'the bobby on the beat', but deployment at industrial disputes during this period often resulted in the police acting in the interests of the State. Strikes (including the General Strike of 1926), marches and demonstrations in London and the often violent struggles between different political movements were a problematic issue for the police, who were commonly seen as a repressive tool of the State during this period. A march to Downing Street in 1920 by unemployed London ex-servicemen was the first serious test for the Metropolitan Police. It earned them much criticism and resentment. A baton charge into the crowd by mounted police was described by the (Labour-supporting) *Daily Herald* as 'charging up and down Whitehall running down and clubbing men, women and children' (Morgan 1987: 235). The response of the police to the 'hunger marches' of the early 1930s perpetuated this friction and during 1931 alone, more than 30 British towns and cities experienced serious battles between police and unemployed demonstrators.

Despite a series of scandals during the interwar period (Wood 2010, 2012b; Shore 2013), calls for investigation into police actions were often brushed aside by both government and police, who argued that actions were justified and there was no case to answer. However, it was the clashes between fascist and anti-fascist agitators in the 1930s, which provided the police with their most decisive test, upon which historians have written extensively. Sir Oswald Mosley formed the British Union of Fascists in 1932. While never coming close to matching the political upheaval created by fascism in Italy and Germany, they were at the centre of some of the worst political violence in Britain in the twentieth century and were a key factor in the introduction of the 1936 Public Order Act. Wearing distinctive uniforms, Mosley's fascists organized huge meetings where inflammatory anti-communist and anti-Semitic speeches were given. Violence often broke out both inside and outside the venues as communist and anti-fascist activists tried to disrupt proceedings. Some historians, such as Robert Benewick (1969) have argued that, because the fascists wore uniforms and marched to and from their meetings in an orderly fashion, the police were inclined to treat them leniently. Others, such as Barbara Weinberger (1991, 1995) have suggested that the police were biased against the political left, deeply distrusted communists and acted harshly against them. Other historians (such as Robert Skidelsky 1990) have argued that the police were in fact merely 'pro-police' – aiming to retain control of the streets with the minimum possible violence. This is a complex debate for which there is not space here. It is certain, however, that during this period the police were often unable to control the huge public demonstrations of the time without resorting to violent, authoritarian tactics. Clearly, however, the notion that policing during the period to 1950 was characterized solely by the cheerful 'bobby on the beat' is erroneous and the National Council for Civil Liberties (now known simply as Liberty) was set up during this period primarily in response to broad concerns over the biased nature of public order policing (Clark 2012).

The outbreak of the Second World War once again placed additional strains on the police. Added to the duties that had characterized policing during the First World War was the considerable extra burden caused by German air raids, including the threat of gas attacks. Broadly speaking, the police benefited from an increase in public esteem and an enhanced self-image because of the role they performed in connection with air raids. They were also the first point of contact for the bereaved, for those searching for missing relatives or for families made homeless. There were also factors that might have lowered public esteem such as the role played by the police in suppressing industrial disputes (which increased during the war) and monitoring unpopular rationing laws. In particular, enforcing restrictions on petrol supplies brought the police into conflict with the motoring middle class. Nevertheless, public opinion surveys conducted at the end of the war indicate a highly positive attitude towards the police. The wartime role and the experiences of police and public alike between 1939 and 1945 did much to shape the image of the English 'bobby' personified in the character of George Dixon in the film *The Blue Lamp* (1950) and later resurrected in the television series *Dixon of Dock Green*.

The manpower problems of the Second World War had been met by calling on reserves, including police pensioners, specials and women. The war also brought into sharp focus the problems of co-ordination and efficiency. With no clear lines of demarcation to establish areas of responsibility and jurisdiction between various agencies the police often found themselves in conflict with the Air Raid Warden and the Home Guard – a situation the Home Office failed to resolve. Women first entered the police during the First World War via a number of competing organizations that grew out of various trends in the suffragette movement. The one that was acceptable to the authorities was the Voluntary Women's Patrols (VWP), perceived by many (including the women who volunteered) as an occupation for gentlewomen (Jackson 2006).

After the war, many women police were axed in the public spending cuts. During the 1930s police forces could afford to be particularly choosy about recruits and most favoured the employment of men who, it was widely believed, could perform 'proper' policing tasks. As Louise Jackson has highlighted (2003, 2006), it was a persistent belief that women were only suited to welfare work within police forces. Despite this, the Home Office did issue regulations in October 1931 to govern the employment of women police. This established a lower rate of pay and stipulated that only unmarried (or widowed) women between the ages of 22 and 35 could be so employed. The matter of employment and the nature of duties were left entirely at the discretion of Chief Constables. The Children and Young Persons Act 1933 required the attendance at court of a woman in cases involving children. While this opened the door a little wider, it also established the nature of women police duties for the next 40 years. With the notable exception of a few detectives in provincial forces such as Lancashire, women police were ascribed tasks that conformed to contemporary gender assumptions: cases involving women and children and being generally subservient to male officers by typing their reports.

The Second World War brought little change. However, the subsequent move towards professionalization resulted in a need to recruit more women after the war when their 'special' role, especially in relation to children, became more valued. In 1948 women were accepted into the Police Federation and the Home Office recognized the term 'police officer' rather than policeman or policewoman. Lifting the marriage ban in 1945, however, did little to attract women recruits and women police remained an unintegrated minority until the Sex Discrimination Act 1975 removed the formal basis for the bias against them.

Modern parallels

It is possible to trace the legacies of many of the changes and trends outlined above in the latter part of the twentieth century and beyond. One key area where historical comparisons can aid contemporary analysis is in the policing of public order. For example, on 1 April 2009 the newspaper vendor Ian Tomlinson collapsed and died after being struck by a police officer during the G-20 summit protests. The officer involved, a constable with the Territorial Support Group of the Metropolitan Police (specialists in public order policing), was subsequently found not guilty on manslaughter charges but was dismissed from his post for gross misconduct. Extensive press coverage of both the police handling of the demonstration (particularly their use of the so-called 'kettling' containment technique) and the officer's violent behaviour led to considerable debate about the state of public order policing in Britain. A range of police actions were subsequently judged 'unlawful' (Dodd 2011), but how can a consideration of the development of policing over the *longue duree* help us understand this complex series of events?

As broad context, it is clear from even a cursory historical analysis that the New Police have always found public order policing something of a problematic issue (Clark 2012). Public order events are, by their nature, not part of 'everyday' duties for the British police. On 1 April 2009, the Metropolitan Police were coping with six distinct protests in London, and 5,500 officers were deployed, working 14 hour shifts and often required to sleep on the floors at police stations before returning to duty. These conditions may have contributed to the tensions on the day, but the 2009 enquiry and report 'Adapting to Protest' (led by the Chief Inspector of Constabulary) acknowledged that rank and file officers had little training in how to effectively facilitate peaceful protest. It was ever thus. Under the Old Police the control of any serious disorder or large crowds almost always involved intervention from the military. Once the New Police were established (and public dismay over the Gordon Riots of 1780 was in fact one of the many spurs for police reform), this duty gradually shifted to them.

Their early performance in this role was not promising. In 1833, clumsy policing at a meeting of the National Union of the Working Classes at Coldbath Fields resulted in hand to hand fighting between the police and the crowds and the death of a police constable from a stab wound to the chest. Tactics were improved and largely successful at controlling major Chartist demonstrations in 1848 and in policing the Great Exhibition of 1851, but a wave of demonstrations by the unemployed in London in 1887 again reignited public debates about the ability of the police to maintain order in the streets. The interwar years saw further accusations of partial and heavy-handed policing of left-wing demonstrations, and the latter half of the twentieth century witnessed major disturbances, such as the Notting Hill Race Riots (1958), the Brixton, Toxteth and Handsworth Riots (1981), the UK Miners' Strike (1984–5) and the Poll Tax Riots (1989–90). These events all had very different causes and dynamics, but all demonstrate how public order policing has always been highly contentious. Those involved in demonstrations or unrest often feel the police react clumsily or in a heavy-handed manner, while other members of the community often do not recognize the legitimacy of the claims of the demonstrators/protestors and believe the police should act more decisively still. While there have been many developments in tactics, uniforms and procedures, the fact remains that the UK still largely uses a non-militarized, civil police to deal with large-scale, violent public disorder.

A further, useful point of historical context involves the use of violence on the part of the police, perceived to be a persistent problem in public order situations. Of course, the use of violence is in some ways an acceptable part of police practice. The state has the monopoly on legal violence and the police are the mechanism via which this is most often employed. Despite a public rhetoric that stressed the unarmed and consensual nature of the British police, officers have been (and still are) armed when their duties require it. More to the point, however, there is evidence from the memoirs and autobiographies written by police officers, but also from more recent criminological studies, that the occupation culture of the police has in the past both legitimized and foregrounded the use of violence as both a marker of masculinity and an integral element of police work. Victor Meek, for example, a police officer during the 1940s noted that a 'wicked feeling of joy and rage' welled up in him whenever a baton charge was ordered at demonstrations, and that 'even the fat old coppers found a burst of speed on these occasions and if the crowd ran too soon there were curses of disappointment' (Meek 1962: 18). Public order events traditionally challenge the authority of the police on the streets, both institutionally and individually, and hence it is perhaps unsurprising that a robust, physical response is often drawn forth.

Finally, the Tomlinson/G-20 events also highlight the complexities of making the police accountable for their operational actions. Police complaints procedures are actually of relatively recent advent. During the nineteenth century, despite fact that officers wore numbers to enable individual officers to be identified, it was very hard to bring individual officers to account. Up until the First World War, procedures were marred by 'highly ineffective accountability mechanisms, strongly biased against complainants' (Johansen 2011: 61). These early complaints mechanisms were almost wholly internal to forces and in fact allowed the police to investigate themselves. As we have seen earlier in this chapter, the civil liberties agenda developed in the 1930s at least partly due to perceptions of police bias and a lack of accountability in relation to the policing of political demonstrations and marches. Following further scandals in the 1970s, the Police Complaints Board (PCB) was set up in 1977. The PCB was independent of any individual force (in theory at least), but continuing dissatisfaction with its actions led (following the Brixton Riots and Scarman Report) to the setting up of the Police Complaints Authority (PCA) in 1985. The PCA was itself perceived to be insufficiently independent (as it reported to the Home Office, which was itself ultimately responsible for the control of police forces) and hence it was replaced in 2002 with the Independent Police Complaints Authority. This current body has also subsequently been criticized both before and after the Tomlinson incident for not being responsive enough to public concerns and for delays in taking decisive action.

Conclusion

As the example above (and this chapter more generally) demonstrates, knowledge of historical antecedents and context can contribute significantly to our analysis of contemporary and recent police practices. Overall, a complex pattern of enforcement and discretion, change and permanence emerges when policing since 1750 is considered. Certainly there were marked developments in the organization of policing in Britain over these two centuries, but it is an oversimplification to trace a line of 'progress' from the amateur patchwork of provision in 1750 to the recognizably 'modern' forces of the latter part of the twentieth century. Recent research has demonstrated that the Old Police were remarkably effective in combating certain types of crime and that there was strong resistance to their replacement. Moreover, the difference in duties between 'old' and 'new' constables was (initially at least) not particularly marked. Equally, it might be argued that, despite changes in the organization and mechanisms of policing, the underlying 'purpose' of the police (to fight crime or to oppress the working class, depending on your point of view) has remained remarkably static. Certainly, the notion of a 'golden age' of consensual policing has now been discredited. Yet even in the twenty-first century, policing remains defined by a mixture of compassion and repression, enforcement and tolerance. The mere existence of legislation means little on its own (unenforced legislation has scant social significance), and police officers have been, and continue to be, crucial in determining which aspects of the law get enforced rigorously and which social groups are the most closely policed. Nowadays, the police are so much a part of the fabric of daily life that their duties and organization often go unexamined. In fact, this arm of the modern state has a long and varied history and understanding of this is vital to knowing how and why the police act today. The study questions and further reading below, along with the references contained within the bibliography at the end of this book, are available to you to follow up any particular questions you may have.

Key questions

An issue that historians have grappled with extensively in recent years concerns the differences between the Old and New Police. Given what we now know, how much of a change was really represented by the introduction of the Metropolitan Police in 1829? On one level, the differences between the older, more piecemeal systems of policing in operation up until 1829 (in London) and 1839–56 (in more provincial areas) seem easy to spot. It might be argued that the 'old' system of police was largely amateur in status. Constables were picked by their community to serve, and could be fined if they refused. While professional law enforcers (the so-called 'acting constables') did exist in many major towns, these were still often more involved with the recovery of private property than the maintenance of civil order. By contrast, the New Police have been depicted as uniformed professionals, received rudimentary training, had a strict set of instructions to follow and got involved in the 'policing' of a much wider range of issues. However, while perhaps broadly true, this picture has since been considerable nuanced. Dodsworth (2008) and Beattie (2012) have shown how many of the most significant initiatives and debates about the police started in the 1780s, rather than the 1820s. Equally, the supposedly professional New Police did not really have much training until the end of the nineteenth century and were often dismissed for drunkenness and discipline offences (Williams, C. A. 2014). Others, such as Churchill (2014) have questioned the very idea that the New Police rapidly developed a monopoly of policing, pointing to the continued existence of private forces and non-official means of conflict resolution.

Another interesting area of recent debate is the extent to which there ever was a 'golden age' of policing (usually imagined to be between c.1890 and c.1950).

Was there really a higher level of acceptance of the police and a greater standard of public orderliness during this period? Emsley (1996), Weinberger (1995) and Gatrell (1990) all have classic, well-known material relevant to this issue but more recent work by, *inter alia*, Clark (2012), Wood (2012a) and Jackson (2008) has also challenged prior assumptions. Yet another recent trend in the field has been to examine the policeman as worker, and to consider the backgrounds and occupational lives of police officers. Shpayer-Makov (2011) has produced a ground-breaking work on detectives, and others such as Klein (2010) and Emsley (2009) have looked closely at the lives of regular constables on the beat.

Chapter 3

The role of the 'victim' since 1750

Introduction

This chapter deals with the role of the victim in the criminal justice process – a pivotal but sometimes nebulous role, which is as critical to the running of a criminal justice system as the police systems described in the last chapter, but which has received little attention until recently. Our contemporary view of the nature of crime usually places the victim in a *passive* role in relation to a criminal act. This is not to say that victims are marginalized or ignored in our current conceptions of crime, but rather that they are not seen to have a particularly proactive role to play in either the prosecution or detection of crime. It is true that, during the 1950s, prominent liberal reformers such as Margery Fry (1951) argued that 'the injured individual [has] rather slipped out of the mind of the criminal court' and successfully campaigned for Criminal Injuries Compensation for the victims of violent crime. However, although this led to a growing interest in the needs of victims, such campaigns were very much based on the view that 'the suffering, and innocent victim of violence' (Rock 1990: 84) should receive redress via the professional criminal justice system. Equally, the rise of 'victimology' (the study of victims of crime) since the 1950s has certainly raised the profile of victims, but has also arguably not altered substantial perceptions of victims as passive actors. As Miers (1978: 15) notes, the very term 'victim' inevitably promotes an image of passivity, where the victim has 'traditionally been viewed as the "sufferer" in a simple "doer–sufferer" model of criminal interaction'. In fact, victims played an active rather than passive role in the prevention, prosecution and detection of crime until the First World War, after which the police acted for victims in the courtroom and the media provided images of victimhood for wider consumption.

At the beginning of our period in 1750 it was largely through individual or private actions that any cases were prosecuted at all. The part played by private action was far greater than is generally believed. This chapter will therefore begin with a consideration of victims, the prosecution of crime and the changing face of the prosecutor. Before the police moved into this area of criminal justice the onus was on the victims to bring prosecutions. These could be expensive as well as difficult and we will examine the various ways by which private individuals were able to bring cases to court. We then discuss the emotive subject of self-defence. 'The Englishman's home is his castle' is not just a modern sentiment but a long-established view. We will take a close look at how the use of 'reasonable force' has been variously interpreted and the underlying causes of any shifts in attitudes. There have always been measures that private individuals could take – and were often expected to take – to safeguard their own property and prevent crime. This *active* role became increasingly important as the government bureaucratic machinery became more efficient at counting crime statistics. Accordingly, the responsibility for crime prevention did not stop with the private individual but infiltrated 'normal' police activity. The third part of this chapter explores the part that the police management of prosecution practices played in directing crime statistics. Lastly, the conclusion shows how the police management of prosecution in the twentieth and twenty-first century has lead to crises in policing, and in public confidence in criminal statistics.

'Victims' and the prosecution of crime

During the eighteenth century the state took a rather detached and piecemeal attitude towards the prosecution of crime. The matter will be dealt with in more detail in the following chapter but, broadly speaking, and in keeping with the *laissez-faire* policies that dominated ideas concerning the role of government, the state was only involved in the prosecution of a limited number of offences. These tended to be offences that directly impinged on the government's ability to run the country. Coinage offences, for example, could attract the attention of the Treasury Solicitor and occasionally resulted in prosecution of offenders. Forgery of paper money was also taken very seriously by government officials. Following the Forgery Act of 1729, there were about 120 statutes against forgery on the books by the 1830s (McGowan 1999: 107). As McGowan has shown, 'judges and the Crown [were] the staunchest advocates of the death penalty for forgery', believing that the seriousness of the offence, warranted the execution of the offender 'even in the face of the uneasiness of those who were victims of the crime' (1999: 140). Similarly, the Attorney General would, from time to time, concern himself with the prosecution of cases of treason or sedition. Another type of case that presented a serious threat to the state was the mutiny of troops. The thought of soldiers – trained and armed – being beyond the control of the state was anathema to all shades of political opinion during the eighteenth century. The danger to society was obvious and the state acted accordingly. At the end of the seventeenth century a mutiny by the Royal Scots Regiment had caused the government of the day to rush through the Mutiny Act 1689, which for the first time empowered the army to try soldiers during peacetime.

But these were the exceptions rather than the rule. What bound all of these together was the seriousness of the threat, which was presented to the running of government either through its finances (coinage offences), rebellion (treason and sedition) or armed insurgency (mutiny). Nevertheless, the government did not itself always directly pursue the prosecution of even these most serious offences. For example, in the late-eighteenth century, magistrates were regularly urged to seek other means to fund the prosecution of sedition cases rather than relying on the Crown Law Officers to finance them (Emsley 2010a: 183). The Bank of England, too, usually financed prosecutions for forgery privately and, indeed, built up a significant body of employees dedicated to this task (McGowan 2005). In the case of ordinary offences against persons or property that did not threaten the existence of the state, the chances of government-funded or conducted prosecutions were minimal. In fact, until the Prosecution of Offences Act of 1879 there was no public prosecutor to take criminal cases to court and even then only significant or important cases were taken forward. The New Police gradually assumed responsibility for the prosecution of most criminal cases but, as has been argued in the previous chapter, the adoption of new forms of policing was still not yet accomplished in many parts of the country by the mid-nineteenth century. This meant that, in the eighteenth century at least, a great many offences were probably dealt with entirely outside of the structures of the criminal justice system with which we are now familiar. Tolerance, 'rough music' (a form of public shaming ritual often associated with the punishment of henpecked husbands or adulterous couples) and community action were all much more common methods for dealing with minor issues than the constable and the courts.

Given the expense and difficulty that prosecution entailed, it is likely that the majority of offences committed early in the period under consideration were never brought to the attention of the courts and were dealt with in some other way. Minor offences would in all likelihood be ignored or even tolerated. These will not show up in criminal statistics and there is, therefore, no way of knowing the real extent to which crime was tolerated. However, some anecdotal evidence does exist that can give us a flavour of public opinion. There are a number of documented instances, for example, where prosecutors were attacked or pressurized in some way for their bringing of cases to court. Sometimes this was a reaction to severe sentencing by the court – especially if the death penalty had been inflicted – but was also motivated, so it seems, by a general community feeling that the case should not have been presented because the circumstances did not warrant it. Often this reflected the status of the offender. Children had a tendency to elicit sympathy, but stories have also survived of adult thieves being assisted by crowds. Clearly, *some* victims were expected to be tolerant of *some* offences. One factor that should perhaps be considered here is changing attitudes towards both property and violence. Levels of interpersonal violence, which would never be accepted today, used to be commonplace. As Emsley (2005a: 10) notes, 'there is a general acknowledgement of an increasing intolerance and general decline of violent behaviour in Europe since the late medieval period'. Accordingly, much that would currently come within the purview of the criminal justice system was in earlier times simply ignored or settled privately between the individuals concerned.

If action was taken in relation to an offence, it was also common during the eighteenth and early nineteenth centuries for victims and communities to deal with offenders by *extra-judicial* means. In the first instance, it was often accepted that justice could be meted out by the victim themselves in regard to certain types of crime – particularly shoplifting and petty thievery. Wood (2003: 114) quotes a mid-nineteenth century boot seller who reported that when he caught young thieves taking boots or shoes he '[gave] them a stirruping [flogging] with whichever it is, and a kick and let them go'. Henry Mayhew, an early investigative journalist, also observed that 'sometimes when these boys are caught pilfering, they are severely beaten especially by the women, who are aided by the men, if the thief offers any formidable resistance' (Wood 2003: 114).

Communities, too, could act to mete out justice on behalf of the victim, although this was by no means always an act of altruism and often the targets of this action were outsiders, or those seen as undesirable (Beattie 1986: 135). For example, a Jewish hawker was ducked in a horse pond at the Huntingdon races in 1753 for trying to steal a ring from a young woman (Emsley 2005a: 182). Of course there is no real way of knowing how many of these cases were genuine acts of meting out 'justice' and how many were simply aimed at misfits or minority groups and justified on some spurious grounds. Nevertheless, the important point here is that this was an accepted practice regardless of its authenticity. This practice appears to have occurred most often in the eighteenth century and the first half of the nineteenth century. Overall, as Wood (2003: 111) has argued, it was relatively common for order to be maintained:

> through a distribution of violence legitimated by a 'customary' mentality that organized retributive, autonomous and disciplinary violence. From neighbourly 'rough music' to direct interpersonal assaults, customary violence marked and defended the boundaries of acceptable behaviour and enforced conformity to community standards (or individual interpretations of those standards).

In the nineteenth century, changes in the level of policing in Britain were part of a wider change in attitudes to violence. At the start of the century there was widespread acceptance that violence was an acceptable way of solving many problems – notably problems between working-class men and within working-class communities more generally. 'Fair fights' with seconds, rounds and the possibility of subsequent reconciliation were a common way for working men to settle disagreements (Wood 2003; Emsley 2010a). People who broke the norms of the community – such as offenders against children – were often glad of the protection that the law offered them against the instant justice that their victims' neighbours were keen to mete out. The mid-nineteenth-century Edinburgh detective James McLevy wrote about the time that he unmasked a gang of women who were stealing clothes from children. When the area's mothers found out, the thieves needed police protection to prevent them from being stripped themselves and badly beaten (McLevy 1975: 204). But during the nineteenth century, more 'civilized' attitudes began to take hold, aided by the arrival for the first time of New Police forces that could enforce a new standard of behaviour. The state began to take note of all violence in public places, with an eye on stopping it. In return, the New Police and the court systems began to stake a claim that they could entirely protect the safety of the citizen. This claim, though, was not total: many police would rather look the other way than interfere in a 'fair fight' – or in any other fight if it looked like the participants and spectators were formidable enough to resist interference.

Thus a significant amount of crime (especially of the more minor type) was probably dealt with outside of the court system for much of the eighteenth and early nineteenth centuries. There was a gradual decline in *reported* occurrences of this type of extra-legal redress, which appears to coincide with the rise of a recognizable prosecution system. However, this does not necessarily imply a causative relationship. It might also be that newspapers – one of the best sources of evidence of this practice – gradually found it easier to glean their copy from the theatricals of the courtroom rather than more mundane human interactions in society itself. The practice did continue alongside the newly emerging professional prosecutors, but only the more sensational appears to have been newsworthy.

Moreover, even during the period since 1750, victims were instrumental in bringing cases to court. As Hay (1989: 24) has noted, private prosecution was the dominant mode in the eighteenth and nineteenth centuries. More than 80 per cent of all criminal cases were prosecuted by private individuals – usually the victim or somewhat less usually an agent acting on his or her behalf – rather than an agent of national or local government during this period (Hay 1983: 167). In Sheffield during the period 1859–62, out of 4,116 court cases of common assault, 3,303 individuals (80 per cent) had been summoned to court by victims under a private warrant rather than being arrested or summoned by the police. Victims thus played an extremely proactive role in the criminal justice process. In the first instance, of course, they were often involved in securing an arrest. With few police officers in many parts of the country, it was often down to victims themselves (particularly in rural areas) to arrange the apprehension of a felon, as the following extract from a theft trial at the Old Bailey in 1790 makes clear:

JOHN ASHWORTH and THOMAS WEBB were indicted for stealing, on the 23rd of December last, two live cocks, value 2 s. and three live hens, value 3 s. the property of Christopher Chapman

CHRISTOPHER CHAPMAN sworn

I live at Sudbury-green, a farmer; on December the 23rd, between five and six, I was alarmed with somebody getting into my yard, and taking my fowls; they roost in an out-house which was open; but the gate of the yard was shut; I found only one dead hen, and a dead turkey; one in the yard, the other in the outhouse: about an hour, or an hour and a quarter after, I went into the adjoining shed, where the cows eat; I found five more; I pursued from information; and going along, two people told me the two prisoners were at the Plow at Kelstone-green, about five miles from Sudbury; I found them about nine the same morning, and seven more of my fowls dead, and hung up for shew and sale, at the public house; they were in their feathers; they were my fowls of different colours; they were clipped in the wing.

(January 1790, trial of John Ashworth and Thomas
Webb t17900113–18 *Old Bailey Proceedings
Online*, www.oldbaileyonline.org)

Clearly, victims of crime in eighteenth-century England could not afford to be passive if their cases were to be dealt with in or outside the courts. The preference for extra-judicial action was in no small part influenced by the anticipated cost of bringing a prosecution. For many this was prohibitive. However, one avenue of assistance with these costs for *some* victims was provided by the so-called 'Associations for the Prosecution of Felons', which had been established in most parts of the country from the 1760s (Gatrell *et al.* 1980: 179). These associations (which would assist fee-paying members with the costs of prosecution and sometimes finance them in full and/or pay a reward) made prosecution possible in many cases where previously it would have been impossible. By the early nineteenth century these associations were firmly established. However, they were formed through private rather than public initiative and as such only served a section of the community. The scope of these associations was therefore limited. They only assisted their own members and had limited financial means at their disposal.

The origins of the Associations for the Prosecution of Felons can be located in informal agreements within communities collectively to contribute towards the costs of 'desirable prosecutions'. It is impossible to be certain of the earliest of these agreements – it is unlikely that records have survived if indeed they were made in the first place – but there is surviving evidence of one in South Yorkshire in 1737. On this occasion 100 parishioners, including 5 women, agreed to contribute to the costs of a prosecution. By the 1790s these agreements were more usually formalized into associations with all the accompanying paraphernalia such as constitutions and rules. Most associations charged their members annual fees to ensure that the association continued and covered all its costs. Normally, the cost of a prosecution entailed hiring counsel to present the case in court and any witness expenses. If it had funded particularly expensive prosecutions then the premiums would have to be raised to recuperate the expenditure. Members, therefore, often saw premiums rise year on year and many associations folded when an insufficient number of members could afford to continue paying the annual fees. At least one association overcame this problem by charging a large joining fee and then smaller subsequent fees, if that was necessary to balance the budget. For example, the Sheffield Association for the Prosecution of Felons charged £3 13s. for initial membership for personal and business premises, and 6s. 10d. annually thereafter. The cost for personal premises only was considerably lower (Thomas 1830: 143). This way, the association secured its money from the outset while members' enthusiasm was greater than their thrift.

Most associations remained relatively informal in so far as they were hardly permanent and were often formed in response to heightened concerns about crime. The associations were often as ephemeral as the feared crime waves that sparked their creation. Rather than representing a shift away from the private prosecution of offenders the formation of these associations actually reinforced – or consolidated – the practice by making the pre-existing system more workable – at least for its members.

But the associations did not limit themselves to expensive court action. First, offenders had to be apprehended and many associations paid rewards for the capture of the perpetrators of crime or the recovery of stolen goods. Some associations even organized local patrols or themselves conducted searches for stolen goods. But these were the minority and the most usual function in most associations was to pay for the advertising of rewards or the printing of handbills. This, of course, had the additional benefit of acting as a deterrent by advertising the fact that the association played such an active role. The impact of this effect cannot be measured but we might safely conclude that it was a cheap by-product of the association's activities.

The ideal association – that is the ones that appear to have functioned most effectively – consisted of between 20 and 60 members, preferably property-holders, from a small area (Philips 1989: 132). Clearly, the cost of belonging to an association was prohibitive for many. According to one historian, members came generally 'from among the middling property owners of a town or parish[es]' who were driven to take action 'by moments of acute anxiety about the level of crime' and concerns that 'crime was being encouraged by the uncertainty of punishment and the failure of victims to prosecute' (Beattie 1986: 48). However, claims that these associations amounted to some form of 'citizen self-policing' are missing the point (Palmer 1988: 148). Associations for the Prosecution of Felons were formed to protect the financial interests of their members. The citizens they were concerned about – and therefore wished to police – were not themselves but others. In fact, it is quite possible to interpret the formation of the associations as those with property protecting themselves against those without property. Even if we put aside any class-based explanation, it is obvious that the associations were not formed for the benefit of the community as a whole, but for a fee-paying section of it.

It could also be argued that there existed a hierarchy among associations, with wealthier ones able to afford to prosecute more often than those that might have been strapped for cash from time to time. The impact of the associations on national prosecution rates was probably negligible at best – again suggesting that they operated in the interests of only a minor section of the community. Beattie (1986: 50) has suggested that they had 'no major effect', while in his study of

Essex King has pointed out their tendency to follow rather than lead the indictment rate (in Hay and Snyder 1989: 202). While their impact as a deterrent – arguably their most significant function – will remain elusive, for the historian they do provide evidence that an important section of society were sufficiently disgruntled about the existing criminal justice system to invest time and money in organizing themselves against the threat of crime.

It is, of course, possible to view the formation of Associations for the Prosecution of Felons as an obstacle to the formation of the New Police. In short, by doing one of the jobs we now associate with the police it removed or at least delayed pressure from the middle classes for the introduction of a new system. Other organizations, such as the Worsted Inspectorate discussed in Chapter 9, may also have had a similar effect (Godfrey 2002). As the upper classes could afford to prosecute in any case and the lower classes lacked influence, only pressure from the middle classes (many of whom were the entrepreneurs who were driving the British economy at this time) would have any impact on government policy. These members of the middle classes had little incentive to change the position – an argument best summed up by David Philips (1977: 133):

> Where property owners had an active Association for the Prosecution of Felons in existence their attitude is easy to understand. They paid their subscription to their association, which protected their property alone. Why, then, choose to pay [presumably much higher] rates for a police force to serve the whole country, which would spend much of its time policing other people's property?

Yet we should also consider the relationship between the associations and the police and point to the many instances when the police developed in parallel with the association, at least up to a point. In fact, there is some evidence to suggest that the New Police benefited from the same movement that had spawned the Associations for the Prosecution of Felons and that counties with most associations were more likely to adopt the New Police if that was an option (Schubert 1981: 36). Where once fears about crime had motivated people to opt for the formation of an association so too could the same fears be expressed by opting to adopt the terms of the County Police Act 1839, but the choice was not limited to one or the other (Philips 1989: 150).

The associations often provided a stepping stone towards establishing the police, although it would be wholly incorrect to suggest that the police were grafted onto pre-existing associations. No doubt the police benefited from rewards offered by the associations, but a more significant legacy was the establishment of the principle of locally funded policing. After the passing of the County and Borough Police Act of 1856 it appears that the police increasingly shouldered the burden of prosecution, thereby eroding this particular role of the victim (Hay and Snyder 1989: 3–52). In addition, the growth of insurance companies eroded other roles of the associations such as the need to recover stolen goods and the offering and payment of rewards. However, conditions had also altered: the widening of summary prosecution had removed the enormous expense of indicting felons in many cases (Schubert 1981: 43). The situation remains blurred. There is no line of demarcation here – the moment of change cannot be pinpointed and is only visible when viewed across a long period of time. While the role of independent action on the part of victims in bringing prosecutions declined over the course of the nineteenth century and into the twentieth, it is important to realize that victims were instrumental to the operation of the criminal justice system for at least a half of the period under consideration here. Even later in the nineteenth century, with the police assuming responsibility for many prosecutions, the expansion of the summary courts (and hence the negation of the expense of a costly jury trial) meant that victims from lower down on the social scale increasingly used the law to mediate disputes. As Jennifer Davis (1984; Hay and Snyder 1989: 413) has shown, working-class prosecutors accounted for between a fifth and a quarter of all prosecutions for theft during the 1860s and 1870s.

Retribution, self-defence and other extra-judicial action

Clearly, then, victims have historically been quite proactive in the prosecution of crime and extra-judicial measures of redress have also often been employed by victims. Another area in which victims have traditionally been less than passive is in the measures that they might take to defend themselves against the perpe-trators of crime, particularly in instances of burglary. Before the emergence of professional law enforcement through the police, one might expect this to be the usual practice. Certainly, it has been argued that the 'right' of self-defence was implicit in the earliest laws of England and was eventually made explicit in the Bill of Rights of 1689 (Malcolm 2002: 4; Malcolm's work addresses an inter-esting topic but should be used with caution as it does contain factual errors and its main premise is seriously flawed; see also Williams 2004). It is difficult to be certain how widespread significant incidents of self-defence have been. Evidence can only be obtained from court records, which record only prosecuted cases and anecdotal or polemical sources such as newspapers. However, the issue of new government guidelines on the use of force against intruders by the Crown Prosecution Service and the Association of Chief Police Officers (ACPO) in 2005 shows that this issue remains contentious. The use of force to defend oneself or one's property is another area that challenges contemporary views of victims as passive actors in any criminal act.

The legal position on self-defence is surprisingly complex and has altered over the centuries. Like many things that are derived from common law, interpretations have varied over time. Broadly speaking, though, it has long been accepted in English law that a person can use *reasonable* force to protect himself or his property (legal language uses the term 'his' to signify both 'his' and 'her'). During the eighteenth century there was considerable debate over the rights and wrongs of self-defence causing Sir William Blackstone, author of one of the most widely read texts on English common law, to consider the problem:

> The law respects the passions of the human mind; and [. . .] makes it lawful in him to do himself that immediate justice, to which he is prompted by nature, and which no prudential motives are strong enough to restrain. It considers that the future process of law is by no means an adequate remedy for injuries accompanied with force.
>
> (Blackstone 1982: 3–4)

Blackstone appears to suggest that not only self-defence, but even retribution by victims of crime was acceptable, provided they acted immediately. If violence was used against a law-abiding citizen, Blackstone proposed, it was perfectly understandable that this individual might not wish to wait for 'the future process of law' and might mete out violence in return immediately. This benign view of *extra-judicial* action by victims of crime can still be detected during the nineteenth century and, most importantly, it appears to have survived beyond the arrival of formal prosecution structures such as the New Police.

During the nineteenth century, however, the widespread ownership of guns was an additional complicating factor and meant that, increasingly, self-defence was synonymous with shooting. Reasonable force, therefore, very often quickly became deadly force. For example, the following cases from the Sheffield area illustrate just how common these occurrences were. In August 1819, a resident at a warehouse fired a pistol at some burglars attempting to enter through a window – one was heard to cry out and fall to the ground. He was not apprehended. Another man 'shot through the thigh' in a similar attempt was convicted the following week. Burglars would often risk facing an armed house owner or at least a mechanical trap. Not always, though, did these have the intended results. In 1837 a spring trap killed its owner after he set it off by accident in his own workshop. In another case in 1841 the victim of a burglar found himself threatened by his own gun (Williams 1998: 278–9).

Public and press alike welcomed rather than condemned the use of weapons against criminals. Williams (1998) has studied the Sheffield press in detail. For example, when a 15-year-old girl in Brightside, Sheffield fought off burglars by shooting at them from the window with a horse pistol, the *Sheffield Independent* commented: 'If all men would act with the same gallantry this young woman did, only taking better aim, burglaries would be less frequent.' In 1839 the same newspaper welcomed the fact that three men had been 'armed and prepared' when they faced down a group of suspected robbers on the town's outskirts one night. In the early nineteenth century it was widely accepted that individuals had a duty to protect themselves. It could even be argued that there was an attitude that *force majeure* would prevail and those who failed to secure their property properly deserved to lose it. An editorial in *The Times* of 1857 noted bluntly that:

> Self-preservation, if not the first instinct of nature, stands very high. Few would hesitate to destroy the highwayman or the burglar, even where property alone was in question. Indeed, in the matter of self-defence we make property part of self, and are all of the opinion [. . .] that life would not be worth living for without that proportion of wealth to which we have been accustomed.
>
> (*The Times*, 28 January 1857, page 6, column b)

The perceived deterrent effect of deadly force was regarded as an essential element of crime prevention. This view was extended to public order and it was not unusual for such force to be threatened during riots – not by the rioters but by those seeking to protect their property and businesses. During the Sheffield election riot of 1832, a crowd attacked the house of lawyer Luke Palfreyman. Palfreyman and one of his clerks fired shots over the crowd's heads in response to their stones, and warned that if they advanced he would fire at them – an act described by the press as 'that defence which is lawful to every Englishmen in his own house'.

The use of 'deadly force' against burglars and other thieves appears to have fallen off after the middle of the century. It is quite possible that this reflects the impact of formalized systems to protect citizens and their property or to prosecute offenders. The most obvious development here was the emergence of police forces in many parts of the country as detailed in the previous chapter, and perhaps there no longer existed a need for private citizens to resort to such extreme measures to protect themselves. But as usual it is important to guard against drawing convenient conclusions from the patchy remnants of primary sources – much of it anecdotal. The apparent downward turn in the 'trend' might reflect nothing more than a difference in survival of the evidence. That in itself, though, might be significant because it could mean that newspapers were less enthusiastic in their reporting of such instances. If that is the case – and it remains a big 'if' – then this suggests that the use of deadly force against criminals had become less socially acceptable later in the nineteenth century, leaving us to ponder the reasons why this could be the case. One obvious argument is that the emergence of a 'proper' system to deal with crime rendered other systems 'improper'.

Whatever the reasons for the apparent decline in use of deadly force, attention turned towards the use of firearms towards the end of the nineteenth century. It was not so much that government was concerned about the 'right sort of people' being allowed to defend themselves and their property, but there developed an increased concern about the availability of firearms to just anyone. Much of this increased concern was linked to the rise of working-class movements such as the trades unions and the Labour Party. Fuelled by industrial unrest across Britain, many commentators were calling for the restriction of firearms. Initially there was public resistance. One letter to *The Times* on the subject of a gun tax suggested that it should only be imposed if a gun was used recreationally. If a man should 'in pure self-defence, be constrained to use the gun for destroying a mad dog on his premises, or the pistol for shooting a burglar in his house', then no fee should be imposed (*The Times*, 27 April 1867, page 10, column b). The comparison of burglars and mad dogs is instructive.

By the time fresh discussions took place in the 1880s, however, (coincident with the rapid spread of cheap revolvers), the prevalent mood was changing somewhat. In contrast to the quotation above, a *Times* leader from 1885 claimed that 'an epidemic of revolvers and the violences attendant on the habit of carrying them has been ravaging the United Kingdom', and that 'peaceable subjects are seriously endangered in life and property by an immoderate toleration of the common use of concealed firearms, of which professional criminals and unruly spirits can always most readily avail themselves' (*The Times*, 26 January 1885, page 9, column e). These concerns continued into the early twentieth century. In a notable event in 1912, members of the Territorial Army were relieved of their rifles when deployed at an industrial dispute in South Wales. The incident, which was reported to Parliament by the Labour MP for Merthyr Tydfil, Keir Hardie, occurred when the owners of the colliery at the centre of the dispute convinced the army commander that his troops – some of whom were also colliers – could not be trusted with firearms. What motivated this action was clearly a concern that in certain circumstances the working classes could not be trusted with firearms – it was not the army's loyalty that was in question, having shot dead two protestors at an industrial dispute at nearby Llanelli only the previous year.

The outbreak of the First World War gave the government an opportunity to tighten control of society in the name of national security. This it did in the form of the Defence of the Realm Act 1914, which gave government sweeping powers to control the labour force, to requisition private property, to carry out surveillance of its own citizens and also to control the availability of firearms. It is debatable whether this was a conscious move on the part of government to legislate against the growing pre-war fears about gun use or whether this part of the legislation would have been swept away after the end of hostilities had circumstances allowed. However, circumstances did not allow and the Bolshevik revolution in Russia in 1917 (followed by post-war revolutions in Germany, Austria and Hungary) meant that fears concerning an armed proletariat or demobilized army were heightened. The 'great fear' that swept Britain was probably out of proportion to the actual likelihood of a Marxist seizure of power, but the raising of the red flag over the town hall in Glasgow in 1919 and another armed rebellion in Ireland (this time successful) merely underlined the potential threat. These incidents and the police strike of 1919 gave an added impetus to the movement to limit and control firearms.

The usual fears of a post-war crime wave – a 'normal' response by governments fearful of desensitized former soldiers who are unable to secure work and unable to re-assimilate into society – combined with ever-increasing concerns about 'political crime' to ensure that gun control became a priority. The resulting Firearms Act 1920 effectively ended the unconditional 'right' of protestant British citizens to possess guns, although they could still be (and often were) acquired for specific purposes. In a bizarre incident in 1930, the Chief Constable of Buckinghamshire granted a permit to hold a revolver to Mark Trower of Taplow, but refused him a permit to purchase ammunition. Trower had suffered two attempts to break into his house and was convinced a revolver was necessary for self-defence. The Chief Constable argued (successfully) in court that Trower was not a suitable man to have a loaded revolver and that, anyway, most burglars would tackle a man even with a revolver (*The Times*, 19 November 1930, page 5, column f). Worse was to follow with the General Strike of 1926, which saw troops deployed on British streets alongside police to deal with a potential working-class revolt. But when the British Union of Fascists, led by Sir Oswald Mosley, took to the streets the prospect of open street war between them and British Communists resulted in a flurry of 'preventative' legislation. The Public Order Act of 1936 was specifically targeted at pacifying the streets, but a number of Firearms Acts (1934, 1936 and 1937) came in quick succession, each designed to tighten up gun control. In the context of warring factions on the streets and elsewhere, guidelines were necessary about the 'right' of self-defence and in 1937 the Home Secretary advised the police:

> As a general rule applications to possess firearms for house or personal protection should be discouraged on the grounds that firearms cannot be regarded as a suitable means of protection and may be a source of danger.
>
> (Malcolm 2002: 157)

After the Second World War, when both fascism and communism were less of a public issue, similar concerns were again raised. An amnesty to recall the very firearms that had been issued to repel enemy troops should they land in Britain was the first step. But a new phenomenon emerged that forced the government to look again at deadly force and how it was often inflicted. Youth gangs had attracted media attention, supposedly terrorizing coastal resorts in particular. The Prevention of Crime Act 1953 outlawed offensive weapons, including objects not intended for offensive use but that might be used as such (a walking stick, for example). The implications for the 'right' to defend oneself were enormous and the ensuing debate a ferocious one. The government's adopted line – that preservation of the peace was principally a police responsibility – was voiced by the Attorney General in Parliament:

> It is the duty of society to protect them [private citizens], and they should not have to do that [carry weapons] [. . .] the argument of self-defence is one to which perhaps we should not attach too much weight.
>
> (Prevention of Crime Act 1953)

The legal definition of 'self-defence' remained but the interpretation of it was, by the end of our period, much different to the understanding that existed at the beginning. Moreover, legislation on firearms and other weapons had diminished the likelihood of deadly force in such cases, once again altering the perceived role of the victim in response to crime.

Victims and 'private' initiatives

Prosecution societies and armed self-defence both serve to dent the image of victims as passive actors in the sphere of criminal justice. However, there were also other means by which individuals, businesses, organizations or communities might defend themselves against crime, or ameliorate its effects once it had occurred. Most of these pre-date the police but many survived the arrival of formal policing. Again, these initiatives mostly reflected people's unwillingness to become victims of crime or at least to resist being merely quiescent victims. The employment of night watchmen, for example, was one way that businesses, associations or even private individuals could protect themselves against the criminal. Then there were a number of ways by which police officials could be encouraged to pay extra attention to a particular district or a particular crime. Paying for additional constables was one such method, offering financial incentives directly to police officers in the form of rewards was another. Predictably, these initiatives caused concerns about conflicts of interest or even outright corruption and eventually had to be supervised.

The payment by private individuals or institutions for the use of police officials in relation to a specific crime was an old practice, but one that survived the arrival of the New Police forces. During the latter half of the eighteenth century, it was common for private individuals to offer rewards or engage thief-takers or police officials directly. Ruth Paley has shown that unofficial thief-takers, many of whom had never served as constables or watchmen, on occasion enticed beginners into crime simply in order to betray them for rewards (Hay and Snyder 1989: 301–40). Many thief-takers (who did not usually devote themselves to the task full time) were often associated with the lower classes and would, for example, also work as the landlords of seedy public houses. Nevertheless, the engagement of a known and respected thief-taker was one of the prerogatives of victims in the later eighteenth century. Recourse to a more respected official body was also open to victims during this period. A system of fixed parliamentary rewards were available for police officials who secured capital convictions, but organizations such as the Bow Street Runners, for example, were available to anyone who could afford the appropriate fee (Cox 2010). John Townsend was one of the most famous of the Bow Street Runners. He was regularly engaged to appear at the Bank of England on Dividend Day, and fashionable people would place on their invitations the words 'Mr Townsend will attend', hiring him to protect their guests from pick-pockets (Tobias 1972: 110). The practice continued until well into the nineteenth century. The Earl of Eustace, for example, employed a Bow Street Runner, George Ledbetter, to prevent an illegal prize fight taking place on the extensive lands belonging to his father, the Duke of Grafton, around the village of Hanslope in Buckinghamshire. The fight between an Irishman called Simon Byrne and the Scottish champion, Alexander McKay, did go ahead on 2 June 1830, but on common land at nearby Salcey Green.

Even after the advent of the New Police, the practice of retaining additional constables – serving policemen paid for by private individuals to watch private premises – was widespread among nineteenth-century police forces and enabled those who could afford it another opportunity to protect themselves further. According to Carolyn Steedman (1984: 45–6): 'In the 1860s and 1870s Additional Constables numbered up to 25 per cent of the northern county and borough forces. They were usually appointed from the ranks of the local force (a plum for the long-serving, deserving man).' More often, though, the private payment for constables was a more mundane and localized affair. In nineteenth-century Sheffield, private individuals and corporations who rented the services of police officers included theatre owners, wine merchants and boiler-founders. About an eighth of the force was employed this way (Williams 1998: 188–91). The 'additional constable' was also specifically used to enforce industrial discipline. When in November 1865 R. T. Eadon, a saw and file manufacturer and member of the Watch Committee, learned that his works was under threat of reprisal from the trade society, he went to the Chief Constable 'and made an arrangement with him to send a policeman to stay from the time the wheel ceased to work until the next morning.' The system of additional constables, therefore, just like the system that preceded it, was a resource available only to those who could afford it.

Victims of crime also often offered rewards as a means of recovering stolen goods or for the apprehension of the offender. With the growth of mass printing, and hence provincial newspapers, from the 1750s, crime advertising (either in newspapers or on specially printed handbills) became very common. As the example given below (from the *Leeds Mercury*, 1784) shows, adverts were most typically related to crimes against property (Hay and Snyder 1989: 60).

Stray'd or Convey'd.

*On Monday Night the 16th February instant out of
a Farm Yard in Ledstone Park.*

A Black Teaming Gelding

Rising Six Years old, about 15 Hands high, a White Face, his Near Eye
Blemished, a short Bob Tail, and three White Legs.

Whoever will bring the said Gelding to Mr. Edward Shirtliff, of
Ledstone; Mr. William Simpson, of Newton; or Mr. John Jackson, of
Fairburn, both near Ferrybridge, shall receive ONE GUINEA, and all
reasonable Expences [*sic*].

Advertisements and rewards were placed by victims of crimes individually, but Associations for the Prosecution of Felons might also investigate this avenue of redress. Levels of success obviously varied, but John Styles' research indicates that, where a crime such as horse stealing was concerned, the practice of advertising a reward was 'an effective and successful instrument of detection, in the sense that it established itself as one of the most important means of bringing suspects to trial and conviction' (Hay and Snyder 1989: 86). Towards the end of the nineteenth century, the dissemination of information about thefts and other crimes became increasingly internalized within the official police service. Initially, however, financial incentives were open to everyone including the police provided it was approved by the Watch Committee. In Sheffield the official granting of rewards became increasingly common during the mid-century (Critchley 1967: 94). This enabled the Watch Committee to exercise subtle control over its officers and reward some while excluding others. For example, in 1865 one major subscription reward – divided among the 'deserving' by the Watch Committee – brought the year's total to £176, of which just £13 6s. went to ordinary constables. Rewards were not significant to more than a minority of policemen, but their discretionary nature again allowed the Watch Committee to exercise paternalistic favour and enabled certain victims to bring their case to prominence. The large-scale use of rewards had a potential drawback. It could weaken the police as an institution and induce the men to compete with each other. In Sheffield in 1858 Inspector Linley was censured for failing to submit proper expense claims for an investigation. His defence was that 'had he succeeded in obtaining any portion of the Reward (£50), he should have said nothing about such sums.' The police subcommittee concluded that one consequence of large rewards was that officers concerned 'withheld their information from the Head of the Police, from the Solicitor for the prosecution, and from each other'. Eventually, the privilege to accept rewards was removed from serving police officers – although many got around this by supplying the information through a third party. Nevertheless, it remained as an incentive to members of the public to assist investigations and victims often put up significant sums of money for recovery of goods or simply to raise the profile of their case.

There was also one other extra-judicial method of dealing with the aftermath of a crime available to victims that should perhaps be mentioned: the controversial 'compounding' of a felony – a private arrangement that often involved the restoration of stolen goods in return for not pressing charges, or the payment of some form of compensation. The practice was illegal, but there is very little record of it being prosecuted. 'Compounding' of even the worst crimes happened sometimes and not always was the practice truly extra-judicial. In 1837 it was reported in the *Sheffield Mercury* that a man who had assaulted, 'with intent to rape', 'a little girl' escaped conviction for this felony when the magistrates decided to 'exercise the discretion vested in them by the law'; and they therefore ordered the prisoner to be discharged 'on paying the prosecutrix £4 costs'. Such arrangements were surprisingly common in Victorian England. Magistrates and judges could also make bargains with offenders brought before them. This might not always have been motivated by ideas of redress (as in the case above) but by those of redemption. Most notably, during the First World War men were often quite literally given a 'get out of jail' option if they enlisted in the armed forces. In one case a convicted housebreaker served with distinction on the Western Front and was awarded the Victoria Cross. This is an exceptional case, however, and most instances were far more mundane involving offenders pledging to leave the area. The problem, therefore, was 'decanted' into another parish or police district. Communities had dealt with persistent offenders or even undesirable types by this method for centuries and it was natural that the police would adopt similar tactics. Vagrants were often targeted and 'moved on', but how much further this practice extended is impossible to tell. Nevertheless, it was a cheap and highly effective method of dealing with crime and its perpetrators.

Throughout our period 'compounding' crime was a widespread practice that was hardly ever recorded. Unfortunately, it is not possible to estimate just how widespread was this type of case nor, therefore, to assess its importance. But we ignore it at our peril because it remains one of the most basic means by which a victim might deal with an offender. The rise in insurance during the late nineteenth and twentieth centuries has made it necessary for more people to report crime when in an earlier time they might not have bothered. The rise in *recorded* crime during the early twentieth century that partly resulted from this provides a glimpse of the possible extent to which crimes used to be dealt with by means such as 'compounding'. In fact 1923 had the highest annual 'crime rate' since records were first officially collated in 1876, but to what extent the apparent inflation in reported crime each year reflected not a rise in actual crime but the lessening impact of unreported crime – or compounding – will remain unclear.

For most of our period, whatever other informal actions were pursued or not (for example, employers often took informal action rather than prosecute workplace theft as Chapter 9 discusses) victims always retained the option of taking offenders to court. The formal prosecution process required a victim to accuse the defendant, and present the case in the courtroom. By the mid-nineteenth century, solicitors could aid the wealthier prosecutors, but the whole system relied mainly on individual victims prosecuting individual offenders. The police still prosecuted serious offences, but, by the 1870s, were adding minor offences to their list too. In England and Wales, the police attempted to control public space and curb drunken disorder in the 1880s and 1890s, which led to a rise in public order prosecutions. They were therefore acting in defence of the public peace or defending a notional community. By 1914 the police led 90 per cent of prosecutions, even in cases where there was a real victim of crime – not just a notional victim. Across all categories of offending, private prosecutions by individuals were becoming ever rarer occurrences (see Godfrey 2014). In their place, aided by media and popular ideas about the most deserving of victims, society came to accept the idea of what we might call 'symbolic victims'. The growth of sensationalist newspapers portrayed deserving victims of crime (usually poor women and children who were victims of violent men). For example, both Florence Maybrick (1889) and Beatrice Pace (1928), two women accused and convicted of murder, became 'celebrity victims' (Wood 2008; Frost 2004). The press, in some of these kinds of notorious or infamous cases became vehicles for the accused to garner sympathy, and for the media to manipulate opinion either in favour or against the accused. Nevertheless, for the bulk of business through the courts, by the end of the First World War, it was accepted that the police were the most appropriate agency to prosecute cases on behalf of victims, or on behalf of a notional law-abiding society. Even when victims were invited back into the courtroom in the late twentieth century through the presentation of 'victim impact statements' (where victims of crime could explain in a written statement how the offence had impacted upon them – making them more fearful, suffering anxiety or loss of sleep, grief, feelings of loss, and so on) the statements were delivered through solicitors not by the victims themselves.

Modern parallels

In 2014 The Home Secretary reported that the criminal statistics were no longer reliable enough to qualify as official governmental statistics (as approved by the UK Statistics Authority).

> Police are failing to record an estimated 20 per cent of crimes, according to a damning watchdog report published today in the wake of allegations that officers fiddle the figures. The under-recording by forces in England and Wales is the equivalent of almost three-quarters of a million offences.
>
> (*The Times*, 1 May 2014)

Criminal statistics, which have been annually published since 1857, were designed to give an accurate reflection of the amount of crime in England and Wales. As shown above, the activities and (and indeed the in-activities) of the police had a great impact over the entire period between 1750 and today, first on apprehensions of criminals and later on the prosecution of offenders. Were they also going to play an important role in shaping the criminal statistics? By the start of the First World War, the police had assumed responsibility in areas that had previously been the domain of individual or collective private action, and victims had become much more marginal to the prosecution of offenders in the courtrooms. Where once victims were in control of their own actions, deciding whether to follow a formal route to redress, or an informal route, which, nevertheless, provided them with the 'justice' they desired. However, as the nineteenth and twentieth centuries progressed, victims became much more marginal in deciding whether and on what terms legal action was taken, they disappeared from the courtroom as vital actors and were replaced by a symbolic vision of victimhood that was wheeled out by police prosecutors to evoke sympathy during court cases. The replacement of the victim with the police officer as the prosecutor in court –

and, let us not forget, the agency that decided whether the perceived offender should be stopped, arrested, as well as prosecuted – created a tool for the police to fashion crime rates. For example, police control over prosecutions gave them the power to drive up crime rates for public order offences and motoring, while driving down the number of prosecuted assaults. Over the period of time that victims were removing themselves or being forced out of the courts, prosecutions for violence especially, fell dramatically. In England and Wales, assault prosecutions fell from 74,985 in 1870 to 22,244 in 1930. Arguably, the ability to manage the number of people prosecuted in court either up or down was increased when the Criminal Prosecution Service was introduced in 1985. This was the first time that gate-keepers officially decided whether a reported offences was 'worth' pursuing in the courts (they decided whether a prosecution was in the public interest, whether it was likely to succeed, and possibly whether it was financially viable too).

The crime figures are subject to widespread distrust by most criminologists today, but for decades they were seen as the best tool for determining how much crime was rising and falling annually, where offending was concentrated, and how the police could be employed to drive offending down. The annually published judicial statistics (from 1857) had numerous faults, some of which were recognized in the 1890s by Home Office statisticians, but were still regularly quoted by the media and politicians whenever they suited a particular political argument. For example, the post-war rise in property crimes, drug-related crimes and, in the 1970s to the 1990s, violent crime, were used by politicians to argue either for harsher sentences and more police resources, or, alternatively, for better welfare, employment and educational opportunities for disadvantaged young people (particularly those living in the inner cities). The election of a Labour government under Tony Blair in 1997 coincided with a long-term fall in crime, which seemed to relate to more inclusive social policy and rising standards of living. That, really, is what criminologists had predicted would happen under less abrasive governments than the previous Conservative administrations. These easy assumptions were challenged in 2014 when the Crown Prosecution Service and the police seemed to be responsible for massaging down crime figures to a completely unacceptable extent – something that could have significant consequences for public confidence in the criminal justice system in the early twenty-first century.

Conclusion

At the start of our period, victims had a role in, and a fair amount of power over, the prosecution of offenders. They could choose to prosecute or not, to ask for other kinds of compensation rather than justice before magistrates, or they could take their own retribution through violence. In the nineteenth century, after the introduction of the New Police, victims of crime had an agency that would assist them, could arrest offenders, and might even take them to court on behalf of a victim. By the First World War the police had become the routine prosecutors of crime (both on behalf of victims, and, for public order offences especially, on behalf of society itself). The police had become a policing power but also a prosecuting agency. When the victims disappeared from the courts, the police were left with the power to define whether an offence was worth prosecuting, and therefore whether it would find itself reported, and, ultimately, whether it was recorded in the official crime statistics. It was really no great shock to historians of crime that the crime statistics were declared to be completely unreliable in 2014, only surprise that it took so long for that fact to be publicly acknowledged.

Key questions

This chapter has raised a large number of questions about the role of police (see the previous chapter), and the role of the victim, in the criminal justice system. What role did the victim have in the prosecution of crime in the late eighteenth century and how did this change over time? Doug Hay and Peter King have debated the power of the state to define crime and to criminalize groups in society (Hay 1975, 1983; King 2000). How has the concept of 'self defence' and the individual's right to defend their property changed over two centuries? There is relatively little written specifically on the right of self-defence. See Malcolm (2002), but be aware that this must be used with caution. See Williams (2004) for an instructive review. Malcolm (1996) is also useful, however, and can be used with more confidence. There are arguments as to why, and what happened when, the police took over the prosecution process in Kearon and Godfrey (2007), Godfrey (2008), and Godfrey (2014) and there is a good overview of why women and men were sentenced differently in the Victorian period in Godfrey *et al.* (2005). Why has there been a resurgence of interest in 'victims' of crime after 1950? The criminological literature relating to this question is voluminous. Fry (1951) is a useful early source, Zedner (2002) provides a useful overview, and the work of Miers (1978, 1990), editor of the *International Review of Victimology*, will provide many further references.

Chapter 4

The law and
the courts

Introduction

The period since 1750 has witnessed far-reaching changes in trial procedures and court jurisdictions and in the administration of justice more generally. In the previous chapter, the gradual decline in the role of private citizens in bringing prosecutions to court was considered. In tandem with this, it is possible to trace the rise of the profession of barrister and an adversarial trial process. Significant change also occurred in the way in which trials were run, with increasing ceremony and more meticulous analysis of evidence becoming the norm. However, as with all historical study, the really interesting questions are not so much concerned with establishing *what* happened, but with *why* it occurred. A key question discussed below (and also touched upon in Chapter 9) is – in whose interests was the judicial system run at this time? Did 'the courts' serve everyone, or just a small, wealthy minority?

The economist and philosopher Adam Smith asserted in 1766 that 'laws and government may be considered [. . .] in every case as a combination of the rich to oppress the poor, and preserve to themselves the inequality of goods', and many historians have subsequently agreed (Hay 1989: 344). There is, however, considerable debate about this issue, and recent research has returned a much more nuanced picture of the use of the criminal law. By the latter part of the nineteenth century, in any case, the role and appearance of the courts within English society had changed considerably. The class strife that had marked much of the early part of century was declining and the courts had arguably become much more accessible to previously marginalized groups such as women and the poor. However, even into the twentieth century, the criminal law and the courts were on occasion operating in a manner suggestive of what, for want of a better term, might be called 'class bias'.

This chapter is divided into three sections. The first provides a broad, largely factual overview of some of the main changes that occurred in the administration of justice during since 1750. The ways in which the courts operated altered considerably during these two centuries, and a firm grasp of major milestones and trends is necessary. The second section considers some of the debates historians

have conducted over the exact role of the court system during the period
c.1750–*c*.1850. It considers how accessible the legal infrastructure actually was
at this time and whether it primarily served the interests of a small, privileged
elite. The third part of the chapter will consider the further development of the
criminal justice system during the period from 1850. Did the image of the courts
as primarily the preserve of a privileged elite change significantly during this
period? The concluding part of the chapter explores what happened to the public
performance of justice in the courtroom in the twentieth and twenty-first centuries.

An overview of the court system from 1750

It is obviously impossible in reality to separate 'the law' (the official, codified
rules of society) from the operation of the court system that enforced and
interpreted it. Clearly, if the courts did not enforce certain aspects of the law, such
legislation was effectively null and void. When the law *per se* is considered,
particularly during the first half of our period, 1750–1850, it can appear a rigid,
imposing apparatus of power. However, recent work on the court system appears
to show that implementation of the law was actually much more variable and fluid
than historians had previously assumed.

It is important, first of all, to realize the extent to which the criminal justice
system and the administration of punishment changed in the two centuries
preceding 1950. The professionalized, bureaucratic courts we know today were
a distant dream in the latter half of the eighteenth century. The lawyer (and later
clergyman) Martin Madan complained in 1785 that the practice of hearing cases
in the afternoon following a lengthy lunch break meant that drunkenness was
'frequently apparent' and that 'the heat of the court, joined to the fumes of the
liquor [. . .] laid many an *honest juryman* into a calm and profound sleep' (Emsley
2010a: 201). Similarly, consider the recollection of a 20-year-old student who had
gone to observe the Oxford Assize court *c*.1800. Even the Assizes, which tried
the most serious criminal cases, were not as solemn as one might expect. On
finding that he 'could not get a tolerable place', the student recorded that he:

> jumped from two men's shoulders and leaped upon the heads of several men
> and then scrambled into the prisoner's place where the judge said I must not
> stay, so one of the counsellors desired me not to make a noise, and he would
> let me have his place, which was immediately under the prisoners and
> opposite the judge.
>
> (King 2000: 253)

Clearly, courts in the eighteenth century were not the havens of procedure and
uniformity they were to become by 1950, and trials could be quite turbulent affairs.
However, this informality and seeming disorder may also have been partly due
to the fact that there was no real 'legal profession' as we would now understand
the term. Hence the participation of the general public in the legal process was

arguably more wide-ranging than it is today. As detailed in the previous chapter, more than 80 per cent of criminal prosecutions in the 1790s were brought by the victims themselves (Emsley 2010a: 183). In other words, the state rarely prosecuted offences – if you had been the victim of a theft or a mugging, it was up to you to bring charges (see Chapter 3). Moreover, while solicitors did exist, they were not often employed in criminal cases, and there was generally no professional representation in court. Trials thus consisted primarily of a face-to-face confrontation between plaintiff and accused, mediated by the judge and the jury (who at this stage were still allowed to ask questions) and could be very short. Trials themselves, particularly those involving magistrates sitting in **petty sessions**, could take place in a number of venues, from the parlour of the county gentry to a private room off the local pub. Thus, as Peter King notes, far from reflecting solely the majesty of the law, 'many assize proceedings may perhaps more fruitfully be seen as "participatory theatre"', a subject we return to in the concluding part of this chapter (King 2000: 255). By the 1950s, of course, following a long period of bureaucratization and rationalization over the course of the nineteenth century, most of this had changed. The judiciary was fully professional (although magistrates were still voluntary), trials took place in purpose-built premises and were conducted by specialist personnel, the state customarily prosecuted criminal offences and legal assistance was available to all under the Legal Aid and Legal Advice Act of 1949, although access to legal aid has now been severely curtailed by the introduction of the Legal Aid, Sentencing and Punishment of Offenders Act of 2012.

Given these broad changes, it might be tempting to read the history of the courts as a gradual change from a chaotic and biased system to the more orderly, representative arrangement we know today. However, it is important to avoid simplistic notions of 'progress' when studying history, and many of the developments in the criminal justice system alluded to above were hotly contested at the time, as can be seen if we consider the operation of the courts in more detail.

Obviously, the further back in time one peers, the more basic the 'official' structures of justice. Rural medieval and early-modern communities had a number of ways of resolving disputes without recourse to law and the courts. Community sanctions (such as **charivari**, for example) could be applied, or mediation by a local person of authority (such as a member of the clergy or a representative from the nobility) could be sought. However, the gradual expansion of the state during the sixteenth and seventeenth centuries meant that the 'rule of law' was becoming increasingly dominant within English society. This was, however, by no means a uniform system. Indeed, a variety of courts were in still in existence in England during the mid-eighteenth century. Ecclesiastical courts, which had once been extremely powerful, still retained vestiges of authority. They could theoretically try certain offences against morality and retained their authority over divorce until the mid-nineteenth century. Military courts were influential, too, particularly during times of war when they exercised virtually sole jurisdiction over large groups of enlisted men. Aside from these, however, the main courts throughout the period in question were the magistrates' courts, the quarter sessions and the **assize courts**. In magistrates' courts, one magistrate sitting in 'petty sessions' decided cases alone and these usually handled the bulk of minor crime. The quarter sessions and assizes tried more serious offences where a jury was present.

Over the course of the eighteenth century, the number of offences that could be heard 'summarily' (by one magistrate sitting alone in 'petty sessions') had increased significantly to embrace the majority of thefts and also minor crimes such as poaching. As noted already, most prosecutions, both criminal and civil, were privately brought. The state had very little role in bringing cases to court, except in a few limited instances, like that of treason. In practice, these two developments meant that, first, the magistrates' courts were the busiest element of the criminal justice system and that, second, the plaintiff bringing the case to court could often decide him/herself whether to opt for a summary trial (which was likely to be quite quick) or press for a trial by jury (where the sentences could be stiffer but which would inevitably take much longer; see Gray 2009). In addition, as Peter King (2000: 8) has noted, it also meant that the boundaries between criminal and civil cases were 'extremely blurred', as legislation usually allowed plaintiffs to opt for either.

More serious trials took place in the higher courts – the quarter sessions and the assizes. Outside of London, quarter sessions only took place four times a year (hence the name) and assizes usually only twice. Bail was rarely granted in such cases and hence the accused was often in gaol for several months *prior* to the trial itself (in the nineteenth-century, a third of all prisoners were on remand, awaiting either their trial or sentence). There is an interesting modern parallel here, with 60 per cent of the defendants remanded into custody awaiting trial never actually receiving a prison sentence in the end. Magistrates have recently (under the 2012 LASPO Act) been directed to only remand those offenders who have a realistic prospect of custody when their case is concluded.

Further, the significant delays between the apprehension of the accused and the administration of justice also added to the costs of justice for the victim/ plaintiff. After bringing a case, the plaintiff would have to travel to attend the court (which was usually held in the county town) and pay to stay for several days while waiting for his case to reach the top of the list (no timetable was drawn up). Those prosecuting might also have to pay the expenses of any witnesses they wished to appear. A consultant before the 1819 Select Committee on Criminal Laws testified that numerous cases seemed to be going unprosecuted due to 'the considerable sacrifice of time, the additional cost, nay the *heavy* load of expense, the tiresomeness of attendance, and keeping witnesses together' (Emsley 2010a: 192). Such concerns eventually resulted in Robert Peel's 1826 Criminal Justice Act, which, among other things, provided for the paying of expenses for some witnesses as well as prosecutors.

Some reformers also concluded in the wake of the 1826 Criminal Justice Act that a system of public prosecutions, as was in fact in operation in Scotland and parts of continental Europe at the time, would be preferable to this private system.

However, this took a long time to introduce. Successive bills failed in the House of Commons in the 1830s, the 1850s and the 1870s, partly due to vested interest on the part of solicitors, partly due to fears of cost and partly because of concerns over the erosion of individual liberties. While a director of public prosecutions was appointed in 1879, this post was mostly advisory for almost 30 years. However, as Emsley notes, and as we discuss in Chapter 3, until recently, 'the increasing role of the police as prosecutors from the middle of the nineteenth century has been largely ignored by historians' (Emsley 2010a: 195). This is despite the considerable impact that the introduction of police prosecutors had on crime (particularly violent crime) statistics. There is a noticeable decline in prosecutions whenever the police – rather than individuals with summonses – were the route to trial.

So, in the mid- to late nineteenth century, most defendants faced a police prosecutor and a single magistrate (or as many who bothered to turn up that day) in provincial police courts. In London, the situation was slightly different. There stipendiary magistrates (professional lawyers who were paid a salary), again sitting in so-called 'police courts', dealt with the large number of petty cases heard in the capital. By 1850 these courts were dealing with over 100,000 cases a year in London alone. As will be discussed in the third section below, they also acted as advice centres and places where the neighbourhood disputes of the poor could be settled swiftly and cheaply (Davis 1984).

The development of the legal system over the course of the nineteenth century is thus a complex one, but by the First World War the courts as we know them today were largely in operation. Of course, there were changes to the system even in the twentieth century, particularly in relation to magistrates' courts. An Act of 1908, for example, known as the 'children's charter', established specialized juvenile courts. Following the Children and Young Persons Act of 1933 magistrates with special qualifications were henceforth selected for this work. The Sex Disqualification (Removal) Act of 1919 ensured that women were able to become magistrates for the first time. The quarter sessions had lost their administrative function in 1888, when the passing of the Local Government Act empowered county councils to take charge of matters such as the upkeep of the roads. However, both the assizes and quarter sessions continued in roughly the same form until 1971, when the Courts Act replaced them with Crown Courts run by central government. We now also have the Supreme Court of the United Kingdom (that began work in 2009) as the court of last resort – established to decide appeals arising from the major courts, and to decide upon general issues of law that are in dispute.

Clearly then, radical changes took place in both the administration of justice and the dispensation of punishment in the period 1750–1950. On the one hand, there was a trend towards increasing uniformity and professionalization. Yet, on the other, there was no real state prosecution or profession of 'barrister' until relatively late in the nineteenth century (Rock 2004). While the Prisoner's Counsel Act of 1836 had recognized the right of a defendant in a felony case to legal representation (and also allowed defence counsel to address the jury for the first time), many lawyers in fact doubted its efficacy in the criminal courts and the public remained sceptical until quite late in the century. Moreover, despite the retrospective pride often taken in the English 'trial by jury' system, the Jervis Acts of 1848 had massively expanded the jurisdiction of the summary courts, and meant that magistrates sitting alone were dealing with twenty times the number of cases dealt with by all the other criminal courts combined (Emsley 2010a). In fact, even trials in the Old Bailey, the foremost criminal court, could be hasty affairs. In 1833 it was calculated that the average trial took under nine minutes, with a trial of several hours being noteworthy (Beattie 1986: 376).

Thus, as with the New Police discussed in Chapter 2, it is too simplistic to view the changes that took place over this period as merely 'progress' or 'professionalization'. Certainly, as Emsley asserts, 'the relaxed, relatively informal magistrates' tribunals of the eighteenth century had little place in the increasingly urbanized England of the nineteenth century with its emphasis on decorum and bureaucratic formality', but change was slow and often contradictory, and the reasons driving it were far from simple (Emsley 2010a: 211). Moreover, as already noted, it is not enough for the historian simply to *narrate* these developments, and it is too simplistic to attribute them merely to 'progress'. Why did these changes occur? What significance did they hold for those involved in reform? Such 'historiographical' questions will be the subject of the chapters that follow.

Historians, law and the courts between 1750 and 1850

There has been considerable debate among historians concerning the evolution of the criminal law and its enforcement in the courts during the period 1750–1850. At a first glance, much legislation passed in the late eighteenth and early nineteenth century appears overly concentrated on property crime and less concerned about violent crime. The so-called '**Bloody Code**' (a series of over 200 statutes via which the death penalty could be applied to relatively minor theft offences) has often been cited as evidence that the criminal law was primarily a mechanism via which class power was maintained. In a fairly typical instance from 1796, for example, a 15-year-old boy from a poor family was sentenced to death for pickpocketing a leather notebook worth two shillings. His situation was characteristic of many thousands of other petty pilferers and thieves who faced capital punishments. By contrast to this ferocious response to a case of petty theft, John Beattie (and many others) have noted that 'there was clearly a high tolerance of violent behaviour in eighteenth-century society' (Beattie 1986: 75). What appear to us as quite shocking instances of violence were often virtually ignored by legislators and the courts. The Old Bailey sessions papers detail quite a number of instances where backstreet fights (often with hundreds of spectators) ended in the death of one participant. In one such case from 1803, the guilty defendant was briefly imprisoned and fined just six shillings.

However, Emsley (2010a) has argued that in fact the 'Bloody Code' of the late-eighteenth century has been somewhat misread by some historians of crime. While it was undoubtedly a harsh and noteworthy set of statutes (over 200 by 1820), there were many overlapping areas covered by separate laws. 'Destroying Westminster Bridge' was one statute, and 'Destroying Fulham Bridge' (to all intents and purposes the same offence) was another. There were 20 separate statutes, for example, protecting trees, hollies, thorns and other types of plants from theft. Thus the sheer number of capital statutes, which might initially appear to indicate an extreme disciplinary code, has to be approached with caution. Moreover, as Emsley notes, there were 'real and heated' debates in Parliament over many aspects of the Bloody Code, and it is certainly not the case that it was an unmitigated attempt to discipline the poorer classes. On occasion, legislation introduced to protect the property of the rich had a hard time passing through the House of Commons (Emsley 2010a: 15). Gatrell, moreover, claims that most of those hanged were convicted under 'straightforward' statutes, which had been capital for centuries and that pardons were the end result in over 90 per cent of cases by 1820 (1994: 7).

The Bloody Code was gradually dismantled from around 1820 onwards. Wiener (1990) has argued persuasively that legal history must be more broadly located within its cultural context, and attributed the dismantling of the Bloody Code to changing Victorian perceptions of offenders, which dictated a rationalization of the criminal law. This idea is covered in greater depth in Chapter 7 but, essentially, Wiener argues that crime came to be seen in the early Victorian period not as an expression of poverty or social circumstances but as the result of 'a fundamental character defect', one which stemmed from 'a refusal or an inability to deny wayward impulses or to make proper calculations of long-run self-interest' (1990: 46). In other words, criminals were simply those who could not control their primitive urges. Thus Victorian reformers aimed to replace the unsystematic and flexible 'Bloody Code' with 'a more defined and impersonal, and thus more predictable, criminal law'. As Wiener notes, the twin aims of 'deterrence and popular character building' dictated that 'the sanctions of the criminal law should be clear, consistent and certain' (Wiener 1990: 61).

However, as Wiener has also noted elsewhere, research among historians has tended to concentrate far more on the criminal law's administration than on changes in the law itself (1990). Most debates about the law during this period have addressed not simply the evolution of statutes and laws *per se*, but the wider context of their administration, focusing on the judges, juries and courts that applied the law. A great deal of attention has been applied to the trial process, particular during the period 1750–1820. More specifically, two models have been debated – a 'consensus' model of the law as a system whereby the accepted norms of a society are expressed and enforced, and a 'conflict' model in which the law is viewed as, essentially, an apparatus that operates in the interests of and for the maintenance of a dominant class. Consensus models of the law were often implicit within the work of early historians of crime and the law, such as Sir Leon Radzinowicz, author of the five-volume *A History of the English Criminal Law and Its Administration from 1750* (begun in 1948). The unproblematic use of the theme of 'progress' meant that the administration of justice was dealt with 'as a self-contained and self-explicable sphere whose history can be best understood by working back from later twentieth-century professional perspectives' (Wiener 1987: 85). Conflict models of the law, often initially associated with the work of Marxist historians, viewed the law as primarily constructed to oppress the poor and the working class, and as a mechanism by which the sanctity of the private property of the rich was ensured. More recent research has sought to mediate these two stark positions, and a more nuanced picture of the use of the courts has emerged. These debates are perhaps best illustrated by reference to some key texts.

As noted, early works of criminal justice history such as Radzinowicz's *History of the English Criminal Law* took a somewhat one-dimensional approach to the subject. To understand this, it is important to understand the context in which books such as this were written. In 1948, when the first volume of Radzinowicz's series appeared, it was practically the first book ever published in the field of British criminal justice history. It appeared at a time when pride in British institutions was at a peak. After all, British democracy in the aftermath of the Second World War stood in stark contrast to the revolutions and dictatorships in evidence throughout much of Europe. As Wiener notes:

> At such a moment, the outlines of the nation's criminal justice history seemed quite clear: a gradual and more or less continuous advance out of a 'medieval' world of disorder and cruelty to the present era, in which serious crime had been largely conquered and criminal justice [had been] made both humane and efficient.
>
> (Wiener 1987: 94)

Such complacent approaches to the history of crime and the law remained popular until the early 1970s, when they began to be challenged by a new generation of Marxist historians (Iggers 1997: 78–94). In relation to the courts, Douglas Hay's now well-known essay 'Property, authority and the criminal law' appeared in an edited collection entitled *Albion's Fatal Tree* (1975). This was a bold statement of the working of the courts and the law during the latter half of the eighteenth century, based on a 'conflict' model. Hay argued that the criminal law of the time was constructed by elite groups to serve their own interests and that, as such, it was primarily concerned with protecting the property of the rich. The harsh use of the gallows combined with *discretion* (the possibility of mercy and a reprieve) gave magistrates and judges (all of whom were drawn from the ruling classes) a tool by which to inspire awe and deference in an age before a regular police force. Hay quoted men like the Oxford Professor of Law William Blackstone, who claimed in 1793 that 'the execution of a needy decrepit assassin is a poor satisfaction for the murder of a nobleman in the bloom of his youth, and full enjoyment of his friends, his honours, and his fortune' (Hay 1975: 19). Clearly, argued Hay, all men were *not* equal before the law in this age.

He then further focused on three particular aspects of the work of the courts – the *majesty* of the law, the notion of *justice* and the prerogative of *mercy*. The ceremonial majesty of the law, typified by the solemn wearing of a black cap when the death sentence was pronounced or the pure white gloves worn after a 'maiden assizes' (one in which no death sentences had been passed), inspired deference and awe in the lower classes. Combined with this, the criminal law seemed to offer justice. It appeared impartial, an appearance sustained by the occasional execution of a minor member of the nobility. In fact, the weight of the law pressed down harder on the poor than on any other group, but this seeming impartiality helped to secure its acceptance. Finally, argued Hay, the prerogative of *mercy* on the part of those bringing the prosecution (by only pressing minor charges, or by dropping the charges altogether) meant that, 'in short, it was in the hands of the gentlemen who went to law to evoke gratitude as well as fear in the maintenance of deference' (1975: 41). Thus, as E. P. Thompson noted in developing Hay's thesis, while it was not the case that the ruling classes could simply do as they pleased (they too were bound by the law that they had constructed to an extent), certainly 'the law did mediate existent class relations to the advantage of the rulers' (Thompson 1975: 264).

However, Langbein (1983) critiqued Hay's essay from a conservative per- spective. He argued that, in fact, while many of the 'accused' appearing in court were drawn from the lower classes, most of the 'victims' pressing charges were not that much better off. Anyone studying the Old Bailey sources, Langbein claimed, 'will conclude that the victims seldom come from the propertied élite' (1983: 101). Moreover, in numerous instances, sentences of death were commuted or lowered not by the judge but by the jury, which was often drawn from men of the more 'middling sort'. Far from the elite bulwark that Hay claimed them to be, Langbein quotes Martin Madan, who worried in 1785 that petty jurors at assizes were usually 'low and ignorant country people' (Langbein 1983: 107). Thus, overall, Langbein maintained that 'the whole of the criminal justice system, especially the prosecutorial system, was principally designed to protect the people, overwhelmingly non-elite, who suffered from crime' (1983: 105). Clearly, this was a much more 'consensual' view of the law than that constructed by Hay.

John Beattie's *Crime and the Courts* contributed significantly to moving this complex debate forward. He looked at assizes and quarter sessions cases (as opposed to very big state trials or magistrates' petty sessions), concentrating on those of Surrey and Sussex. Beattie agreed with Hay that the preponderance of offences against property in the courts was striking, and noted that violence that did not cause death was rarely the subject of successful prosecution. However, he went on to argue convincingly that the criminal law was by no means simply a tool fashioned to maintain the power of the propertied classes. Gentlemen, in fact, were the smallest group of prosecutors in his sample, while 14–18 per cent of prosecutions were initiated by labourers or servants. The criminal law was used by all classes but did not, of course, treat all with equality.

These debates continued, in one form or another, for some time. It is important to realize, as Peter King noted:

> The development of an increasingly subtle and detailed picture of how the administration of the criminal justice system worked has not [. . .] always led to greater agreement among historians about who controlled the law [. . .] or about the extent to which the law [. . .] underpinned and legitimized the rule of the eighteenth-century elite.
>
> (King 2000: 3)

That said, King does provide a near definitive (or at least highly convincing) statement on the matter. He adopted a pluralistic view of the criminal law of the period, proposing neither a wholly consensual or an entirely conflict driven model, and questioning the very idea that 'the law' can be considered as a unified concept. Rather, he argued, 'the law held different meanings for different people and its pluralistic nature meant that each individual or social group might have a range of often contradictory experiences of legal institutions' (King 2000: 3).

More specifically, King asserted initially that the law *was* applied unequally within late eighteenth-century society. Wealthy individuals who purloined money or property (either by weights and measures fraud or tax evasion) were rarely branded as criminals, but rather usually faced a *civil* case. By contrast, those among the poorer classes accused of theft were routinely dealt with via the *criminal* law, with all the stigma this held. However, it is important, he argued, to move beyond this assumption of inequality to a more nuanced picture. Historical evidence shows that a substantial number of labourers brought prosecutions to the courts, thus using the law for their own protection. Only 5–10 per cent of prosecutions involved the gentry or professional classes as victims/plaintiffs (King 2000: 3). Moreover, members of the lower classes bringing cases to court often used *discretion* themselves, by initiating a prosecution but not actually turning up for the trial. The case was then dismissed, but they had the satisfaction of knowing that the accused had suffered a lengthy period of pre-trial imprisonment. Thus as King argued, 'the decisions that pulled the levers of fear and mercy were not taken by propertied men alone' (2000: 358). The concept of discretion thus tempers straightforward class views of the operation of the criminal justice system during the period 1750–1850.

Of course, this debate is just one among many you may encounter in studying the courts and the development of the criminal justice system. Most discussions, however, start from the assumption that the law favoured some groups in society more than others, and then argue about the precise extent of this bias and the timing of its erosion. Most historians would probably agree that by 1850 the application of the law was more consensual than it was in 1750. However, did that continue in the following century?

Historians, law and the courts since 1850

The first half of the nineteenth century had witnessed a huge increase in the use of the courts. Gatrell and Hadden claim that while around 4,500 men and women had been prosecuted in assizes and quarter sessions in 1805, this figure had risen to over 30,000 by 1842 (1972: 293–4). The expansion of the jurisdiction of the summary courts via statutes such as the Criminal Justice Act of 1855 meant that the lower courts (arguably more accessible to the ordinary member of the public) also witnessed a great rise in business. By 1857, justices sitting in petty sessions had to cope with over twenty times the total number of cases dealt with by all other courts combined (Emsley 2005a: 210). Partly, this development can be seen as a reflection of the increased expansion of the state into everyday life throughout English society. As the jurist J. F. Stephen noted in 1863, 'the administration of criminal justice is the commonest, the most striking, and the most interesting shape, in which the sovereign power of the state manifests itself to the great bulk of its subjects' (Gatrell 1990: 239). Thus again the question arises – in whose interests did this growing use of the courts operate? The extent to which different groups within society were able to access and use the legal system has already been debated in the second section above. Current thinking emphasizes the way in which the law and the courts, while expressive of an elite perspective, were also used artfully by a broad cross-section of individuals to obtain what they felt to be 'justice'. This mixture of partiality and even-handedness is also in evidence later in the century in, for example, London's police courts. The rapid growth of London at the end of the eighteenth century had led to calls for stipendiary (salaried) magistrates. In 1792 a system of paid magistrates for London was set up. Initially, these officials sat in police offices and even had certain investigative powers. The posts were further reformed in the 1820s and 1830s, and after 1839 lost their police functions and became attached to the newly established Metropolitan Police Courts (Davis 1984, 1989a). By mid-century there were 13 such courts with 26 magistrates dispensing rapid justice on all manner of small misdemeanours. By 1855 the courts were handling around 100,000 cases per annum (Davis 1984: 312). If an individual was arrested on a minor matter (including offences such as being drunk and disorderly, petty theft and **vagrancy**), they were likely to be held in the cells overnight and to appear before the police court magistrate the following morning. The police courts handled a vast range of business and, as Davis notes, 'at mid-century, the stipendiary magistrate probably wielded more unsupervised power then any other paid functionary of the legal system' (1984: 311). Police court magistrates were highly paid (deliberately so, to avoid attracting merely rejects from the bar) and were often both socially and professionally prominent. How then did they deal with those who came before them, who were overwhelmingly (but not entirely) drawn from the working class?

According to Davis and others, stipendiary magistrates often went beyond a strict enforcement of the law. They also distributed financial relief to destitute supplicants, used their 'enormous' discretion to arbitrate disputes between the poor and 'offered a wide range of individual advice to their predominantly working-class clientele' (1984: 309). In the words of a witness to the 1837 Select Committee on Metropolitan Police Offices the police courts came to be seen as 'a poor man's system of justice'. The police and the propertied classes certainly used the police courts to prosecute members of the lower classes, but they were not solely an apparatus of social discipline. A fifth of all larceny charges heard by the police courts were brought by working-class prosecutors. Although most assault charges were presented by the police, it was also relatively common for residents of working-class neighbourhoods to bring assault charges, or for women to seek redress for violence perpetrated on them by their husbands. Overall, the police courts have been represented by historians as an arena in which family and neighbourhood disputes could be arbitrated and free legal advice received.

However, while many justices were no doubt sympathetic towards their clientele, part of the rationale behind the police courts (as Davis makes clear) was to win working-class support for the law. The Metropolitan Police were, during the latter part of the century, still immensely unpopular with the working class. An explicit motivation behind the setting up of the police courts was 'not merely to suppress law breaking but also to win lower-class acceptance of the law and, thus, implicitly of the social order' (Davis 1984: 315). Certain types of cases, particularly those that might be seen as challenging to the existing social order (such as complaints of police brutality and mistreatment while in custody), generally received an unsympathetic hearing. Thus, as during the earlier period under discussion in the second section above, it is clear that the law and the courts were not entirely consensual, nor yet entirely a mechanism of social control, but rather an admixture of both fairness and support for the existing social order.

The role of the criminal justice system in supporting the existing status quo (both social and political) is quite evident during the period 1850–1950, albeit not perhaps as clearly as a century before, and is worth exploring in rather more detail. Arguably, there was a marked decline in 'class strife' by the end of the nineteenth century and recorded crime rates dropped year on year between 1850 and 1900. This is not to say that there were not moments of real public concern over the threat of disorder. During the mid-1880s, for example, following a severe economic depression, unemployed workers had taken to sleeping in large numbers in Trafalgar Square. A series of mass demonstrations were clumsily handled by the police, who vastly underestimated the manpower required for the job, and prolonged rioting broke out. A thick fog descended on London and for several days looting and disorder swept the West End (Stedman Jones 1971). However, in general, historians believe that the bulk of the working class was gradually co-opted into mainstream society during the latter half of the nineteenth century. By the end of the period, only the '**residuum**' (a derogatory term for the poorest, roughest and most unproductive element of the working class) and incorrigible habitual offenders (Godfrey *et al.* 2007, 2010; and Chapter 9) were feared.

However, these social changes do not mean that the 'class' bias in the use of the law and the courts necessarily disappeared. The growth of general consent to the rule of law and the gradual acceptance of the role of the police and the courts by the majority of the population did not end the suppression of certain forms of public dissent. It is possible to argue that the law and the courts were, until well into the twentieth century, still a vehicle for the suppression of dissatisfaction with the status quo, particularly on the part of the working class and the political left (which were often virtually synonymous). As Gatrell notes:

> The construction of consent through more or less concealed forms of coercion remained an option with which the liberal state could no more dispense than could the totalitarian. For it was an inevitable corollary of consent-building that *dissent* should come to be invested in the liberal state with new, increasing and peculiar significance.
>
> (Gatrell 1990: 265)

The judiciary, and magistrates in particular, had a role in the suppression of political unrest and the maintenance of public order throughout the nineteenth century. In the first half of the century, especially before the establishment of the New Police, magistrates and troops combined to suppress disorder. If a disturbance (or potential disturbance) was brought to the attention of a magistrate, it was generally his responsibility to decide how to handle the matter. Under common law a 'riot' (sometimes involving only two or three people) was a minor matter, punishable only by prison or a fine. In such circumstances the magistrate might just ask the local sheriff or constable to deal with the situation. However, if a more serious disturbance seemed to be on the horizon, the magistrate could 'read the Riot Act' (or rather, a small section of it) – as detailed below:

> Our Sovereign Lord the King chargeth and commandeth all Persons, being assembled, immediately to disperse themselves, and peaceably to depart to their Habitations, or to their lawful Business, upon the Pains contained in the Act made in the first year of King *George*, for preventing Tumults and riotous Assemblies – God Save the King.
>
> (Proclamation of the Riot Act 1715)

Once the Riot Act had been read out at the scene in a loud voice, the offence of 'riot' became a felony, punishable by death. Thus any individuals who failed to leave the area within an hour could be subdued by force (as opposed to the 'reasonable means' which applied to the offence as a misdemeanour). In the case of a major disturbance, the magistrate was likely either to seek assistance from troops or to enrol special constables (or 'specials') – local men of property sworn in for a limited period to help keep the peace.

Once the New Police had been established, magistrates often requested their assistance rather than resort to the use of troops or special constables. Obviously, between 1829 and about 1839, the Metropolitan Police were the sole New Police force. As such, their assistance was often requested by local magistrates who feared unrest. Between 1830 and 1838 a total of 2,246 officers from London were sent to the provinces to quell rioting (Vogler 1991: 97). These forays were generally successful. Aided by the new inventions of the telegraph and (particularly) the railway, officers were now able to move around the country swiftly in response to the threat of disturbance, often arriving in hours rather than days. The fact that London was the hub of the new rail network bolstered this process. In some cases police squads sent to the provinces worked alongside the military and cooperated successfully with them.

During the early part of the twentieth century, the responsibility of magistrates to quell public dissent was gradually shifted to Chief Constables and to central government. Vogler (1991) argues that the direct intervention by the Home Secretary (Winston Churchill) at the Tonypandy strike disturbances in 1910 was crucial in this regard. However, the judiciary remained a core element in the suppression of political and labour unrest until well into the twentieth century. Fears over the rising influence of the political left and the possibilities for public disorder that might ensue led to the passing of several statutes (including the Emergency Powers Act of 1920 and the Public Order Act of 1936), which were enforced via the courts. The case of *Duncan* v. *Jones*, for example (actually just prior to the passing of the Public Order Act) concerned the power of the police to stop meetings even where no obstruction or disorder was apparent. The police case was upheld by the High Court. As Barbara Weinberger notes, 'in other words, the police were granted the right to ban any political meeting in the street, where previously they had only been able to intervene if an immediate breach of the peace was threatened' (Weinberger 1995: 174). Thus it is possible to argue that one of the principal activities of magistrates, the courts and the law throughout this period was the maintenance of the status quo in the face of demands for the reordering of society from below.

Once again, then, it is apparent that the law and the courts (although they had changed considerably from the 1750s) were not necessarily the wholly consensual system we might like to imagine. Changes in the role of women within society, and in relation to the law and the courts in particular, serve to underline this further. Perceptions of women as criminals and the role of women as offenders are discussed later in this book. However, what about the involvement of women in the criminal justice system from the other side, as prosecutors, witnesses – even as magistrates and judges? To what extent did the courts consider and satisfy the needs of women? A brief consideration of the issue of domestic violence can perhaps illustrate the now familiar picture of use of the courts by a group within society, but only within a set of constraints not always particularly favourable to or understanding of the needs of that group.

During the seventeenth and eighteenth centuries, the physical chastisement of women by their husbands was generally accepted by the courts. However, by the mid-nineteenth century, this was becoming less and less publicly acceptable. By the start of the twentieth century, notions of 'reasonable chastisement' had all but disappeared. This changing tolerance of violence against women was mirrored by legislative changes. The Matrimonial Causes Act of 1878 gave magistrates the power to order separations and insist that husbands paid a weekly sum for the maintenance of their wife and children. The Summary Jurisdiction (Married Women) Act of 1895 allowed women to make the decision to separate from their husbands themselves. As Shani D'Cruze notes, 'this legislation meant that the magistrates' courts became a more frequent resort of women subject to violence by their husbands, and magistrates took on the role of both "marriage menders", and overseers of separations' (D'Cruze 1998: 11). Given this, it is tempting to see here gradual 'progress' and the evolution of a more civilized vision of society. However, on closer inspection the picture is, perhaps not unexpectedly, more complex than that.

On the one hand, it is undeniable that the courts increasingly sought to protect women from violence, and to stiffen the sentences given to those who transgressed. Martin Wiener has dissected the case of George Hall, tried in 1864 for shooting his new bride Sarah (Wiener 1999b). After courting for three and a half years George married Sarah (with whom he had sung for years in a church choir) on Christmas Day 1863. Shortly afterwards, Sarah left the marital home. Her parents brought her back and she stayed a few more weeks before leaving again – almost certainly because of her infatuation with a young Irishman with whom she had been sleeping all along. George purchased a set of pistols, called on Sarah and took her for a walk, shot her in the head and turned himself in. The fact that Hall was convicted of murder despite 'enormous popular sympathy' does indicate the fact that 'judges and other officials were attempting to place violence against wives – regardless of provocation, and despite the lowliness of social position of the perpetrator and victim – beyond the pale of acceptability' (Wiener 1990: 186). However, the scale of the appeals for clemency attached to Hall's case (and his eventual reprieve) perhaps demonstrate that there was still a discrepancy between juries and the public who often advocated leniency, and the judges and officials determined to make a stand on this issue.

Moreover, even in the final quarter of the nineteenth century, if a wife was seen to have 'aggravated' the situation, via nagging, taunts, insults or wilful behaviour, then the verdict of the law could still appear harsh. D'Cruze notes that 'magistrates used the courts to discipline the perceived "rough" elements, particularly among working-class men given to drunkenness and violence. Women whose sexuality was seen to be lax could also receive the opprobrium of the court' (1998: 4). Adverse assumptions about the evidence of women in such cases remained common among the judiciary. A handbook on sentencing published by Edward Cox in 1877 argued that:

> In the vast majority of these cases the suffering angel of the sensation 'leader' [newspaper article] is found to be rather an angel of the fallen class, who has made her husband's home an earthly hell, who spends his earning in drink, pawns his furniture, starves her children, provides for him no meals, lashes

him with her tongue when sober and with her fists when drunk, and if he tries to restrain her fits of passion, resists with a fierceness and a strength for which he is no match.

(Tomes 1978: 339)

Thus, while women gradually (and increasingly) grew to use the law and the courts to protect themselves from violence and to seek redress, even at the start of the twentieth century the protection afforded by the courts only really reflected changing conceptions of what *men* thought was acceptable. It is an obvious point, but one worth making, that women were not actually involved in the courts as representatives of the state until very late in the period. Judicial appointments were only opened to women in 1919 (coincident with granting of the franchise). The first female magistrates were appointed in 1919 and the first female barrister in 1922. However, it was not until 1945 that the first female judge (Sybil Campbell) was appointed. Obviously there is a limit to how 'consensual' a system that excluded approximately half of the population from direct participation could ever have been.

Modern parallels

In 2014 the trial of former Paralympic champion athlete Oscar Pistorius was broadcast in his home country of South Africa.

The high court judge, Dunstan Mlambo, granted permission to South African media groups to install the cameras in 'unobtrusive' locations [. . .] He said opening arguments by the prosecution and the defence could be shown live, along with the presiding judge's decision and the sentencing should Pistorius be convicted.

(*The Guardian*, 25 February 2014)

The cameras are still banned from courts in England and Wales, but there is ever-greater demand for justice to 'be seen to be done' (with, for example, police constables being fitted with cameras in order to reveal how they go about their daily interactions with the public). This chapter has discussed the longer history of access to justice, questioned whether the courts were delivering partial justice, or justice for everyone in society, and this section will now examine how the courts have tried to both demonstrate their impartiality and also reinforce the authority of the law.

While changing significantly in appearance and usage over the period 1750–1950, the law and the courts can essentially be viewed as arenas where competing social demands are exercised. As Wiener has argued:

'Courts' have been regarded as a single thing – the 'courts' did this or that. Yet, before they produced verdicts and rulings, courts were settings for events – arenas where competing narratives were in play, sites of contestation where values and beliefs were not only declared but shaped.

(Wiener 1990: 469–70)

They were also heavily contested. The magistrates and judges expressed the views of the propertied classes not only through the severity of the sentences handed down, but also, much more directly, in speeches and courtroom declarations.

The real audience for the moral messages were the, sometimes tens, sometimes hundreds, of people sitting in the public galleries (the Liverpool newspaper *The Porcupine* talked of hundreds of people assembling every morning, and spending the greater part of the day there, 14 November 1868, p.315). Those galleries were often filled to capacity, particularly if the trial involved local 'celebrities', or might involve entertaining accounts of neighbourhood disturbances. As D'Cruze (1998) has shown, the reputation of (especially female) witnesses could be paraded through the courts, and successively renegotiated with the evidence of each witness. An appearance in court was a chance to refute allegations and secure freedom; protect one's reputation and prevent damaging rumours from gaining common currency; or to attack rivals, former lovers, or competitors of one kind or another.

> The outcome of these public evaluations could result in ostracism from social contacts, friends or acquaintances; and restrictions of opportunity on employability, or marriage prospects (particularly if the case involved sexual promiscuity). For, although the courts tended to be an insular and almost self-contained forum, the presence of the public meant that information about the case (and therefore the people involved in it) could leak through to the wider community. There were, therefore, considerable risks involved for those caught up in litigation. However, the courtroom also provided an opportunity to defend one's honour, and to assert a counter dialogue in which to present a more favourable image of oneself to the world. In this way the communicative power of the court was appropriated by the witnesses themselves, and the magistrates became more marginal to the process. For example, many women came to court to allege brutality by their husbands, in the course of which the drunken and loutish spouse would be shown to have failed in his duties as a husband, perhaps even as a man.
>
> (Godfrey 2003c: 168–9)

However, as the many newspaper court reports and the memoirs of justices and legal officers for the 1930s and 1940s reveal, the courts were often in uproar and chaos. Magistrates had to contend with disturbances, counter-statements, arguments and disputes erupting from time to time. Witnesses argued with each other, the public galleries reverberated with hisses and boos for unpopular witnesses, victims and defendants. However, in the post-Second World War period, the gradual withdrawal of general public participation in the trial process changed the atmosphere of the courts. By the 1960s the numbers of people in the public galleries had dwindled to very few indeed. The courts' appeal as a venue of entertainment had declined rapidly in the face of the growth of easily obtainable alternative leisure activities – radio, then television. In the twenty-first century the public galleries in magistrates' courts are virtually empty although the Crown Courts, which try more serious cases, have more visitors (and murder trials can still draw large numbers of spectators).

The major obstacle to justice being seen to be done in today's courts is the massive programme of court closures currently in progress. Between 2008 and today over one-third of the magistrates' courts in England and Wales have been closed in an attempt to save money. The unfortunate consequence, or perhaps we should say, one of many unfortunate consequences, of this cost-cutting exercise, is that the work of the courts has become even more distant, withdrawn and inaccessible, than ever before. Certainly the Victorian and Edwardian public had an easier time witnessing justice being done, than the public does today.

Conclusion

Clearly, 'the law and the courts' is too big a topic to discuss comprehensively in a single chapter. However, a number of issues have hopefully been clarified somewhat. In conclusion, a wide range of debates have been conducted by historians researching the courts. Many of them, however, have focused on the extent to which the law and the courts acted more in the interests of some groups within society than others. As Gatrell notes: 'The question of how poorer people regarded the law and its enforcers – the question of consent itself – is central to all assessments of the legitimacy of the state. It is a question on which opinions divide' (Gatrell 1990: 281). Historians have sought to show how poorer members of society (and other groups such as women, trade unionists and those on the political left) sought to use the law, often in ways which confounded the intentions of those shaping legislation. It is clear that the law and the courts were not entirely consensual, nor yet entirely a mechanism of social control, but rather an admixture of both fairness and support for the existing social order. It would be hard to argue that law did not become any more consensual during the period 1750–1950, but it perhaps did not change as quickly or as completely as might initially be imagined.

Key questions

This chapter raises some questions about the ways that justice was organized and performed throughout 1750 to the present day. More fundamentally, it has questioned who the courts provided justice for, which groups benefitted and which were disadvantaged: a pertinent question that the remainder of this book will also attempt to answer. So, to what extent did the law and the courts reflect the needs of the whole of English society during the period since 1750? This is a vast period of time, and any answer must take account of the significant changes that took place in the administration of justice during these nearly three centuries. Broadly speaking, there was a shift from a lively, contested, amateur court system where prosecution was usually initiated by the aggrieved party (at their own expense) to a more professional, orderly system where the police were responsible for bringing most cases to court with the aid of full-time lawyers and judges. It is tempting to view the development of the modern court system as 'progress' and to make glib assumptions as to the extent to which courts gradually came to work more efficiently and to serve all members of English society equally. There is some basic truth in this portrait, but it needs to be nuanced considerably. In the first instance, there is much historical evidence to suggest that, if not solely a vehicle for elite repression of the masses, the law and the courts in the period to 1850 by no means represented all members of society equally. Women were often absent from the courts, and the poorer classes often found that the system did not work to their advantage. Violent crime was often sidelined by legislators in favour of a concentration on property crime. That said, recent research by King and others into the use of *discretion* has strengthened the notion that all but the poorest were able to use the law to further their aims, albeit often not in the ways those in authority intended. In the period after 1850, while it might be argued that London's police courts did function as a 'poor man's system of justice', the role of the law and the courts in maintaining the social and economic status quo (often by marginalizing the needs and demands of women, trade unionists and those on the political left) should not be underestimated. There is, of course, a tightly focused body of historical work that can offer perspectives on these questions and issues. See Hay (1975), Thompson (1975), Brewer and Styles (1980), Davis (1984, 1989a), Beattie (1986), in the first instance. This early work has been enriched by King (2000), Hitchcock and Shoemaker (2014), and particularly by research on the petty sessions courts by D'Cruze (1999) and Gray (2009).

Chapter 5

Punishment
since 1750

Introduction

The contrast between the punishments dispensed by the courts in 1750 and 1950 is, if anything, even starker than the changes in the judicial system outlined in the previous chapter. In the late eighteenth century, execution or transportation (initially to America and then to Australia) were the norm for all serious (and many more minor) offences. Prisons were used primarily to detain offenders before and after trial, and to imprison debtors who could not pay their fines. Executions were public and regularly drew crowds numbering in their thousands. While it is true that many of those condemned to death received reprieves, many thousands did not (Gatrell 1994: 7). Even young teenagers were, on occasion, executed. While more serious non-fatal mutilations (such as the burning of the hands for thieves) were declining by c.1750, whipping (in public, too, for men until c.1830) remained 'a common punishment for petty offences' (Emsley 2010a: 254). The offender, male or female, was 'stripped to the waist and flogged along a public street'. As late as 1820 men convicted of treason could have their heads cut off and held up to the crowd.

By the latter half of the twentieth century, however, this system of bodily punishment had been wholly replaced by the almost exclusive use of the prison in serious criminal cases. While the death penalty was not finally abolished until 1969 (with the last person hanged in 1964), transportation had ended in the 1860s (the last transport ship sailed to Western Australia in 1868; see Godfrey and Cox 2008) along with public executions, court-ordered corporal punishment had ceased in 1948 and the prison had long been the primary punishment inflicted by the courts. While discussions about the purpose of prisons had been raised by books such as John Howard's 1777 treatise *The State of the Prisons in England and Wales* it was during the nineteenth century, and particularly during the relatively short period c.1830–c.1880, that the prison rose to prominence.

This change, and indeed almost all of the changes outlined above, have been the subject of heated debate among historians. Does the rise of the prison indicate a growth of 'humanitarianism', or just a switch to a different (but similarly severe) method of discipline? Was there a relationship between changing modes of punishment and the rise of industrial society and (later) the welfare state? When precisely did the 'rise of the prison' occur? Some of these debates will be explored later in this chapter. First of all, however, we need a clearer idea of how and when all these changes occurred.

Changing patterns of punishment since 1750

The period from 1750 witnessed a profound shift in the forms of punishment most commonly dispensed by the courts. Essentially, there was a gradual but comprehensive change from 'punishments of the body' (corporal punishment, including the death penalty, and transportation overseas) as the primary sanction for serious offences to incarceration. These two and a half centuries also witnessed significant fluctuations in the aims and social meanings of punishment. Clearly, the death penalty was a purely *retributive* punishment, at least for the individual on the receiving end (it was, however, supposed to deter others). Prisons, by contrast, were (and indeed are) at least partly associated with a belief in *reformative* punishment, although the expression of this changed over time. Training in the virtue of work and frequent visits by the clergy featured heavily in early Victorian regimes, while the period *c.*1865–*c.*1895 was marked by the return of harsh prison conditions imbued with a significant deterrent intent.

After 1895 the pendulum swung the other way again and the early twentieth century witnessed the rise of what David Garland has termed a 'penal-welfare complex'. The prison was arguably *decentred* from punitive policy in the early part of the twentieth century, and became 'one institution among many in an extended grid of penal sanctions' (Garland 1985a: 23). Britain in fact closed 15 out of 26 local prisons between 1914 and 1930, and the daily average prison population remained between 9,000 and 13,000 throughout the interwar period, roughly half that at the start of the century (Emsley 2005a: 21). The rise of penal welfarism is considered in more detail below but, as stressed in previous chapters, it is important not to see the historical development of the prison and the end of punishments of the body as a smooth continuum of 'progress'. The changing nature of punishment (and the causes behind these changes), have been the subject of many debates among historians. Before considering these debates, however, it is important first to map out the main trends in punishment. Three interlinked and overlapping forms of punishment must be considered – the death penalty, transportation and the prison.

Capital punishment (the death sentence) was still an active penalty for many offences, not just murder, until at least 1830. As discussed in the previous chapter, it was once common for historians to point towards the eighteenth-century Bloody Code (a long series of capital statutes, many of which applied to relatively minor offences) and to assume that punishment in the period was inevitably harsh and unfair. After all, capital offences in the 'Bloody Code' included 'being in the company of gypsies for one month', 'vagrancy for soldiers and sailors' and 'strong evidence of malice in children aged 7–14 years of age'. However, while there were certainly a lot of executions in the period 1750–1850, many for quite minor offences, the code itself has often been misinterpreted. While voluminous, many of its statutes overlap considerably, merely outlawing the same offence in different areas of the country, for example. Moreover, by the end of the Napoleonic Wars in 1815, around 90 per cent of those condemned to death were receiving pardons or having their sentence commuted to transportation. Juries appear to have been increasingly unwilling to convict on an array of more minor capital charges. As Emsley notes, many in authority began to worry that this tendency was 'making the judicial system appear an unsustainable lottery' (Emsley 2005a: 258).

However, while there was increasing debate about the efficacy of the death penalty as a deterrent, there is another side to this picture of gradual decline in usage. Gatrell, among others, has noted that there was actually an overall rise in executions during the early part of the nineteenth century, claiming that:

> as many were hanged in London in the 1820s as in the 1790s, and twice as many hanged in London in the 30 years 1801–30 as hanged in the 50 years 1701–50. How easily has this extraordinary fact been forgotten – that the noose was at its most active on the very eve of capital law repeal.
>
> (Gatrell 1994: 7)

The picture towards the end of the eighteenth century and the start of the nineteenth is thus a complex one. On the one hand, the 'Bloody Code' was still enforced to some extent. On the other hand, actual executions did not match sentences and calls for change were growing. Reform itself was slow in arriving, however. It was only between 1832 and 1834 that Parliament abolished the death penalty for shoplifting goods worth five shillings or less, returning from transportation, letter-stealing and sacrilege. It was not until 1861 that the number of capital crimes was reduced to just four: murder, treason, arson in royal dockyards and piracy with violence. Moreover, attitudes towards the death penalty, even in the mid-nineteenth century, can seem quite alien to us today. Consider, for example, the following report from *The Times* in 1831 on the execution of John Any Bird Bell:

> MAIDSTONE, Aug. 1. – The execution of this wretched youth, who was convicted at our assizes, on Friday last, of the murder of the boy Taylor in a wood near Rochester, took place over the Turnkey's lodge, in the front of the county gaol. The tender age of the culprit, for he was not yet 14, and the circumstances under which the atrocious crime was perpetrated, drew together an immense concourse of people to witness the sad spectacle. [. . .] by half past 7 o'clock, at least 10,000 persons had congregated near the gaol. [. . .]
>
> At half past 11 o'clock, the solemn peals of the prison bell announced the preparations for the execution. After the operation of the pinioning, &c had been completed, the culprit, attended by the chaplain, &c., walked steadily to the platform. When he appeared there, he gazed steadily around him, but

his eye did not quail, nor was his cheek blanched. After the rope was adjusted around his neck, he exclaimed in a firm and loud tone of voice, 'Lord have mercy upon us. Lord have mercy upon us. All the people before me take warning by me!' [. . .] At the appointed signal, the bolt was withdrawn, and in a minute or two the wretched malefactor ceased to exist.

(*The Times*, 2 August 1831: 4)

The execution of John Bell was actually the last of a boy that age. However, it is revealing on a number of counts. First, the reporting of the conduct of the condemned is interesting. This was a significant feature in newspaper accounts of executions, and was often (as here) worded to support the legitimacy of the punishment. Executions were carried out in public due to the perceived 'example' they set, and for the condemned to ask for mercy (and preferably repent) seen as a good thing. Second, it reveals the extent to which public executions did draw very large crowds. Executions continued in public until 1868, providing a popular 'thrill' for thousands in a way which seems abhorrent to us now. Martin Wiener argues that the enjoyment seemingly gained by crowds and the fears of the authorities that onlookers were failing to draw the correct message from executions (but were rather being corrupted by them) were both important factors in the ending of public executions (Wiener 1990).

The novelist Charles Dickens attended the execution in 1849 of the notorious husband and wife murderers Mr and Mrs George Manning (even hiring a room with a good view of the gallows for ten guineas). He later described vividly the disorderly crowd and noted (perhaps somewhat hypocritically for he too had come to watch) that:

a sight so inconceivably awful as the wickedness and levity of the immense crowd collected [. . .] could be imagined by no man [. . .] The horrors of the gibbet and of the crime which brought the wretched murderers to it faded in my mind before the atrocious bearing, looks, and language of the assembled spectators. When I came upon the scene at midnight, the *shrillness* of the cries and howls that were raised from time to time, denoting that they came from a concourse of boys and girls already assembled in the best places, made my blood run cold.

(Quoted in Wiener 1990: 97)

Dickens's fear and distaste of the mob are readily apparent. Thus, as Gatrell notes, 'if there was any single reason why executions were hidden behind prison walls from 1868 onwards it was because the crowd's sardonic commentaries could no longer be borne. Too often that despised crowd denounced justice as murderous in itself' (Gatrell 1994: viii). The gradual decline of capital punishment was thus a far from straightforward story. While no longer, by the 1860s, the default punishment for a wide range of crimes, change had been slow in arriving and was not always prompted by the motives that might be expected.

The punishment of transportation shows a similar boom and decline over roughly the same period. Transportation – the removal overseas of offenders not warranting the death penalty but deserving of something more than whipping and a discharge – began following the Transportation Act of 1718. Initially convicts were sent to America, for periods of 7 or 14 years, or for life. Transportation to America was stopped by the outbreak of the War of Independence and the British government looked for another destination. Australia had been claimed as a British territory in 1770 and hence in 1787 the first 778 convicts set sail for Botany Bay in Australia. Convicts sentenced to transportation were initially held on 'hulks' – disused warships. Harsh conditions prevailed even here, and death rates prior to transportation were high. The voyage to Australia was routinely at least six months, and some died *en route* – locked below decks. On arrival, convicts lived in barracks and were sent out to work for local farmers. As in England, their sentence could be reduced by the granting of a **'ticket of leave'** for good behaviour (see later in this chapter).

As with the death penalty, transportation (which had declined following the American War of Independence) increased during the early part of the nineteenth century. By the 1830s around 5,000 prisoners per annum were being forcibly removed to Australia (Hughes 1987). Between 1787 and 1857 around 160,000 convicts were transported to Australia, the vast majority of them male. Transportees could be as young as 10 or as old as 80, and political prisoners were also transported. Emsley notes that from the beginning of the 1820s to the mid-1830s, 'about one-third of all those convicted at assizes or quarter sessions were either sentenced, or had a death sentence commuted, to transportation' (Emsley 2005a: 275). By the mid-nineteenth century, however, public opinion began to turn against the use of transportation as a punishment. Not only were there doubts as to its deterrent efficacy (particularly given that most convicts chose to remain in Australia after the end of the sentence), the system also gradually came under increasing pressure from colonial groups unhappy at the use of their locale for the dumping of dangerous offenders. Both types of views were aired in front of the Select Committee on Transportation that met between 1837 and 1838 (chaired by Sir William Molesworth) and, following prolonged debate, transportation was abolished as a judicial sentence in 1857.

Thus there was a gradual decline in the use of both transportation and the death penalty during the first half of the nineteenth century. Both came gradually to be replaced by the sanction of the prison. Here too, however, developments were by no means sudden. As touched upon above, concerns over the ineffectiveness of the death penalty had been discussed since the English publication of Cesare Beccaria's *Dei Delitti e delle Pene* (*On Crimes and Punishments*) in 1767. Beccaria had argued that punishment should be more rational and that, rather than relying mainly on the death penalty, it would be more sensible to deprive offenders of their liberty and put them to work. Continuing this debate, the reform advocate John Howard published his treatise *The State of the Prisons in England and Wales* in 1777. Drawing on a study of a number of local prisons, where he had 'beheld scenes of calamity', this text condemned the existing use of prisons in England (largely for the pre-trial detention of offenders) and contributed to arguments that punishment should be both more humane and more consistent (Howard 1929: xix).

Certainly then, by the nineteenth century, there was a growing interest in the prison as an effective deterrent alternative to the death penalty. It is by no means certain however that this reform movement was solely (or even primarily) motivated by humanitarian concerns. Partly, perhaps, it grew out of fears that the huge crowds attending executions were not drawing the appropriate lessons from the spectacle and partly it was prompted by a growing desire for a more *effective* and *uniform* system of punishment. Regardless of intent, however, there was a swathe of prison building in the early part of the nineteenth century, and a concomitant decline in the numbers of those being sentenced to death. Construction work on Millbank prison began in 1812 and it was the largest in Europe when it opened in 1816. Pentonville, with its innovative 'separate system' of solitary confinement, was opened in 1842. By the 1830s it was rare for the death sentence to be applied for anything except murder and by the 1850s, imprisonment had become the norm for almost all serious crimes. During the 1860s, over 90 per cent of those convicted of indictable offences went to prison (Wiener 1990: 308). Thus, as Emsley notes:

> If controversy continued to remain about sentencing policy a significant change had taken place. In the space of 100 years a custodial sentence had become virtually the only punishment that the courts could award; fines continued to be imposed for many petty offences, but with the proviso that failure to pay would lead to imprisonment.
>
> (Emsley 2005a: 287)

Early prison regimes had a clear reformative intent, based on the understanding that habits of good behaviour could be learnt, principally via strict discipline, hard work and silence. This interest in reform was, however, largely abandoned in the period 1865–95, for reasons that are debated below. Conditions during this period were such that it has been described as 'the most deterrent period in the history of the modern prison' (Brown 2003: 83). There was a clear increase in the intensity of the punishment of penal servitude (imprisonment with hard labour). Each day was a monotonous and lonely repetition of the one before. Florence Maybrick, for instance, convicted in 1899 of the poisoning her husband with arsenic, spoke of 'the voiceless solitude, the hopeless monotony, the long vista of tomorrow, tomorrow, tomorrow' (Brown 2003: 17; see also Chapter 3). Towards the end of the century, however, the pendulum swung the other way again. A series of social surveys by investigators such as Charles Booth revealed the extent of social deprivation in England, and a succession of economic crises in London meant that:

By the 1890s it was becoming apparent to all but the most reactionary sections of the bourgeoisie that any adequate solution to the social problem would involve large-scale intervention in the shape of welfare provision, housing improvements, medical care and unemployment relief.

(Garland 1985a: 56)

This, coupled with a general recognition of the failure of the prison as a disciplinary institution, meant a refocusing of punishment. Prison was still the default sanction, but was bolstered by an array of welfare and medical interventions by the interwar period. The first decade of the twentieth century, for example, saw the rise of the probation service. The origins of probation go back to the nineteenth-century practice, whereby members of the clergy would agree to take responsibility for young offenders in order to prevent them entering the prison system. However, closely allied to the growth of the discipline of psychology, this charitable system gained official status in 1907 following the Probation of Offenders Act, which enabled courts to assist and advise offenders via specially appointed probation officers. Like the Prison Service, the Probation Service developed locally within regional law enforcement structures like local councils. In this, as in many other new agencies, control and reform were gradually linked to welfare and rehabilitation (Vanstone 2004).

During the First and Second World Wars, millions of enlisted and conscripted men under arms became subject to military discipline, and the punishments (usually corporal) meted out by Courts Martial could often be severe (Emsley 2013). Possibly as a reaction to the experience of both combat and military discipline, the long debates about corporal punishment came to fruition in aftermath of the Second World War, with corporal punishment finally ending in 1948 (Gard 2009). The abolition of capital punishment took somewhat longer, however. Despite the fact that a majority of the House of Commons had been in favour of ending the death penalty in 1945, it took a further two decades of debate and political manoeuvre before abolition in 1965. Even then, the Abolition of the Death Penalty Act sharply divided press and public opinion (Twitchell 2012).

It is important to note that this chapter is primarily focused on *state-sanctioned* punishment. While harder to research, there were undoubtedly 'private' responses to crime that involved punishment. These became less common closer to the present but during the nineteenth century community interventions to remedy criminal acts or punish offenders were not uncommon (Churchill 2012). The workplace, too, was often an arena in which punishments or sanctions were enforced which stood wholly outside the criminal justice system (see Locker 2005, and Chapter 9 of this book). Moreover, while debates about punishment naturally focus on those applied to major offences (as these drove policy reform discussions) it is important also to recall that the majority of all offences resulted in the application of fines or other more minor sanctions.

This aside, it is clear that radical changes took place in the State's dispensation of punishment in the period since 1750. However, as already noted, it is not enough for the historian simply to *narrate* these developments, and it is too simplistic to attribute them merely to 'progress'. *Why* did these changes occur? What significance did they hold for those involved in reform? Such 'historiographical' questions will be the subject of the sections that follow.

Historians, sociologists and the rise of the prison

There has been a multiplicity of debates among historians, sociologists and criminologists about the changing nature of punishment in the period since 1750. Many, however, have the same starting point – how can we account for the sudden dismantling of a system of capital and corporal punishment (executions, whippings and the 'Bloody Code') and its replacement with the prison as the main viable penal sanction? As we have already seen, this change was (in historical terms) rapid. Gatrell notes than 'there has been no greater nor more sudden revolution in English penal history than this retreat from hanging in the 1830s' (Gatrell 1994: 10). It was also very complete. In less than 100 years, a largely novel system of punishment supplanted one that had been in place for centuries. Why was this?

Older, traditional views of this shift (typified by the work of historical criminologists like Sir Leon Radzinowicz) focused on the idea of 'progress', this time in relation to the growth of 'humanitarian' ideas and the spread of liberalism. For Radzinowicz, the 'march of penal progress' was seen as the result of far-sighted policy-makers implementing steadily more rational and effective forms of punishment in response to increasing levels of crime (which eventually declined at the end of the nineteenth century, thus demonstrating the effectiveness of their choices) (Wiener 1987). Certainly, considerations of 'humanitarianism' need to be taken into account when the retreat from the death penalty is analysed. Beccaria and Howard have already been considered above and other philanthropist reformers, such as Sir Samuel Romilly, campaigned vociferously for the end of the 'Bloody Code' from the start of the nineteenth century. However, this 'humanitarian progress' argument cannot simply be taken at face value. As Randall McGowan has noted, Radzinowicz's depiction of a battle between far-sighted reformers and blinkered reactionaries is too simplistic (McGowan 1983). Wider social and political factors have customarily been ignored by proponents of the 'progress' argument but need, equally, to be taken into account.

Consider, for example, the ending of public executions in 1868. In Radzinowicz's eyes, this might be seen as a triumph of human sensibility over irrational barbarism. In fact, both the political climate of the time and changes in broader social sensibilities need to be considered. Fear of the huge, unruly crowds attending executions troubled many in 'polite society' and certainly contributed to the debate. This is not, strictly speaking, a 'humanitarian' concern. Equally, Gatrell notes that it is likely that the liberal government only agreed to the ending of public executions in 1868 in order to outflank the abolitionist camp. In other words, by agreeing to conduct executions in private, the government actually guaranteed that prisoners *could* still be executed. Again, this is hardly a 'humanitarian' motive. Thus older views of changes in punishment find it hard to account for the specific 'timing' of the shift to the prison that, as we have seen, happened quickly, primarily between *c.*1820 and *c.*1870.

Leaving 'humanitarian' concerns to one side, there have been a number of attempts to provide explanations of 'punishment' that, by reference to deeper, structural 'causes', can better account for the specific timing of the rise of the prison. Most notable among these are the work of the Marxist scholars Georg Rusche and Otto Kirchheimer in the 1930s, and the ideas of Michel Foucault and Michael Ignatieff in the 1970s (Rusche and Kirchheimer 1968; Foucault 1991; Ignatieff 1978). All these accounts primarily try to link changes in punishment during the nineteenth century to the Industrial Revolution and the development of modern, capitalist society. Rusche and Kirchheimer argued that there was a relationship between certain forms of punishment and certain 'modes of production'. They claimed that there was little point studying nineteenth-century penal theory, or the intentions and work of humanitarian reforms, because it was the underlying *economic structure* of society that held the key to the rise of the prison. There is not space to outline these ideas at length, but basically the Marxist approach to punishment held that 'every system of production tends to discover punishments which correspond to its productive relationships' (Rusche and Kirchheimer 1968: 5). The agricultural, medieval economy favoured capital punishment because there was plenty of available labour, and hence some could be wastefully executed as 'examples'. However, during periods of labour shortage, such as in the seventeenth century, the labour of convicts could not be wasted and was instead exploited in 'houses of correction'. Such views can easily be criticized as 'reductionist'. In other words, Marxist analyses tend to reduce complex changes to a single driving factor – the economy. Hence they are unlikely to be particularly subtle and are usually no more convincing than the 'progress' view already considered.

However, the works of Foucault (and, to some extent, of Ignatieff), while taking a similar 'structural' approach to the history of punishment (seeking the *underlying* causes of change), were in some ways far more ingenious. Foucault's work in particular is hard to summarize, but his central concern is perhaps with 'power'. Where Rusche and Kirchheimer related punishment to economic production, Foucault linked it to forms of government. He began *Discipline and Punish* with a contrast between a state execution for attempted regicide (killing of the King) in France in 1757 and daily life in prison 80 years later. The plan for the execution specified that:

> On a scaffold that will be erected there, the flesh will be torn from his breasts, arms, thighs and calves with red-hot pincers, his right hand, holding the knife with which he committed the said parricide, burnt with sulphur [. . .] and then

his body drawn and quartered by four horses and his limbs and body consumed by fire [. . .] and his ashes thrown to the winds.

(Foucault 1991: 3)

By contrast, the prison rules from 1838 are a model of uniformity and order. It was decreed that:

The prisoners' day will begin at six in the morning [. . .] They will work for nine hours a day throughout the year. Two hours a day will be devoted to instruction [. . .]. At the first drum-roll, the prisoners must rise and dress in silence [. . .]. At the second drum-roll, they must be dressed and make their beds.

(Foucault 1991: 6)

Foucault believed that the huge contrast between these two forms of punishment could be explained by a consideration of changing forms of government. The harsh public execution was linked to the early-modern absolutist monarchy. The king personally had 'absolute' power over his subjects in all matters, and demonstrated this 'ownership' by punishments effected visibly on their bodies. In the new, increasingly democratic nation-states of the nineteenth century, the individual was the 'property' of society as a whole, and hence punishments were designed not to damage individuals, but to set them to productive work, to reform them, to make them more 'useful' to society.

Foucault also considered a wide range of institutions in addition to the prison, including hospitals, workhouses and army barracks. He regarded all of these as 'mechanisms of control', where new types of 'bureaucratic' discipline were vested. Whereas power in pre-industrial societies was largely individual and hence variable (in other words, it was vested in the *person* of the king or his representatives), power in industrial society resided more in *institutions*. The complexities of modern capitalist society meant that it could not function adequately by relying on the authority of individuals, who could, after all, die or change the way they did things. Rather, power in the nineteenth century rested not with specific individuals but with specific institutions and their abstract knowledge. One prison governor could be replaced by another, who would fulfil the post in the same manner because the 'system' would remain the same. As he expressed it:

The power in the hierarchized surveillance of the disciplines is not possessed as a thing, or transferred as a property; it functions like a piece of machinery [. . .] it is the apparatus as a whole that produces 'power' [. . .] the disciplinary principle [. . .] constantly supervises the very individuals who are entrusted with the task of supervising.

(Foucault 1991: 177)

Hence, for Foucault, the key to an understanding of the prison was primarily a consideration of the changing nature of politics and society in the nineteenth century. Many of his ideas are hard to grasp, especially when described so briefly. The bibliography gives some indications as to further reading.

However, Foucault can be criticized on a number of counts. Specifically, historians such as Peter Spierenburg have condemned his lack of historical method. Foucault did not work from archives, by looking at original documents. Rather, he constructed his theory primarily from printed texts. Spierenburg (1991), attempting to assess the changing nature of punishment by a consideration of a wide range of archival sources, dates the rise of the prison much earlier than Foucault, claiming that he (Foucault) merely provides an 'ideal type', which does not stand up to scrutiny. It has also been observed that while Foucault *describes* the transformation in punishment rather well, he does not really provide any convincing *explanation* of it.

However, once explanations of punishment based on the economy, on politics and on notions of 'progress' have been considered but found flawed, what else remains? Some historians stress the need to consider broader social and cultural trends as a way of illuminating changes in punishment. David Garland has pointed to the work of Émile Durkheim (one of the founders of modern sociology) as giving useful insights to any historical criminologist (Garland 1990: 47–83). In his 1925 work *L'Education morale* (*A Moral Education*), Durkheim was one of the first to consider the moral and social-psychological roots of punishment. He was especially interested in what he termed the 'collective conscience'. In other words, rather than focus on the administrative and managerial aspects of punishment, Durkheim was more interested in its functional role within society, and concluded that it acted to produce solidarity. A re-reading of Durkheim's work can thus help the modern criminologist to understand the importance of the symbolic and emotive roots of punishment, and the wider social context of changing methods of punishment.

One historian who has placed particular emphasis on this wider social context is Martin Wiener. Wiener explicitly rejects explanations of changes in the law and punishment based on what he calls 'internalism' and 'pragmatism'. In other words, nothing is gained (in his view) from writing legal history from an 'internal' standpoint – relating it primarily to the legislation that preceded it and that came after. Equally, an approach based on 'pragmatism' – the assumption that changes in punishment were primarily the result of short-term pressures – reveals little. Rather, he argues, it is vital to take a broad, *cultural* approach to the history of punishment. Wiener focuses primarily on changing Victorian notions of the body and of the individual in an attempt to account for both the rise of the prison and increasing dissatisfaction with it by the end of the nineteenth century. He claims that in the early Victorian period there was a decline in the religious view of crime as 'sin', and a rise in the notion that it was caused by a deficiency of character, by a crack in the thin veneer of civilization, which covered man's primitive and selfish desires. Once this idea had arisen, public executions (which were seen to inflame the baser instincts of the watching crowd) and a discretionary justice system (which was sometimes severe and sometimes lenient) had to be replaced.

Instead, there was a need to inculcate responsibility and forward planning in individuals, and hence the use of the 'Bloody Code' gradually declined and its place was taken by the rise of a reformist prison agenda based on solitude and hard work. The following quotation by the Radical MP Charles Pearson (made in 1857) illustrates the way in which criminality was now believed to stem from wayward desires rather than logical calculation. Base instincts could, it was felt, be quashed via a combination of repression and rewards.

> Labour should be made to feed the appetite, or the appetite should be made to enforce the labour. Nine times out of ten the irregular indulgence of appetite will be found either the proximate or the remote cause both of the commission of crime and the suffering of punishment amongst our prison population. Appetite has been to the criminal outside of the prison both a tempter and a traitor; within the walls it should be made his teacher or his tormentor [. . .] the right hand of industry, long neglected and despised by the idle criminal, will then be taken into his confidence as the only friend that can save him in the hour of distress [. . .] [It] shall be the instrument of his restoration to freedom, not by being put forth by fits and starts of exciting activity, but by constant and continuous exertion, cancelling hour by hour the sentence under which he is confined.
>
> (Wiener 1990: 120)

It can easily be seen from even this brief survey that a wide range of explanations have been advanced to account for the decline of capital punishment and the rise of the prison. Politics, the economy and prevalent trends of social thought have all been cited as key factors driving major shifts in punishment that occurred during the nineteenth century. While complex, you can follow up any (or all) of these debates by doing some further reading. Details of the most relevant works can be found in the bibliography. However, it is important to bear in mind Garland's point that punishment often puzzles us primarily because we have 'tried to convert a deeply social issue into a technical task for specialist institutions' (Garland 1990: 1). Explanations of punishment that focus exclusively on one particular factor are unlikely to prove convincing. What is necessary is 'a multidimensional interpretative approach', which combines study of a number of different factors (Garland 1990: 2).

Debates over punishment and welfare since 1850

The decline of hanging and transportation, the end of corporal punishments such as flogging and the rise of the prison have been quite well researched in recent decades. Discussions continue among historians, but it seems unlikely that any major new interpretations will be advanced. However, while the prison was to remain the pre-eminent punishment within English society, it was by no means unchanging. While the period 1850–1950 witnessed no change in punishment quite so dramatic as the initial rise of the prison, there were big differences between the harsh penal regime of the late Victorian period and the combination of welfare, punishment and reform, which were the norm by 1950. Consider, for example, the case of 15-year-old Edward Andrews, who committed suicide in Birmingham borough prison in 1854. The governor at the prison routinely kept petty offenders in solitary confinement where they had to turn a hand crank weighted at 30 pounds pressure 10,000 times every 10 hours. Should they refuse (as Andrews did) they were soaked with cold water, put into a straitjacket and fed only on bread and water. After two months of this treatment, Andrews eventually hanged himself in his cell. The prison schoolmaster was the last to see him alive:

> going up the steps to his cell; had the straitjacket last Sunday morning two hours. It made shrivelled marks on his arm and body. A bucket of water stood by him in case of exhaustion. He stood with cold, red, bare feet soaked in water. He looked very deathly and reeled with weakness. Had been sent regularly to the crank except when confined in the jacket [. . .] Food, usually bread and water.
>
> (Quoted in Ignatieff 1978: 208)

Yet, by the early part of the twentieth century, a very different approach was taken to young offenders. By the interwar period it is likely that a young offender such as Andrews would either have received a short spell in a specialist reformatory **Borstal**, or would have been assigned a probation officer to work with him and his parents in an effort to foster more positive social mores. As a **Fabian** tract from 1912 noted:

> The parents quite as much as the children are 'put on probation': Working through the family and the home, the system gives the unfortunate a strong friend from the outside who can provide education and training and employment.
>
> (Quoted in Garland 1985a: 240)

Clearly then, while prison remained the primary sanction for most offences, very big changes in the administration of (and social attitudes towards) punishment took place during the period c.1850–c.1950, the causes of which have also been debated by historians and criminologists alike.

The historical criminologist David Garland (1985a) has provided one of the most convincing investigations of the rise of what he terms our modern 'penal-welfare complex'. In *Punishment and Welfare* he noted the striking differences between late Victorian penal policy (typified by the widespread use of harsh sentences of penal servitude) and the softer, more nuanced approach to punishment of the twentieth century (characterized by probation and aftercare, institutions with a reformist agenda and the rise of specialist detention centres for problematic cases such as persistent drunks and the 'feeble-minded'), and sought to consider how this change came about.

The centralized and harsh late Victorian penal system (1865–95) was characterized by what the historians Beatrice and Sydney Webb once called 'the fetish of uniformity'. As Garland notes:

> The primary concern was with the production of a disciplined and orderly regime, a regime which enforced an intense form of obedience through a number of uniformly distributed conditions and procedures.
>
> (Garland 1985a: 12)

Such an approach to the use of the prison was very much based on what Garland calls 'classical criminology' – the idea that 'all individuals are free, equal, rational and responsible' and that criminals, therefore, had made a rational choice to commit crime based on a desire for short-term gain. Given such a view of criminality, the Victorians believed that prison should give offenders their just deserts in the form of a proportional measure of retribution. Thus, arguably, *retribution* and *deterrence* were the keystones of penal policy.

All this changed rapidly around the turn of the century. Garland dates the formation of our modern system of penal punishment to the period between the Gladstone Committee Report of 1895 (which recommended modifications to the existing prison system) and the outbreak of the First World War in 1914. During this relatively short period, the range of sanctions available to the criminal court almost doubled. For example, the 1907 Probation of Offenders Act introduced probation orders, thereby establishing 'a non-custodial, supervisory sanction for both juveniles and adults, which was to be used in cases where the character of the offender or the nature of the offence made "punishment" inexpedient' (Garland 1985a: 19). Similarly, the Prevention of Crime Act of 1908 introduced Borstal training provision for young offenders and also dealt with 'habitual offenders'. Preventive forms of detention, such as detention in an inebriate reformatory, were also introduced (Godfrey *et al.* 2010). The Mental Deficiency Act of 1913, for example, gave the courts the authority to detain in a specialist institution for the mentally defective anyone found guilty of a criminal offence and who met the rather loose definition of 'mentally defective'. In addition, supervised fines were introduced through the Criminal Justice Supervision Act of 1914. Thus the prison quite quickly became just one of a range of interventions aimed at modifying behaviour not sanctioned by society.

Garland cites a number of factors in an effort to explain why this happened and, in particular, why this happened so suddenly. The end of the nineteenth century was a period of rapid change and, arguably, crisis in England. Economic and political structures underwent transformation as the liberal, *laissez-faire* capitalism of the mid-Victorian period gave way to monopoly capitalism and cyclical depressions between 1873 and 1896 led to calls for state intervention in the economic sphere. There was also a growing awareness of the persistence of poverty. The social investigator Charles Booth published his seventeen-volume *Life and Labour of the People* in London between 1889 and 1903, with detailed colour-coded maps showing the extent of poverty in the capital. By the 1890s, therefore, many members of the middle and upper classes had come to believe that any solution to 'the social question' would have to involve state intervention on an unprecedented scale. This awareness coincided with a general recognition of the failure of the prison as a disciplinary institution and 'a remarkable public outburst, which severely criticized the penal system, its institutions, principles and authorities' (Garland 1985a: 64). This period of turmoil was resolved, according to Garland, by the piecemeal development of the 'welfare state' and the 'welfare sanction'.

In England, the involvement of non-governmental agencies (including both the philanthropic organizations set up by the middle classes and the mutual assistance schemes set up by workers themselves) remained crucial to welfare provision at the turn of the century. However, while a mix of state/private agencies continued to administer welfare, state provision gradually rose to the fore. Britain introduced the first compulsory unemployment insurance scheme in 1911, pensions were administered by the government from their introduction in 1908, and local authorities were empowered to build and manage council housing. By 1939, 12 per cent of housing stock was owned by the government (Hohenberg and Lees 1985: 314). According to Garland, this 'welfare state' (together with the expanding franchise) gave the working classes a 'stake' in English society, which they never previously had. Acceptable social behaviour – working hard, acting in a orderly manner, maintaining allegiance to the existing social structure – was reinforced and ensured by the positive rewards of the welfare state.

In tandem with this, however, a new range of penal practices and institutions was assembled (as outlined above). These new sanctions served as a 'back-up mechanism' for the small minority of obdurate deviants and recidivists. Garland divides the new policies and procedures into three sectors. The *normalizing* sector included initiatives such as probation and the aftercare of offenders. This shallow end of penality was intended to 'normalize' minor misbehaviours and to correct offenders within society. The *correctional* sector (which included new institutions such as Borstals and reformatory schools, described in Chapter 8) was institutionally based, but still correctional in intent via training and education. Finally, the *segregative* sector (including the prison, but also new state reformatories for the mentally deficient) was intended to provide for long-term removal from society of its most troublesome elements. The development of this new range of sanctions was sponsored by the newly emerging discipline of criminology.

Criminology as a discipline aimed to *individualize* the criminal. By contrast with prior thinking, which aimed to treat all offenders as equal, rational beings before the law, criminologists sought to explain what predisposed specific individuals towards criminality. As Garland notes:

> Perhaps the major implication of the criminological programme was th[e] social-engineering capability which it claimed to offer. Criminology would replace the ineffectual niceties of legal punishment by practical technologies involving diagnostic, preventive and curative instruments and institutions.
>
> (Garland 1985a: 106)

By shifting attention away from specific *criminal acts* (which might be explained by environmental factors such as poverty) to criminals themselves, and by claiming a competence beyond the legal sphere (for example by analysing vagrants, the 'feeble-minded' and inebriates as *potential* criminals), criminology was thus conceivably another mechanism that enabled the continued association of the poor with crime.

Thus the 'penal-welfare complex' with which we are familiar today evolved as an amalgam of a diverse range of social trends and forces, including the birth of criminology itself. Despite its changed role, however, the prison remained the dominant mode of punishment until 1950 and beyond. Moreover, it is also important (as ever) to guard against interpretations of change in the sphere of punishment, which focus solely on 'progress', 'humanitarianism' or 'welfare'. The riots that took place at Dartmoor Convict Prison in 1932 (Brown 2013) and in Hull Prison in the 1970s (Emsley 2011) both demonstrate how poor conditions repeatedly led prison inmates to violent protest disorders. Moreover, it is a mistake to look back at punishment in the first half of the twentieth century and see *only* the genesis of our present system. It is clear (as Garland and others acknowledge) that there were a number of competing interests and programmes at work during the period. Many of the ideas being discussed may appear strange to us now, and even those elements that were eventually successful were clearly not based solely on compassion and consideration but were in fact simply different, more subtle mechanisms of power and control. Two examples can perhaps serve to illustrate this.

Traditional histories of the probation service, for instance, tend to depict its development as the history of a 'moral good' driven by 'humanitarian concern' (Vanstone 2004: 34). However, another case could be made. It might be argued that the early twentieth century was marked in England by an expanding franchise, by a growth in the power of organized labour and by a better educated and more vocal working class. Hence, it became increasingly less easy for social elites to adopt openly repressive policies towards the poor (as had arguably been the case in the nineteenth century). Thus new initiatives such as probation helped to enable the continued regulation of the poor. As Vanstone notes:

> Each attempt to control the behaviour of others requires 'experts' who have a key role in moulding the problems to be dealt with and regulated, and who constitute the connection between government and the 'sites' where behaviour is processed and responded to.
>
> (Vanstone 2004: 38)

The development of the probation service was strongly influenced by the development of eugenic thought. Indeed, **eugenics** was (as Garland and others argue) a crucial factor in the development of the penal-welfare complex, even if the project was ultimately unsuccessful. Ideas of **'degeneration'** – the notion that the health (both mental and physical) of the English 'race' was declining due to the unhealthy conditions of modern, urban life – had permeated the last decades of the nineteenth century. Such ideas remained persistent well into the twentieth century, where concerns were often focused on the degenerate physical and moral condition of the urban poor. Charles Masterman, for example, writing in the wake of the shock revelation of the poor health of the urban working class during recruitment of soldiers for the Boer War, described the characteristic physical type of a town dweller as '[s]tunted, narrow-chested, easily wearied; yet voluble, excitable, with little ballast, stamina, or endurance – seeking stimulus in drink' (Masterman 1901: 8).

This theme of actual *physical* difference declined as the century progressed but was replaced by a focus on the poor standard of mental health of the lowest segment of the population and on the social problems (alcoholism, vagrancy, petty criminality) seen to be associated with this. The Report of the Women's Group on Public Welfare, from as late as 1943, identified a putative 'submerged tenth' – a strata of 'problem families' at the bottom end of the social spectrum – 'always at the edge of pauperism and crime, riddled with mental and physical defects, in and out of the courts for child neglect' (Macnicol 1987: 297). Eugenicist organizations developed throughout Europe, which proposed radical solutions to these perceived problems. Those set up in Nazi Germany are perhaps the most well known but England, too, had a thriving Eugenics Society (Dikötter 1998; Stone 2001). The English Eugenics Society proposed a range of options for problem groups within society, including permanent removal from society in specialist institutions. Some, such as Anthony Ludovici, went further, proposing involuntary sterilization. He argued that reformers had to 'do what no society hitherto has ventured to do, i.e., they must determine by law beforehand who is and who is not to be sacrificed', believing that 'where they [governments] take over the whole burden, as they do in this country, of indigent lunatics and other degenerates, they have the right to exercise all the means at their disposal for preventing degenerates from being born' (quoted in Stone 2001: 401). Ludovici was no mere crank. His books were discussed favourably in *Eugenics Review* and, indeed, the views of the Eugenics Society more generally informed government reports and scientific publications.

In the end, England escaped the sterilization legislation that was implemented upon the mentally unwell (associated with social problems such as alcoholism, vagrancy and petty criminality) in many other European countries (Dikötter 1998). During the 1920s and 1930s, however, this was by no means a foregone conclusion. Thus, these examples serve perhaps to show that the development of our modern penal-welfare complex, as with the rise of the prison before it, should not be read simply as a function of the growth of compassionate approaches to individuals and to punishment. While it is true that punishment in the twentieth century developed a greater understanding of (and focus on) the diversity of individual experiences and needs, it remained very much grounded in control via the prison and the new adjuncts of medicine and scientific knowledge.

In the latter part of the twentieth century, most criminologists agree that penal welfarism was eroded in the UK and replaced with a new 'culture of control' (Garland 2002b). The period from the 1980s onwards witnessed both a decline of the rehabilitative ideal and the re-emergence of punitive and expressive justice. A further interesting development during the latter part of the twentieth century was the way in which criminal justice policy came to be of far greater interest to public opinion, and a far more 'political' matter, than had been in the period to mid-century. While Home Office officials during the 1950s and 1960s had regarded 'untutored public sentiment towards crime' as 'a dangerous thing – an object to be monitored and contained [. . .] but not to be followed' (Loader, 2006: 568), the decades from the 1980s onwards have arguably been an era of increasing punitiveness (Farrall and Jennings 2012) with the UK prison population reaching the record level of 80,000 in December 2006.

Modern parallels

In May 2014 the UK press reported that Michael Wheatley had absconded from HMP Standford Hill in Kent. In fact, he had simply not returned to the prison after being released on temporary leave from the **open prison**. He was eventually recaptured after three days on the run. Aside from the inevitable media uproar that accompanies escapes from prison, the newspapers and TV media questioned why a man like Wheatley, nicknamed 'Skullcrusher' because of the violent robberies he was imprisoned for, was allowed out of prison at all. He was serving thirteen life sentences for armed robbery, so why was he released on licence? The answer to these questions, and the origins of the licence system, can be found on the other side of the world over 200 years ago.

When convicts were transported to Australia as a punishment for their crime, they only served a small proportion of their sentence imprisoned in convict barracks. They were quickly given probation, which allowed them to earn a living, or work for local employers. They were released on a 'ticket of leave', a licence to be free as long as they did not infringe certain conditions (or commit new offences). The convicts were required to produce their 'ticket' whenever challenged by a police constable, and eventually 'earning your ticket' became a common part of the Australian convict system.

When the convict period was coming to an end in the 1850s (Australian transportation did not finally end until 1868) the British government set about building a number of convict prisons. Originally they thought that about 3,000 prison beds would be needed, but very quickly the number of British convicts grew. The licence system, which had been established in Australia, was now considered essential in managing a growing British penal estate.

After 1853 approximately 3,000 licences a year were granted to prisoners who had served approximately half of their prison sentence. Even the most serious offenders (many of whom had committed much more serious offences than Michael Wheatley) were licensed, and very few prisoners served the entirety of their sentence in prison. For example, in 1857, Sarah Jemmison was sentenced to death for the infanticide of her 3-year-old son, with the sentence later commuted to a life term in prison. Sarah was perhaps fortunate not to hang for her offence because the court had heard disturbing stories of how her son's body had been found in several pieces on the Yorkshire moors, with the body showing signs of considerable brutality. The conditions of her life perhaps shed some light on how this situation had arisen:

> After gaining a job in domestic service, Sarah had arranged for a nurse to look after her child while she was at work, the child residing with the nurse. However, she could not keep up the payments and she was forced to take the child to live with her in service. When her employer objected to this arrangement she offered to take the child to a nurse. She set out with the child on a donkey across the moors, and returned alone. When a dog discovered a child's leg, an attending constable dug around the moors until he found a child's skull, thigh, and some ribs. Sarah's defence was that she had abandoned the child on the moors hoping that someone would find him, and take him in. She maintained that she had not killed him, the environment has, and wild animals must have disfigured the body post mortem. Considerable legal and medical debate followed as to how the child received his injuries, and there was enough sympathy both for Sarah's explanation and for circumstances that her sentence was commuted.
>
> (Cox *et al.* 2014)

She was released on licence in 1870 having served 13 years in a series of British convict prisons. The 1871 census records her as working as a domestic servant to a widower in Yorkshire. She was employed as a nanny to his four small children, and she continued to be employed in domestic service until she died in Yorkshire in 1898 aged 65. She never married, she never gave birth to another child, and she was never prosecuted for any other offences, let alone anything as serious as the offence that had so blighted her and her son's life.

Unfortunately, unlike Sarah and Michael, some other prisoners have had their licences revoked. Nevertheless, there were a number of reasons to keep this system intact. The majority of prisoners did not (and do not) re-offend while on licence. The system gave some hope to prisoners who might therefore behave themselves better inside prison on the expectation that they would get early release if they 'kept their noses clean'. Lastly, the system saved a considerable amount of money for the government without which the prison system might actually have been unviable. For those reasons the system was extended from convict prisoners to all prisoners in the late nineteenth century, and the system still continues to run today. The odd escape by a licence holder still seems to be a price worth paying.

Conclusion

Significant changes occurred in the way punishment was both conceived of and administered after 1750. First, there was a rapid decline in the use of capital and severe corporal punishment, although it must be remembered that the death penalty lingered for a long time. Moreover, even at the time of its abolition in 1965 (by a temporary act, made permanent 10 years later) a majority of the public remained in favour. Second, the nineteenth century witnessed the ending of transportation, the removal of convicts to lands that were, at the time, immeasurably far away and required a sea voyage of many months to reach. Finally, this period witnessed the rise and entrenchment of the prison. Debates continue over the precise chronology, but it is impossible to dispute the fact that between 1800 and 1850 the prison became the default sanction for all but the most serious of crimes. Controversy as to the social role and purpose of the prison, have continued ever since. The reasons behind these broad changes are complex. One thing, however, is certain. Any convincing explanation of punishment needs to consider the interplay of a wide range of social, cultural, economic and political factors.

Key questions

Punishment is such a socially significant marker of state power that an analysis of the practice of punishment throws up important questions. How do dominant systems of punishment arise, how to do they change over time, and how are they accepted by the public? In Britain, as in the rest of Europe, there was a shift in the way punishment was administered, primarily between about 1800 and about 1840. At first, the main punishment for almost all felonies (serious offences) was death. Gradually, however, the death penalty was abandoned, except for the crime of murder, to which it applied until the 1960s, and transportation became the main way of disposing with offenders. Was transportation more than simply a punishment? The history of transportation has now been quite well researched. A good overview is provided by Hughes (1987). Emsley (2005a) also provides some information regarding transportation. More specialist literature includes Neal (1987), Duffield and Bradley (1997), Nicholas (1988), Shaw (1966), Godfrey and Cox (2008) and Godfrey (2012). The experiences of female transportees are considered specifically by Daniels (1998) and Oxley (1997).

Transportation, too, came to an end around the middle of the century. The reasons behind the ending of transportation are relatively straightforward. Throughout the first half of the nineteenth century Australian lobby groups, unhappy with the dumping of convicts on their doorstep, sought to put pressure on the British government to end transportation. This pressure, coupled with public suspicions that transportation was not an unpleasant enough experience to deter crime, led to its abolition as a judicial sentence in 1857. The gradual decline in the use of capital punishment is a more complex phenomenon, however, and is intrinsically bound up with the rise of the prison.

Certainly, it might be argued that the ending of *public* executions (in 1868) was due to fears that the watching crowds were deriving vicarious excitement (rather than moral instruction) from the spectacle. However, executions had declined massively as a judicial sanction significantly prior to the 1860s, and it would appear that this decline had more to do with the growing enthusiasm for the sanction of the prison than with 'humanitarianism' or 'progress'. Explanations for the rise of the prison are varied. Certainly, the desire of reformers such as John Howard for a more humane form of punishment must not be discounted. However, as Foucault has argued most strongly, the rise of the prison in the nineteenth century did not necessarily lead to a diminution of punishment, but rather to a new type of agony and one more fitted to an industrial society. The obvious starting point in examining the concepts behind punishment in the industrial age is the work of Garland (1985a, 1985b, 1990). In addition, useful information can be found in Wiener (1987) and Vanstone (2004). The significance of eugenic thought in England is covered by Stone (2001) and Dikötter (1998). Debates concerning a putative underclass during the twentieth century and its influence on penal policy, can be found within Macnicol (1987), Morris (1994) and Welshman (2005). While penal policy was often (and in fact usually) national, there are always interesting variations in sentencing practices in different areas of the country. A useful case study of this in relation to the application of the death sentence in peripheral areas of Great Britain is provided by King (2010, 2011).

Part 2

Crime and criminals

Chapter 6

Violence, war and terrorism

Introduction

Some of the most important and interesting questions that we can ask about ourselves involve violence. How violent are we as a society, and how do we compare with other countries? Is violent crime rising or falling? Is aggression against others innate – a biological imperative – or an effective and convenient means of communicating power and authority over others? Who can use legitimate violence and does violence have 'rules', as some suggest? Does the experience of war make society more violent in the aftermath? Is terrorist violence qualitatively different from other types of violent crime? The list does not stop there, but this chapter will provide a broad historical analysis of questions to do with violence and its control in the nineteenth and twentieth centuries.

The first section of the chapter consists of a consideration of changing rates of violent crime over time. The media and older generations of society often tell us that violent crime and public disorder are now much higher than they were at some (usually undefined) point in the past, but myths of a putative 'golden age' in the 'peaceable kingdom' are never entirely convincing or particularly analytical. This chapter will take a more rigorous approach, taking the statistics of violent crime from 1857 (when annual statistical measures started) and asking when the figures rose or fell.

After discussing whether the level of violence in society has changed (and most researchers agree that it has), the second part of this chapter will discuss why this might be, and whether the 'meaning' of violence has also changed. After this review of a number of the different theoretical and empirical explanations for changing levels of violent crime, the final section of the chapter will offer some historical perspectives on two very specific aspects of violence, both closely related to any consideration of the criminal justice system – war and terrorism.

Measuring levels of violence

In the Middle Ages, lethal interpersonal violence was 'a relatively common element in medieval life, compared to later periods of European history'

(Spierenburg 2008: 17). Among other topics, social historians have extensively researched the feud – the complex rules and social customs governing retribution for real or perceived slights – and concluded that violent feuds were not uncommon and were associated with the maintenance of elite status and also with social cohesion. As Pieter Spierenburg put it – 'families that slayed together, stayed together' (2008: 22). This is interesting as current criminological research tends to see violence as dysfunctional and mainly committed by those who fail educationally and/or economically. Historical evidence shows that this association with marginality was much more variable prior to the nineteenth century and that high-homicide societies were generally ones with high levels of elite violence. Gradually, however, mechanisms for private reconciliation and recompense were introduced (encouraged at times by nascent states) and by c.1600, a significant decline in homicide rates was under way (Eisner 2003). This may have been driven by (and be indicative of) declining rates of male-on-male violence, but may also, of course, have been affected by better medical care (meaning fewer attacks were lethal) and the way in which the feud became stylized among elite members of society in the duel. But for how long did that era last? What was happening to rates of interpersonal violence in 1750?

While office statistics for all offences prosecuted at magistrates' and quarter sessions' courts were only collected nationally from 1857, most historians believe that murder rates had actually steadily fallen between 1750 and 1850. The crime of murder, in particular, has often been the focus of historical research into violent crime. As 'the most dramatic crime of violence', it has often been assumed to be 'among the most frequently reported offences [. . .] and therefore probably closer to the real level of the offence' (Emsley 2005a: 41–2). Ted Gurr, for example, author of a ground-breaking study of violent crime over the *longue durée*, argued that:

> from a methodological viewpoint, when dealing with data on homicide in particular we can be more confident that trends reflect real changes in social behaviour rather than changes in the practices of criminal justice systems. There is some discernible correspondence between trends in some kinds of official data on crimes against persons and real changes in the incidence of interpersonal violence in society [. . .] it is possible to overcome the limitations of official data by focusing on the most serious offences and by obtaining converging or parallel evidence on trends in different types of offences and from different jurisdiction.
>
> (Gurr 1981: 266–7)

The reliability of even murder statistics (particularly historical ones) are not uniformly accepted, of course. Howard Taylor (1998b), for example, has argued that murder investigations and trials were too expensive for the authorities to prosecute and were deliberately reduced in number over the course of the nineteenth century. Taylor argues that the statistics of murder remained suspiciously constant (a cumulative average of about 150 a year, plus or minus 20 per cent) from the latter part of the nineteenth century until 1966. While this has traditionally been represented as a beneficial effect of the creation of the New Police, Taylor's view is that there was political pressure to reduce both the number and cost of prosecutions and that 'it was an open secret that most murders and suspicious deaths went uninvestigated'.

Other historians, too, have pointed to some rather 'strange' decisions taken by the authorities when presented with a dead body. John Archer (1999: 171–90) summarizes the attitudes of investigating officials in relation to two dead bodies discovered in Kent in 1859:

> Both the magistrate and the coroner felt [the first dead body] was that of a foreigner and hence not worth the taxpayers' expense of an investigation. The verdict of suicide passed by the coroner's jury seems strange given that the corpse had stab wounds in its back. It would appear that just a few weeks later another body was found naked at the foot of some cliffs at Ramsgate. In this case the German had been staying at a local hotel where a porter recalled him with a heavily bandaged left hand. This led some to argue that his death was suicide, and that 'in a fit of frenzy, (he) first chopped off his hand and then stabbed himself in the heart'. In this state, it was claimed, he then threw himself off the cliff.

Clearly, in these instances at least, murders were not recorded as such in the official record. However, Archer goes on to debate whether this was common practice, and whether the homicide rate was really severely depleted by administrators and politicians 'cooking the books'. It would obviously be over-optimistic in the extreme to hope that official murder statistics accurately captured the number of murders committed. There is clearly an argument over whether the number of homicides in the nineteenth century is accurate and it may be that administrative and political influences combined to reduce the number of murders that were reported, investigated and prosecuted. That said, it is probably correct to say that murder statistics are likely to have at least a reasonably close correlative relationship to the number of murders committed.

And these statistics, as noted above, do demonstrate a steady decline in the murder rate from c.1750 until around the 1970s. The period from 1750 until 1857 is not covered by a single set of annual statistics, but historians generally believe (from a range of other judicial sources) that the nineteenth century began with a modest rise in homicide rates from 1.4 per 100,000 population before 1800 to about 1.7 in the period 1825–50 (Eisner 2003: 99). In Victorian England the homicide rate only reached 2 per 100,000 of population once (in 1865), and generally it remained around 1.5 per 100,000 before declining gradually over the period to the 1960s. Table 6.1 sets out the changes that occurred over the period 1861–2011.

The 1960s do appear to have been an historical low for murders, and rates during the twentieth century seem to have remained relatively stable bar the modest

Table 6.1 Homicide rate in England and Wales, 1861–2011

Year	Number of homicides	Population of England and Wales	Homicide rate per 100,000 of population
1861	274	20,228,497	1.36
1871	403	22,704,108	1.78
1881	418	25,974,105	1.61
1891	295	29,002,550	1.02
1901	341	32,527,843	1.05
1911	291	36,003,276	0.81
1921	251	37,886,699	0.66
1931	287	39,952,377	0.72
1941	315	41,261,192	0.76
1951	328	43,757,888	0.75
1961	265	46,104,548	0.58
1971	459	48,707,471	0.94
1981	559	48,517,707	1.15
1991	766	51,088,277	1.50
2001	891	52,041,916	1.71
2011	553	56,075,900	0.99

Source: Annual judicial statistics and decennial census data.

rise at the end. Care should be taken with these, as with all, statistics. However, despite more people reporting victimization, the vast increase in crime reportage and higher levels of policing and surveillance in society, rates of murder seem to have remained predictable and relatively low. Thus, the historical record seems to indicate fairly conclusively that lethal violence declined massively from 1600, and then continued to decline during the nineteenth century, and remained low until *c.*1970. The modest rise since then, which seems now to be falling off again, is inconsequential when set against prior falls. The homicide rate for 2011 was again down to 0.986 per 100,000 population.

A quick glance beneath these bare statistics reveals certain obvious patterns of offending. The great majority of lethal violence was perpetrated by young men, who usually knew each other, and were often in pubs. This pattern holds true across all known statistics of murder. As Eisner has put it, consistently throughout recent centuries, 'the majority of cases are male-to-male encounters, often between people of similar social status, arising out of situational conflicts involving clashes over honour, property, or other entitlements' (2003: 123). Of course, part of this trend can be accounted for by the increasing absence of women in the criminal justice processes from the eighteenth century onwards. The murder of newborn babies by desperate young women (infanticide), for example, was usually punished by hanging in the early part of the nineteenth century and would have been included in homicide statistics. However, by the mid-nineteenth century, juries were becoming increasingly sympathetic to the plight of some women charged with infanticide (usually servants who had become pregnant by their employers), and were reluctant to bring in guilty verdicts. Instead, it became common to record verdicts for the crime of 'Concealment of Birth', which did not carry a capital sentence. Generally, however, as will be explored more fully below (and in Chapter 8), lethal violence has been much more closely associated with men than with women.

But what about non-lethal violent crimes such as assault and robbery? Do similar patterns emerge here also? The numbers of assaults, domestic attacks, street fights and drunken brawls dwarfs the number of murders committed each year and always has done. Can a study of minor acts of aggression tell us something about changing levels of violence in society?

Contemporary opinion formers in the newspapers, pamphlets and parliamentary speech believed that society was becoming more violent in the early to mid-nineteenth century. Judicial or criminal statistics confirmed a rise in prosecutions between 1857 and 1880. Although the early nineteenth century saw increasing physical restraint among the propertied classes, with notions of honour moving away from an emphasis on physicality, it was not until the end of the nineteenth century that notions of 'respectability' and a 'fair fight' became prevalent among the working class (Wood 2004). In his well-known 1980 study, Vic Gatrell stated that the growth of industrial and urban-based capitalism in nineteenth-century England had fostered criminal acts through the impact of social alienation, the anonymity of urban dwelling and the opportunities the city provided for crossing the invitational threshold to crime. Although Gatrell also believed that industrial prosperity, for those in work, mitigated the conditions that fostered crime, he takes the view that industrialization created the preconditions for a general rise in crime. Yet after 1880 the statistics of violence began to decline rapidly, falling away to an all-time low by the 1920s. From this time, recorded violent crime, as with most types of offences, began to rise again, with a particularly rapid increase in the 1990s, tempered by a significant (and, at the time, unexpected) fall in the early twenty-first century (see Table 6.2).

A broad snapshot like this cannot reveal much about patterns of offending, and we might even question whether it can indicate anything at all beyond a broad rise. And even that assertion has to be nuanced. The data could, of course, give us an indication that violence declined during the early part of the twentieth century, then increased towards the end, and has now gone down again. Or, it could tell us that the assiduousness with which police have recorded crimes has waxed and waned. Or, it could demonstrate that the public has become much less tolerant of violent behaviour, and is now much more likely to report it as an offence than deal with it privately. All these are tenable explanations for this data.

Looking in a bit more detail at the fall to the 1920s can perhaps help illuminate some general problems with this type of statistical data. It has always been thought that the New Police were anxious to demonstrate their worth by arresting as many offenders as possible. However, Howard Taylor (among others) has argued that the nineteenth-century police in fact walked a thin line – too few arrests demonstrated inactivity, but too many proved they lacked deterrent impact. Chief

Table 6.2 Rate of violence against the person in England and Wales, 1901–2011

Year	Total violence against the person	Population of England and Wales	Rate of violence against the person per 100,000
1901	2,068	32,527,843	6.36
1911	2,113	36,003,276	5.87
1921	1,992	37,886,699	5.26
1931	2,727	39,952,377	6.83
1941	6,516	41,261,192	15.79
1951	17,601	43,757,888	40.22
1961	47,036	46,104,548	102.02
1971	100,207	48,707,471	205.73
1981	139,913	48,517,707	288.38
1991	190,339	51,088,277	372.57
2001	650,330	52,041,916	1,249.63
2011	601,134	56,075,900	1,072.00

constables themselves were probably adept at massaging figures down (to show their effectiveness) or up (in order to argue for an increase in police resources). Certainly it is the case that as soon as police officers overtook the magistrate as the most approachable official agency for victims to report crimes, the crime rates for violence fell. One reason may have been because the police often viewed time spent in court as a waste of time: it took men from the streets and left the 'thieving magpies' without street scarecrows to warn them away. Moreover, it was having a deleterious effect on police budgets. Prosecutions were useful propaganda tools – magistrates could make homilies in the press about how crime did not pay; the punishments meted out may also have deterred potential offenders – but too many prosecutions could have an unfortunate effect: they reduced police staffing at street level (because officers were tied up in court) and therefore helped negate preventative policing.

Historical evidence suggests that, in the nineteenth and early part of the twentieth centuries, the number of physical punishments, cautions and admonishments meted out on the streets by the police may have far outnumbered the times they actively sought the prosecution of offenders. For any violent incident to end in the conviction of an offender, or even their appearance in court, it had to pass through a number of processes – a victim willing to report it, police action taken to apprehend the accused and a court case where all the injured parties turned up (many prosecutors agreed to settle minor cases of violence before trial started – particularly in cases of domestic violence where husbands and wives were reconciled before trial). If we look at police reports from the period 1880–1920, we can see that the difficulties of finding and apprehending people accused of violence also might have caused a shortfall between real and reported levels of crime. Consider, for example, the following extract:

[The victim said] [s]he was in Rose Barn Lane with master's child in a perambulator when a woman followed her and asked her for some money. [S]he told her that she had got none. [T]he woman then took her by the arms from behind, put her hand into the pocket and took out her purse (there was nothing in it) and would not let her go, or give up the purse, before a soldier and another woman came and made her let the girl go. [T]he servant describes the woman as about from 30 to 40 years of age, medium build dressed in an old black dress, black jacket and black hat.

(Exeter City Police, Occurrence Books, 1889 Report
of 25 October 1889, Devon Archives)

In this example, while the incident was reported to the police, bystanders in fact intervened to see off the offender. No prosecution resulted from this incident of violent crime (and hence it, and many more like it, would not have appeared in the official statistics) but the willingness or otherwise of bystanders to inter-vene is yet another variable that can affect the incidence of recorded violent crime. If no assistance had been forthcoming, this particular incident could have ended more seriously, and hence made it into the official crime statistics. The description of the offender in this case from Exeter was broad and must have matched hundreds of similarly dressed people. At least with property crime, the police had a chance to catch the offender with the stolen goods, thereby providing some linkage between the accused and the crime. With cases of violence, the police officer could only arrest the suspect if they had actually witnessed the assault, otherwise they could only arrest the suspect for a breach of the peace (in which case the incident would never be recorded as an assault) or advise the victim to bring the offender to court on a summons. Many have critiqued the reliability of criminal statistics for these reasons. As Godfrey (2003a) has pointed out, since a vast number of violent incidents were not reported (and we know this from oral history testimony), it is not possible even to say with certainty that violence fell in the 1880–1920 period. He has argued that the 'U-curve' might be flattened out to produce more of a continuous level of violence per population across the nineteenth and twentieth centuries.

With violent crime in particular, it was often the credibility of the victim and their witnesses pitched against the credibility of the accused, which determined whether a conviction was achieved. In court, the police usually prosecuted the case until lawyers were introduced to put the evidence to the defendant, as discussed in Chapters 3 and 4. Only in the nineteenth century was the defendant legally represented – and only then by the relatively few that could afford their services. The 'character' (as well as gender and class) of the defendant, and to some extent the complainant, has long played a part in the prosecution process, and it is easy to see how class and gender might have played a part in determining the outcome of trials for assault and threatening behaviour. If a working man assaulted a social superior, he was more likely to be convicted than for an incident between social equals. How much validity would a Victorian magistrate give, for example, to the word of a prostitute complaining about an assault committed by a client – conversely, would a magistrate doubt the word of a police constable who said he had been assaulted while arresting a drunk man?

There are thus huge questions to be asked before any set of statistical data about violence and violent crime are accepted as even a rough approximation of reality. Some suggestions for further reading on this topic are presented in the 'Key questions' section at the end of this chapter. However, it seems likely that the homicide rate fell significantly to the period *c.*1950, rose somewhat at the end of the twentieth century, and has now begun to decline again (although it will be interesting to see whether this decline continues). Less serious violent offences against the person also declined significantly in the period between 1750 and *c.*1920, then rose over the course of the twentieth century (markedly so during its final decades) and have also begun a recent decline. Changes in public attitudes to violence, police recording procedures and mechanisms, the operation of the criminal justice system, and in actual levels of offending are all likely to be involved in any explanation of the changing nature of violent crime. The following section will consider in more detail some of the primary explanations advanced by historians, criminologists and evolutionary psychologists for both the persistence of, and the fluctuating level, violence in society.

Explaining violence and violent crime

If, as argued above, even the most unambiguous of violent offences – murder – is not simple to measure, can it also be that the importance of that most decisive of acts seems to change over time? For most people 'murder' is simply the unlawful killing of one person by another and is not layered with ambiguities, as are offences like theft and other types of property crime. Murder is often termed 'the ultimate crime', and depriving a person of their life is, in every society for many hundreds of years, viewed as the most serious offence. It always attracts the heaviest penalties given out by the courts and is usually reported in the popular press. Has that always been the case – does 'murder' have a universal and unchanging value – or is it historically contingent – does murder have a historical 'meaning'? Did a murder committed in 1750 when people were accustomed to a high rate of infant mortality, deadly epidemics like cholera sweeping the cities, and thousands of husbands and lovers perishing in wars across Europe and the empire, mean the same as one committed two hundred years later? Why do some murders seem to be timeless in their impact, attracting a greater level of speculation and public interest than others? An appropriate example might be the Whitechapel ('Jack the Ripper') murders of 1888, possibly the most infamous series of murders in history.

While a series of relatively small newspaper reports over three months in 1888 are almost all the remaining evidence of the events, the murders of 1888 collectively became a cultural phenomenon, which has become emblematic of Victorian society. Both Walkovitz (1992) and Leps (1992) have described how stories woven around the Whitechapel murders contributed to and were located within existing social anxieties. 'Jack the Ripper' and his work personified sexual danger and fears about sexual freedom, the dangers that lurked in the working-class districts and the physical and moral degeneration of the species. He was also the embodiment of fictional gothic terrors that were current in the popular imagination – the similarities between Jack the Ripper and Dracula are unmistakable. The huge amount of both accurate and wildly inaccurate information about the murders published both at the time and later encouraged speculation in a way that made the story seem 'bigger' than it was and allowed myths and stories to grow up around it. Coming at a time when English people seemed very anxious about the way the world was changing, Jack the Ripper was newsworthy in a number of ways.

First, he committed his crimes in London, the national capital and symbol of the British Empire. Events in London 'mattered' in a way that provincial capitals or towns did not. In Shropshire, for example, at about the same time as the Ripper murders, the parents of a small child murdered and beheaded their daughter, and the mother wrapped the head in brown paper and threw the parcel in the village pond while the father remained behind to burn the body on the family hearth. The local newspapers reported the case in detail but *The Times* afforded it just a small report tucked away on an inside page. In the same region and in the same month, an elderly couple were brutally slain in their home and a mother and child were kicked to death so violently that their faces were unrecognizable. Neither case was reported in any of the national newspapers. However, the Whitechapel murders struck at the image of Britain, and so they were regarded as being of national importance.

Second, the true identity of Jack the Ripper remains unknown to this day. A faceless man can always have identities superimposed upon him – the degenerate East End criminal, the Jewish ritualist, the respectable man turned sexual deviant (all of which were suggested at the time); a member of the Royal family, or a woman (both of which have subsequently been suggested) – all stoked up the story and kept it playing in the public eye. At least it did while the media agenda chimed with contemporary concerns. While anxieties about the moral and physical decline of urban areas were high enough in 1888 to propel a few gruesome murders to national notoriety, but by 1891 the news agenda and public concern had moved on to other matters. Thus, across time, the cultural significance of any given violent act will differ but that said, there are a number of theoretical models and approaches that can be useful in a consideration of changing patterns of violence.

A major influence on those considering violence over the *longue durée* has been Norbert Elias' *The Civilising Process*. Originally published in German in 1939, this work was not translated into English until 1969, and has since been drawn on extensively by historians and criminologists concerned with violence. Elias did not write about crime (and only tangentially about violence) but argued that, starting within the court and the practice of courtly etiquette, European standards regarding violence, sexual behaviour, bodily functions, table manners and forms of speech were gradually transformed by increasing thresholds of shame and repugnance (mental and physical aversion to certain types of actions). Elias considered the causes of these changes to be rooted in the increasingly centralized early-modern state and the increasingly differentiated and interconnected web of society. As the state established itself as the legitimate source of power and lawful authority over a territory (a nation) and became stable (as happened in Europe in the late seventeenth and early eighteenth centuries), the citizens of that state developed manners and sets of practices, which assisted in the formation of a capitalistic economy. People had to interact socially with neighbours, strangers and foreign traders. In doing so, they adopted common understandings of how to behave and less aggressive ways of settling disputes – usually bringing in state agencies such as the police or taking civil action in the courts. Over time, societal norms became internalized. As Pratt comments (2002: 5):

> As these internalised controls on an individual's behaviour became more automatic and pervasive [. . .] they eventually helped to produce the ideal of the fully rational, reflective and responsible citizen of the civilised world in the nineteenth and twentieth centuries: one who would be sickened by the sight of suffering and, with their own emotions under control, one who respected the authority of the state to resolve disputes on their behalf.

This theory could be employed to explain both the fall in recorded violent crime in the period to 1920 and the increase at the end of the twentieth century. Certainly, historians of the early-modern period generally note, as Beattie (1986: 112) does of the period 1660–1800 that:

> men and women seem to have become more controlled, less likely to strike out when annoyed or challenged, less likely to settle an argument or assert their will by recourse to a knife of their fists, a pistol, or a sword. The court record suggests that other ways of resolving conflicts became increasingly favoured and that men became more prepared to negotiate and to talk out their differences.

Where the twentieth century is considered, one could argue that actually it was the decreasing level of tolerance to violent acts among the general population (rather than an increase in violence *per se*), which led to the increase in reported offences.

Consider, for example, the changing ways in which newspapers reported extremely violent crimes. Early reports could be very short and usually confined themselves to brief details of the offence, victim and defendant. Do they possibly reveal a level of indifference (or at least a lack of surprise) in relation to serious violence, compared to our present-day mores? Compare the first newspaper report below ('The murder by boys in Liverpool') from 1895 with the reporting of the murder of James Bulger nearly a century later:

Manslaughter by a Lad – George Best, a lad of 11 years of age pleaded guilty to a charge of killing and slaying George Davis, another lad, on 4th July, at the township of Wolverhampton. It seems that death had ensued in consequence of the prisoner striking the deceased with a constable's staff. His LORDSHIP, in sentencing the prisoner to a week's imprisonment, trusted that he would never be guilty of a mischievous act again, seeing the disgrace he had brought upon himself, and the unhappiness upon his family.

Manslaughter at Wolverhampton – John Fletcher, 44, was charged with the manslaughter of Thomas Lowe, at the borough of Wolverhampton, on the 9th of April. The prisoner, who pleaded guilty, was sentenced to two months' imprisonment.

At the Liverpool Police Court on Monday, the boys named Samuel Crawford, aged nine, and Robert Shearon, aged eight, were brought up on remand and charged with causing the death of another boy named David Dawson Becks, aged eight, on 7th inst. by drowning him in some water in the foundations of an unfinished building in Victoria St. A Coroner's jury had already found a verdict of 'Wilful Murder' against the boys as they had confessed to the crime. The evidence given before the Coroner was repeated and the boys were committed on the capital charge by the Magistrates.

(*Crewe and Nantwich Chronicle*, 11 September 1895)

Jon Venables and Robert Thompson, both aged 11, became the youngest convicted murderers in Britain for almost 250 years when a jury [. . .] found them guilty yesterday of abducting and murdering two-year-old James Bulger. They were sentenced [. . .] and were expected to be kept locked up for at least 20 years.

(Sharrock *et al.*, *The Guardian*, 25 November 1993: 1)

Of course, we should not assume that the different style of news reporting reflects a heightened sensitivity to violence, or that there was not a growing interest in sensationalist reporting from the mid-nineteenth century onwards (see Archer and Jones 2003; Sindall 1990). Modern media comment on violent crime may seem disproportionate to the amount of actual violent offending, and to portray the details of violent offences in vivid and exaggerated style (see Soothill and Walby 1991; Jewkes 2004). However, it is certainly possible to argue that one component of the recent rise in violent crime is a decreasing public tolerance to violent acts of all kinds.

Historians and criminologists have drawn on Elias' work in two particular ways in recent decades. Some researchers have focused on issues around urbanization and increasing state intervention when seeking to explain the decline in violence over the long term. Others have focused more closely on Elias' thinking about affect and emotion, considering the role of changing notions of honour and masculinity in violent behaviours. Taking urbanization and the state first, Manuel Eisner (2003, 2008, 2011) has provided detailed and nuanced assemblies of all available data to conclude that homicides declined first in countries that modernized early – England, Belgium and the Netherlands. Moreover, by the 1880s, homicide rates were very low in all the highly industrialized countries of northern Europe but were much higher on the eastern and southern rim of Europe, leading him to conclude that 'homicide was low in the centres of modernization characterized by high urbanization, industrialization, literacy and education', while 'elevated levels of violence were found throughout the peripheral areas' (Eisner 2003: 105–6). This neat picture of gradually declining violence has been challenged by Peter King (2010, 2011), who has demonstrated that, in fact, some areas of Western Europe (such as Scotland) experienced increasing levels of lethal violence in the first half of the nineteenth century. In fact, for King, in certain geographical areas there was 'a clear correlation between urbanization and higher rates of lethal violence' (King 2011: 258).

Aside from urbanization, other historians have noted the increasing intervention of the state (as another intrinsic component of modernization) in conflict resolution, and have attributed changes in violence to this. Martin Wiener (1998: 230) has argued specifically that, 'in virtually all times and places, violent behaviour has been highly gendered, far more characteristic of males than of females'. In the eighteenth century and before, traditional values of aggression and competitiveness were deeply rooted in the male identity. When these values caused excessive violence or challenged public or social order, the authorities stepped in to enforce control and this naturally resulted in large numbers of men being indicted for homicide and other forms of violence. Martin Wiener argues that, in the nineteenth century, legislators and moral entrepreneurs accelerated and mobilized the civilizing influences that Elias and others have described into a concerted assault on male aggression. The de-capitalization of offences for various categories of property offences (for which women were mainly prosecuted), and the increasing intolerance of the public towards violence in public and (increasingly) private spaces (such as the armed forces, the workplace and the domestic household) caused three effects. First, the law acted mainly against men (who held positions of power in the military, the workplace and the home). Second, men suffered relatively harsh penalties because of the type of violent offences they committed, or, as D'Cruze (1998, 1999) stated, 'public court hearings undertook surveillance of disorderly working-class masculinity, principally by adjudicating what were acceptable boundaries of conduct' and imposing suitable punishments accordingly. Lastly, because more and more men were flowing through the courts, there was a 'masculinization' of the social perception of 'the criminal' (Wiener 1998: 197–231).

Turning now to consider the role of affect and emotion in the civilizing process, Pieter Spierenburg in particular has drawn on Elias' work to identify connections between masculinity, honour and violence. As Spierenburg (1998: 2) writes:

For one thing, in societies with pronounced notions of honor and shame, a person's reputation often depends on physical bravery and a forceful response to insults. Second, notions of honor and shame are characteristically gendered. In almost every society, male honor is considered to be quite different from female honor. Men may take pride in attacking fellow men, whether they use this force to protect women or for other reasons. Passivity, in violent and peaceful situations, is a cardinal feminine virtue.

As Wood (2004) has shown, violence (both ritualized and otherwise) remained an integral feature of working-class culture for much of the nineteenth century. Spierenburg (2001) argued that Elias' theory was convincing but required further elaboration in relation to issues of honour and ritual. Honour contests and the preservation of status could explain many of the street fights, drunken brawls and spousal assaults, which characterize much of male violence in the nineteenth century.

Moving away from Elias' theory and influence, a very recent trend in violence studies has been to incorporate perspectives from evolutionary psychology. Pioneering work in this field was provided by Wood (2007, 2011) but, essentially, evolutionary psychology argues that while not necessarily adaptive (conveying advantage) in modern times, some aspects of modern human behaviour are evolutionarily patterned. In other words, to oversimplify crudely, some of our behaviour traits are 'hard-wired' rather than culturally specific. Until very recently, cultural and social historians largely ignored biological explanations of human behaviour. Evolutionary theory was seen as reductive, deterministic and threatening to historical studies. That said, some historians have now begun to consider the notion that some aspects of human behaviour that appear relatively constant (young men, impulsivity and violence, for example) are patterned in some way by evolution.

To give a concrete example, Randolph Roth's *American Homicide* (2009) considered murder in the USA from colonial times to the present. Roth argued that homicide rates in the US correlate entirely with four phenomena: political instability; a loss of government legitimacy; a loss of fellow-feeling among members of society caused by racial, religious, or political antagonism; and a loss of faith in the social hierarchy. Essentially, his argument is that when people are discontented with the societies in which they live, violence levels go up. He draws on evolutionary psychology here in proposing a concept of facultative adaptions – claiming that we possess evolved mechanisms, which are only triggered under certain environmental circumstances. Briefly, under supportive environmental circumstances, biological processes promote thought and behaviour characterized by trust and cooperation. Low levels of political legitimacy (interpreted as adverse environmental circumstances) promote anger, retaliation and aggression. While still controversial, work drawing on evolutionary theory to explain violence is opening up promising new avenues of research.

Overall, all arguments that attempt to make sense of a decline (or otherwise) in violence of a long time frame always and inevitably break down under the pressure of empirical detail. No 'theory' can be all encompassing and changing rates of violence and violent crime are always likely to be influenced by mixture of biology, culture, local circumstance and contingency. Neither a bird's-eye theory nor a microscopic empirical study has all the answers – both give different, and useful, perspectives depending on the questions being asked. Moreover, this chapter has thus far only considered what we might term 'ordinary' violence (if such a thing can be said to exist) – murder, robbery and assault. Historians have recently come to realize that two very significant forms of violence – war and terrorism – both demand consideration in any analysis of violence and violent crime. It is to these that we now turn.

Terrorism and war

This chapter has thus far considered violence and crime in the context of the criminal justice system. There are, however, forms of violence that are not always considered 'criminal' (at least not necessarily by those who perpetrate them) but which do nonetheless overlap with the concerns of the criminal justice system. War, for example, is state-sponsored violence, usually on a massive scale. Deaths in wartime are not usually considered 'murder' (although the International Criminal Court, set up in 2002 under the Rome Statute, does have the authority to try individuals for war crimes). Casualties in war are not usually included in criminal statistics, and would obviously massively skew them for certain years if they were. However, wars do have an effect on criminal statistics – partly, perhaps, because of the number of young men removed from the home territory and partly, perhaps, because of the extraordinary social conditions they generate. Equally, terrorism sits somewhat awkwardly alongside discussions of criminal violence. Terrorist violence is, obviously, a criminal act but is it qualitatively different from other forms of violence? It is often perceived as such, and hence demands action and legislation in ways in which more 'ordinary' crimes do not. Thus the state response to terrorism also often has an effect on the day-to-day operation of the criminal justice system – either by giving the police and other authorities additional powers that they can use in other spheres, or by leading to a heightened sense of anxiety in the population, which can spill over into fears over 'suspected' populations or groups.

Chapter 2 has already detailed briefly how the First and Second World Wars led to unprecedented numbers of men being conscripted. Although the military and civilian criminal codes move closer together over the course of the twentieth century (Emsley 2013), the army still retained its own disciplinary structures (courts martial of various levels). These were more concerned with the maintenance of the fighting capabilities of the army that with 'justice' *per se*, but by 1950 the military's use of capital and corporal punishment was far more in line with civilian usage than it had been a century before. That said, courts martial still dealt out punishments to conscripted men for a wide range of offences, some of which were obviously 'military' (such as insubordination and desertion) but others (such as theft and black marketeering) were analogous to civilian offences. It would appear that making use of wartime conditions to make a profit was common to both soldiers and civilians (Roodhouse 2013).

Leaving aside the topic of crime in the armed forces during wartime, however, which is a huge topic only just beginning to be explored, is clear that wars have often been perceived to have an impact on offending rates on the Home Front, too. Wars have tended to produce fears (both during wartime and particularly in the aftermath) of a violent crime wave, perpetrated by the sudden demobilization of large numbers of brutalized soldiers returning from service overseas. In 1749, for example, there were widespread fears of a crime wave following the discharge of 70,000 men in the aftermath of the War of Austrian Succession. Indictments for theft in some counties rose dramatically in the years following the war, resulting in a striking increase in the number hanged (Rogers 1992: 78). It is likely that these fears contributed to Fielding's 1751 *Enquiry* which (as discussed in Chapter 2) was influential in starting debates over police reform. In 1815, similar fears can be discerned in the aftermath of the war with France, which again gave an impetus to police reform debates of the time.

It is hard to tell in these early examples whether or not violent crime really did increase during and after these conflicts. Certainly contemporaries believed that it did, and acted accordingly. A more accurate assessment is possible during and after the First World War. It appears that overall levels of recorded crime went down in England and Wales, but increased in Scotland during the war (Emsley 2013). There were great concerns about crimes that might be perpetrated by the 'brutalized veteran' in the aftermath (Emsley 2010b) but these proved unfounded. As the statistical discussion above has shown, the 1920s were in fact a period of unprecedented orderliness. Press reports about crime and veterans quickly shifted tone to foreground shell-shock (a form of post-traumatic stress disorder), which was coming to be understood more clearly at this time. During the final years of the Second World War, crime appears to have increased across the UK but statistics (from both military and civilian courts) 'do not provide [. . .] any clear indication of how far war and, particularly, the recruitment of large numbers of the most criminogenic section of the population influenced the overall patterns of criminal offending' (Emsley 2013: 82–3). By 1960 the UK had moved from a conscription-based National Service to an all-volunteer force, so there have been no subsequent conflicts involving sufficient numbers of men to generate a sound statistical comparison. That said, recent statistics show that up to 10 per cent of the UK prison population have served in the armed forces, indicating that the legacy of war in the criminal justice system is not negligible (*The Guardian*, 25 July 2012).

Terrorism on the UK mainland is a further form of violent crime, which often seems to sit outside of discussions of the criminal justice system. In fact, the historical influence of terrorism on UK policing strategies and penal policy is noteworthy and deserving of further attention. Terrorism in a UK historical context has been most closely associated with Irish Nationalism (Hassett 2007). Fenian attacks on the mainland began in 1867 with three 'outrages' (as the press termed them at the time) in Chester, Manchester and Clerkenwell, London. 'Fenian' was an umbrella term used to cover the Fenian Brotherhood and the Irish Republican Brotherhood, both organizations dedicated to the establishment of an independent Irish Republic, free from British rule. A more sustained campaign of bomb attacks took place between 1881 and 1885, which resulted in 12 civilian deaths (and the deaths of 7 bombers – 3 hanged and 4 during a failed bombing at London Bridge). According to Bernard Porter (1987) the origins of Special Branch (intelligence gathering police units charged with protecting national security) can be traced to this campaign. Despite repeated Home Secretaries asserting that Britain had no 'political police', Special Branch became in effect just that – using plain clothes techniques and informants to gather information at political meetings of all kinds.

The next terrorist campaign began after the First World War when Sinn Feiners, as they became known in the press, attacked 23 buildings in November 1920 at the start of a campaign that would last for 7 months. Sensitivities on the mainland were already heightened as a result of the Easter Rising in 1916 and the Anglo-Irish War of 1919–21. As a direct result of the mainland campaigns, however, the Restoration of Order in Ireland Act (ROIA) was passed in 1920, giving the government controversial powers to deport suspected individuals from the mainland back to Ireland. In 1939, new campaign of bombings when IRA carried out attacks in all major cities resulting in explosions in stations, telephone boxes, railway cloakrooms and cinemas. In the first half of 1939 police recorded 127 separate incidents (Hassett 2007: 2). Once again, the result of this was government legislation (the 1939 Prevention of Terrorism Temporary Provisions Act – PTA), which continued to be used into the 1950s. In the 1970s, further well-known IRA campaigns led to similar legislation (the PTAs of 1974 and 1976), which also served temporarily to set aside traditional safeguards and due process.

Thus, while terrorism is by no means an 'ordinary' or 'everyday' violent crime, historical analysis shows that it has had a significant influence in generating new powers of policing and prosecution, which perhaps inevitably, are used in relation to other types of criminal activity. Most recently, for example, the Anti-terrorism, Crime and Security Act of 2001, passed as a rapid response to the 11 September attacks in New York, was widely criticized for the broad powers of indefinite detention it gave the Home Secretary in respect of non-British citizens. Part 4 of the Act, which contained these provisions, were replaced by the Prevention of Terrorism Act (2005), which allowed the imposition of 'control orders' (effectively, a form of house arrest) to be applied to terrorism suspects on the basis of 'reasonable grounds of suspicions' (a much lower burden of proof than in other criminal legislation). It further introduced controversial procedures whereby classified evidence not available to the accused or their counsel could be introduced in court. In 2011 the Act was deemed to infringe human rights and was repealed. It has now been replaced by the Terrorism Prevention and Investigation Measures

Act (2011), but the history of terrorism on the UK mainland demonstrates how this particular form of violence often results in legislation that tends to subvert due process and increase executive authority. Terrorist violence is exceptional, but the wider use of the legislative precedents it engenders is not.

Modern parallels

The police are given the authority to use violence in the execution of their duties. Perhaps because of the trust placed in them in this regard, when police officers employ violence in an unexpected or disproportionate manner, or against groups or individuals we believe they should not target, police use of violence seems particularly shocking. But should we be so surprised? Are we justified in feeling outraged when the police use what seems to be excessive force? What can the consideration of violent crime in a historical context tell us about the police's own use of force?

Well, to start with, as argued above, at all times and in all places, young men are the demographic group most likely to be associated with violent acts of aggression. Given that historically most beat police officers are younger men, then the insights of evolutionary psychology would seem to suggest a predisposition to aggression in certain situations. While most police officers act with professionalism and in accordance with the rules, at times the occupational or professional culture of the police can favour violence. During the last 15 years, there has been a resurgence of research by criminologists into 'cop culture' – the notion that police forces in liberal democracies face similar basic pressures that shape a distinctive and characteristic culture (Chan 1997). The concept has generated significant debate, but there is broad agreement on certain general characteristics. Peter Waddington, for example, asserts that the 'core referents of police sub-culture are clear enough' and that they include 'the desire for action and excitement, especially the glorification of violence' and an 'Us/Them division of the social world' (Waddington 1999). Most authors would concur with Robert Reiner's claim that other defining elements of police culture include a sense of mission, a love of action, the prevalence of machismo, a sense of solidarity and a 'pragmatic, concrete, down-to-earth, anti-theoretical perspective' (Reiner 2010: 86). While variations must be considered, 'the general characteristics of the dominant police culture [. . .] appear to be common for most, if not all, officers' (Foster 2003: 208). So, if we employ young men, endow them with the authority to use force legitimately, place them in difficult situations within an occupational culture, which foregrounds masculine notions of physicality and strength, should we be surprised that on occasion the force employed is beyond set boundaries?

However, it has been argued in this chapter that general levels of violence within society have largely declined over time (bar a rise in the last few decades). It would appear that a similar trend can be discerned where the police's own use of violence is concerned. Violence was still an integral part of daily police work even in the mid-twentieth century. Paul Bennett, for example, a police magistrate during the 1950s, noted that it was common for magistrates to arrive at court to find 'the prisoner with a black eye, torn coat, shirt in ribbons and covered with blood' and 'in the witness box the officer, arm in sling, an angry large scratch all down his cheek and his thumb in plaster, where he had been bitten' (cited in Meek 1962: 6). Victor Meek's approving comments on baton charges during the 1930s (cited in Chapter 2) closely echo the remarks of an officer involved in a riot situation in 1983, who noted 'it was a great day out [. . .] I thoroughly enjoyed myself' (Smith and Gray 1983: 88). However, it also seems likely that violence on the part of the police shifted during the period 1850–1950 from being 'personal' to 'institutional'.

In the nineteenth and early twentieth centuries, beat police officers felt it important (and a mark of prestige) to stamp their physical authority on the areas they policed. Ginger Mullins, a PC covering the notorious Campbell Bunk in Islington, felt it important to stamp his authority on his beat by intervening decisively. He would fold his tunic carefully, put his helmet on top and then wade in. As he put it 'although our training manual said that we should only use suffi-cient force as necessary, we knew that speed and the first good blow would always do the trick' (cited in Emsley 2009: 213–14). He further noted 'if we ever did come off second best, we never complained of assault because it was looked upon as a sign of weakness to be beaten'. As Arthur Pickering, an officer who joined a city force in 1932, described it, 'in them days I was rough and ready [. . .] if we hadn't got no audience we could settle it around the corner. That's how I tried to do most of my work'. Another constable noted that 'I used to like night duty best, you could give it to 'em hotter than by day'. Chief-Superintendent Tom Andrews, recalling the 1940s, noted that 'in my earlier days [. . .] you might get assaulted, and you'd assault them back!' Not only that but 'you'd get away with it and you'd have a mutual respect for each other' (Open University Archive, Police Collections, typed transcripts of recorded interviews with Arthur Pickering and Tom Andrews).

This sense of the necessity of personal violence to establish authority has gradually declined over the course of the twentieth century. The use of violence remains an integral and constant part of police work and culture and hence there will always be actions and decisions that are seen later as controversial, but the police use of violence in the day to day execution of their duties is now far less prevalent (both in incidence and severity) than in previous centuries.

Conclusion

This chapter has been, more than others perhaps, speculative. It has dealt with big themes, broad theoretical approaches and problematic data. It is clear that historians and criminologists are by no means agreed on the extent or meaning of violence and violent crime in history. This chapter has challenged the validity of statistics to accurately measure violence in society, suggesting that they can only be a rough estimation of the amount of prosecuted violence and that there is a large amount of daily violence that never reaches the courts. It has not, however, tried to suggest that (whatever you think of statistics) the civilizing effects of social processes of education, commerce, trust and manners have not curbed the amount of violence in daily life. British citizens are much less likely to be subject to violence, lethal or otherwise, than at almost any other point in recorded history. It is true that (statistically) Britain does appear to be marginally more violent than (say) 40 years ago, but whether these most recent figures represent changing levels of public sensitivity to violence, variation in reporting practices, or real changes in patterns of offending is hard to establish with any degree of certainty. The sustained attack on patterns of male violence by the courts, the increased capability of the state to survey and control its population and changing public sensibilities towards inappropriate aggression all have a part to play in explaining changing patterns of violent crime.

Key questions

One of the most interesting aspects of the debates about violence and violent crime is how qualitative they have been. Statistics are an important part of any argument about levels of violent crime and a summary of the key issues can be found in Chapter 2 of Godfrey *et al.* (2007b). Few now believe that crime statistics bear a particularly close association with the real incidence. Some, such as Gatrell (1980) believe if the various forces that control fluctuations in prosecution policy/practice can be accounted for, then the statistics can be useful. In other words, if we can identify changes in legislation, police campaigns that 'target' particular crimes, practices that inhibit or encourage prosecution, judicial biases in favour of prosecution and so on, then we can strip these away to reveal a rate of real incidence of offending behaviour. Others such as Taylor (1998b) are more sceptical. The majority ('interactionalist') view is probably that statistics tell us most about the operation of the criminal justice system, rather than the 'state of crime'.

Of course, statistical returns are not the only way we can investigate violent crime in the past. Both newspapers and oral interviews have been used by historians, but how helpful and reliable are these as sources? In answering this question, a good place to start is Sindall (1990) for a discussion of how newspapers helped to develop a panic over 'garrotting' in the mid-nineteenth century; also see Godfrey (2003a) for a discussion of oral sources of historical evidence.

As this chapter has shown, there have been a range of theoretical debates over the changing nature and level of violence, both in the UK and the wider world. Which of these are the most convincing? Well, this is a question you will have to decide for yourself, but good starting points are John Pratt's introduction to *Punishment and Civilization* (2002), Spierenburg's (2001) article, Eisner (2001, 2008, 2011) and Wood (2007, 2011). On the question of police violence, as touched upon in the 'Modern parallels' section, an interesting look at perceptions of police practices in the 1920s can be found in Wood (2010).

Chapter 7

Criminal others

Introduction

One constant in discussions of criminality over time has been the view that crime is usually committed by 'others'. Specific (often marginal) groups within society have often been particularly associated with criminal behaviour. Often this has been the young (the focus of the following chapter) but crime has also been associated with migrant/immigrant groups, with a professional 'criminal class', or with an 'underclass' drawn from the lower socio-economic reaches of society. The idea of crime as something as an act committed by 'ordinary' citizens has been slow to develop. While the prevalence of so-called **'white-collar' crime** is now widely recognized, there is still a tendency (or perhaps a desire) among the bulk of the population to view crime as an activity engaged in by 'other people' who are somehow 'different' from the rest of society.

This chapter will consider the different ways in which criminals and criminality have been conceptualized and represented since 1750. Although complex, it is important to consider these developments, as the views that prevail in society regarding the essential nature of criminality have a strong influence on the ways in which laws are written and policing is organized. The chapter will initially look at nineteenth-century views of a criminal class, and investigate why some groups (particularly among the poor) were often perceived to be inherently 'criminal'. It will then trace the development of new 'biological' and 'criminological' approaches to the identification of criminals during the later nineteenth and twentieth centuries. Finally, it will consider the stereotypes applied to women and ethnic minorities in relation to crime, and assess how these have informed the development of criminal justice policy.

Poverty, crime and the 'criminal class'

As a general rule, the earlier the period under consideration, the more likely we are to encounter a 'moral' view of crime, based on a religious view of crime as 'sin' – the inability to resist temptation. The further we move towards the present, the greater the prevalence of quasi-scientific explanations of criminality, which focus less on apportioning individual blame and more on the role of physiology, environment and social pressures in predisposing certain individuals to crime. Throughout, however, we can identify a tendency to identify criminality as with particular sub-groups within society, rather than seeing it as an attribute equally distributed among the population. Consider, for example, the following quotation.

> Idleness is a never-failing road to criminality [. . .] And when it has unfortunately taken hold of the human mind, unnecessary wants and improper gratifications, not known or thought of by persons in a course of industry, are constantly generated: hence it is, that crimes are resorted to, and every kind of violence, hostile to the laws, and to peace and good order, is perpetrated.
>
> (Colquhoun 1800: 94–5)

Colquhoun was one of the first stipendiary magistrates. His influential *Treatise on the Police of the Metropolis* went through numerous editions, and he has frequently been cited as a key thinker behind the 'New Police' (Neocleous 2000). It is clear from the above quotation that, for Colquhoun, crime was primarily a *moral* issue. He connects criminality with 'idleness' and 'unnecessary wants'. By implication, criminals are individuals with deficient 'character' or 'moral fibre', who are lazy, greedy and unable to stick to 'a course of industry'. Criminals are seen as rational individuals who 'choose' to commit crime rather than work for a living.

Colquhoun readily connected crimes of all kinds with the 'poorer classes', with little recognition in his works of the ways in which poverty might lead to crime through need.

Colquhoun was not alone. During the latter half of the eighteenth century and the first half of the nineteenth, crime was essentially seen as a moral issue, and the stereotypical criminal was poor and indolent. While Victor Bailey (1993) has claimed that the notion of 'the dangerous classes' and the threat of social revolution found limited purchase in England, it is certainly the case that the responsibility for the bulk of crime was readily associated with the poor. The 1839 Royal Commission on a Constabulary Force, for example, concluded that 'the notion that any considerable proportion of the crimes against property are caused by *blameless* poverty we find disproved at every step'. Immorality and vice (particularly alcoholism) were seen to lead the poor inexorably towards crime. As one prison chaplain noted, 'the passion for intoxicating drink is the cause of almost all the crime and misery done or suffered by the working classes' (Clay 1853: 34).

Fears about crime were thus focused primarily on poor, adult men. The 'sturdy beggars' seen to terrorize farmers, the 'dangerous classes' demanding political reform and wealth redistribution, the 'habitual criminals' and 'ticket of leave men', mobile and vicious – all were male, adult and poor. However, from the mid-nineteenth century onwards, fears over criminality among the lower classes came to be focused on the notion of a secretive, professional 'criminal class' (as well as on the young – the subject of the following chapter). The Leeds reformer Thomas Plint, in his 1851 book *Crime in England*, described them succinctly thus:

> The criminal class lives amongst [. . .] the operative [working] classes, whereby they constitute so many points of vicious contact with those classes – so many ducts by which the virus of a moral poison circulates through and around them. They constitute a pestiferous canker [an infectious sore] in the heart of every locality where they congregate, offending the sight, revolting the sensibilities, and lowering, more or less, the moral status of all who come into contact with them.
>
> (Cited in Himmelfarb 1984: 387)

While hard to define precisely, the term generally referred to a rather nebulous group of individuals (not just the poor or the working classes *en masse*, but rather a sub-group of these) who made their *living* from crime. The criminal classes were those who had foresworn the world of labour totally and dedicated themselves wholly to crime and vice of all kinds. Very often seen to be steeped in criminality from childhood, it was often claimed that the criminal classes had their own *argot* (or slang language), their own meeting places and their own customs and rituals. They were thus, in every sense of the word, 'separate' from respectable society – 'the enemies of the human race' as *The Times* put it.

While alienated from the society within which they lived – '*in* the community, but neither *of* it, nor *from* it', as Plint (1851: 153) put it – it was nonetheless a common fear that the deep-rooted criminality they embodied would spread to other groups at the lower end of the social spectrum. Metaphors of contagion (note Plint's use of the terms 'pestiferous canker' and 'moral poison', for example) were common, and it can be argued that anxieties over the 'criminal classes' were readily transformed into policy. The Habitual Criminals Act of 1869 and the

n of Crime Act   dentified repeat offenders as the primary

low and order   ), and Edmund du Cane (director of the

hat 'we have in principle recognized the

cted the operations of the law towards

or bringing those who belong to it under

y held ideas about a criminal class should

ss' ever actually existed. In fact, most

993: 246) does that 'whatever Victorians

were full-time "professionals"'. Emsley

rians probe the reality of such a class, the

er than the bulk of crime being committed

more probable that most crimes were

committed by ordinary working people who needed to supplement their paltry wages. It is also unlikely that most offenders were culturally or socially very different from other members of the working class.

From the mid-nineteenth century onwards, prevalent attitudes to criminality began to undergo modification. Individualistic explanations of poverty and crime were increasingly ceding ground to more collective theories of 'degeneration' and urban decay. Although most commonly associated with the work of the Italian criminologist Cesare Lombroso, Daniel Pick (1989) has demonstrated that this diffuse and ill-defined discourse had a European-wide impact. Degeneration theory placed emphasis on the detrimental effects of modern, urban life (both the effete luxury of the aristocracy and the squalid, filthy existence of the poor) on the physical and mental health of individuals. Adverse environmental conditions not only led individuals towards physical and mental infirmities, but also pre-disposed them to criminality and vice. Moreover, many late nineteenth-century scientists and criminologists came to believe that such defects could then become hereditary, leading to an inexorable decline in the overall health of the nation. As Pick (1989: 21) expressed it, 'degeneration was increasingly seen by medical and other writers not as the social condition of the poor, but as a self-reproducing force; not the effect but the cause of crime, destitution and disease'.

Consider, for example, the quotation below, and compare it to the one from Colquhoun at the start of this section.

> Many unfortunate persons have bequeathed to them by their parents morbid affections of the brain which compel some to homicide, some to suicide, some to drunkenness and its consequent vicious and degraded mode of life, reducing others to idiocy or raving madness. In this sad class of cases, it is obvious enough to any one that the criminal should be no less an object of our deep commiseration than the man who has been seized by a loathsome and painful disease.
>
> (Rylands 1889: 35)

The quotation from Gordon Rylands stands in contrast to that of Colquhoun. Rylands was one of the first generation of 'criminological' writers, who were interested in taking a 'scientific' approach to crime and its causes. Rather than seeing crime as a 'moral issue', it became increasingly common towards the end of the nineteenth century to focus less on the will and personality of the criminal offender and more on the impersonal conditions from which he was manufactured. As Martin Wiener (1990) notes, the criminal thus became 'less a moral actor and more a point of conjunction of forces larger than individuals, a sign of weak spots in the human (and, to a lesser degree, social) constitution. Far from being rational actors 'choosing' the easy life of crime, criminals, for Rylands and other early criminologists, were thus 'destined' to a life of crime by deficient breeding or degenerating living conditions. As we will see, such changing perceptions had important implications for criminal justice policy, which was of course not made in an intellectual vacuum but rather drew upon such implicit, contemporary assumptions.

Attention gradually shifted, therefore, from the will/culpability of the individual criminal to the hereditary influences or environmental factors that shaped his/her destiny. As an idea, degeneration wove itself through fiction (such as *Dr Jekyll and Mr Hyde*, published in 1886), popular discourse and political and scientific thought. Medical writings, in particular within the new discipline of psychiatry, also often referred to the notion of declining genetic stock and the influence of hereditary factors in mental deficiency and criminality. The psychologist Henry Maudsley (1873: 76) noted, for example:

> in consequences of evil ancestral influences, individuals are born with such a flaw or warp of nature that all the care in the world will not prevent them from being vicious or criminal, or becoming insane [. . .] No one can escape the tyranny of his organisation; no one can elude the destiny that is innate in him, and which unconsciously and irresistibly shapes his ends, even when he believes that he is determining them with consummate foresight and skill.

Writers from the new 'science' of criminology often also sought to forge links between modern living, vice and crime (Garland 1985b). The intention of the individual was downplayed and the force of 'hereditary impulses' stressed. For example, when writing about juvenile delinquents, William Morrison (1896: 109–10) claimed that:

> We may [. . .] say on the grounds of heredity that a considerable proportion of juvenile offenders come into the world with defective moral instincts, and that their deficiencies in this respect, combined with external circumstances of a more or less unfavourable character, have the effect of making these juveniles what they are.

Martin Wiener (19[   ]   nat these develo   tific discourse
led to a fundamental c
seen, at the start of
rational, responsible
choices. However, Wi
extending the scale at
vidual weakened'. Ind
described by science
environmental influen
of crime as a wave o
'society of ineffectua
environmental and bi

None of this means, of course, that we should discount and ignore the whole Victorian notion of a 'criminal class'. As with many issues in the sphere of crime and policing, *perceptions of crime* (on the part of the public and government officials) were just as important for the formation of policy (and for our subsequent investigations of this) as 'reality'. The notion of a separate 'class' of criminals allowed crime to be defined as 'other' – in other words, as divergent from, and not really a product of, respectable society. An examination of the evolution of the concept can therefore tell us a lot about both patterns of crime and theories of deviance. For example, it is perhaps instructive that, while the 'criminal classes' were always drawn from the poor in nineteenth-century discourse, the perceived relationship between the two groups (as well as the terminology used to describe them) changed over time. While at the end of the eighteenth century, the 'dangerous classes' were virtually synonymous with the poor, gradually more and more elements of the working class were accepted into respectable society, and the 'criminal classes' shrunk to a small and easily managed 'residuum' – a term that passed into common usage from the 1880s onwards. The 'residuum' was seen to be comprised of the lowest and most unproductive members of society – criminals, but also vagrants, lunatics and paupers – who were seen as 'inherently unable to help themselves, because of biological and physical degeneracy' (Harris 1995: 67).

There are debates over the extent to which the 'residuum' was seen by late nineteenth- and early twentieth-century commentators as 'redeemable', but the idea of an unproductive 'social problem group', which included the mentally ill, the criminally divergent and the physically disabled, continued in one form or another up until the Second World War. For example, the Wood Committee on Mental Deficiency concluded in 1929 that, while 'low grade defectives' (defined as idiots and imbeciles) were evenly distributed throughout society, what it termed 'higher-grade feeble minded' were concentrated at the bottom of society, in a 'social problem group' clearly distinct from the bulk of the working class (Macnicol 1987: 302). As late as the 1980s, Charles Murray's research into the

pers   ni-criminal 'un   fficient purcha
ima   rant serializatio   *Times* (1990

Wc

Whi
und
syst
incr
(and
offi
liter
adu
'abs

a lack of criminal behaviour among the female population? What were the specific constructions of female deviance employed during the nineteenth century, and how do they influence our thinking today?

Some historians have claimed that the late eighteenth and early nineteenth centuries witnessed a significant change in gender roles in Britain. New definitions of public and private space led to the emergence of 'separate spheres' of social action for men and women, with women withdrawing more to the private spaces of the home and the church. As a result of this, it has been argued that women's involvement in crime and criminality also declined significantly during this period. In an influential article, Feeley and Little (1991) cite the marginalization of women in relation to the manufacturing base, and the growing social control of women within private spheres (through increasing patriarchal control and perhaps through greater surveillance in the new forms of work organization) as contributory factors in the decline of female crime rates (Godfrey and Cox 2013).

Towards the end of the nineteenth century, Zedner (1991) has argued that the 'medicalization' of certain female behaviours also led to a shift in the control mechanisms surrounding women. As the regulatory mechanisms applied to women shifted from the public law courts to relative privacy of the hospital and the psychiatrist's office, women continued to vanish from the criminal statistics. Contemporary commentators have discussed the 'double deviancy' stigmatization of women who have offended against both the law and the defining social constructions of femininity (Heidensohn 1981, 1996; Carlen 1983, 1985; Gelsthorpe 1989; Cain 1990; Worrall 1990; Zedner 1991; Lloyd 1995; D'Cruze 1998, 1999). It would appear from recent historical work, however, that women may have received more lenient sentences than men for certain offences when they were convicted. Godfrey, Farrall and Karstedt's (2005) study of men and women convicted of assault between 1880 and 1920 was able to isolate gender from all other contextual factors of the crime (how severe the assault was, the relationship between victim and assailant, and so on) and showed that men rather than women bore the brunt of the civilizing mission and reformative zeal:

> Magistrates might have seen men as the more important gender on whose shoulders the Empire rested, as did its industrial wealth and its capacity to maintain power. Civilising efforts therefore needed to target masculinities. The apparent 'leniency' towards female offenders does not reflect a particular empathy with the situation of working-class women, but rather the contrary. It seems to reflect a more 'dismissive' and perhaps 'contemptuous' attitude toward women.
>
> (Godfrey et al. 2005: 716–17)

It would appear therefore that women's involvement in the criminal justice system fell markedly from the eighteenth to the twentieth centuries (see also Smith 1981; Emsley 2005a, 2010). Certainly, the nineteenth century saw a steady fall in the numbers of women passing through the courts. As Emsley (2005a: 155) notes, 'from the late seventeenth to the early twentieth centuries the percentage of women tried at the Old Bailey fell from roughly 45 to 12 per cent'. However, some researchers remain sceptical as to the real significance of this, arguing that a statistical decline does not necessarily indicate a diminution in rates of offending. It is possible, for example, that the general move towards summary processes in the mid- to late nineteenth century took female offenders out of the records consulted by Feeley and Little (the Old Bailey session papers) and replaced them in the records of the minor courts. Also, as King (1996) reveals, the starting point for Feeley and Little's statistical run was a period when large numbers of men were abroad fighting wars and therefore the proportion of female offenders would have been artificially inflated. Moreover, Feeley and Little concentrated primarily on property offences – for violent offences the rates were very different. Zedner (1991) maintains that women convicted of violence (or other 'masculine offences' such as drunkenness) had a greater presence in the courts – with women making up a third of assault prosecutions in the late nineteenth century.

Thus, there are debates over the level of female offending in a historical context. Although women's offending overall may have been lower than that of men, many women were still convicted of both violent and property crimes. Moreover, there were certain crimes – such as infanticide, abortion, poisoning and prostitution that became particularly associated with women. The official (and public) reactions to these different crimes, and the women who committed them, varied according to prevalent perceptions of femininity.

Infanticide by legal definition was an offence that could only be committed by a mother. Despite the moral overtones (the 1624 Infanticide Act specified that it was an offence committed by an unmarried woman) and the seriousness of the offence, eighteenth-century juries were often sympathetic to women charged with this offence (see Chapter 6). So much so in fact that the legislation became untenable and in 1803 a new act was passed that placed the burden on the prosecution to prove that the child had been killed by its mother rather than the child dying of unintentional neglect. Nineteenth-century juries remained sympathetic to the (usually) poor, young women in the dock, and were reluctant to convict even when the evidence was overwhelming. Many blamed the bastardy laws for creating a situation that drove desperate women to such extreme acts in order to preserve their jobs or reputation. The effect of this was that prosecutions for infanticide dropped by roughly 40 per cent during the nineteenth century and by the early twentieth century it was widely recognized that new mothers often acted out of character because of post-natal depression. The Infanticide Act of 1938 acknowledged this by separating infanticide from the more serious crime of murder on the grounds that mothers found guilty of the offence were often disturbed by reason of not having fully recovered from the effect of giving birth.

There was also a surprisingly tolerant attitude towards abortion. Abortion was not legalized in Britain until 1967, but the law turned a blind eye to its illicit practice at least until the late nineteenth century when a scandal forced Parliament

hundreds of letters from women sympathizing with the treatment she had received (Wood 2012b).

But the crime most synonymous with disreputable, criminal or sexually provocative women was prostitution. Just as with other crimes discussed above, prostitution was widely regarded as unnatural and 'un-feminine'. Again, it was a type of behaviour that amounted to a negation of the idea of womanhood; in this case unnatural sexual urges – a dangerous sexuality – and a growing social problem. By 1857 there were reputed to be 3,325 brothels and 8,600 prostitutes in the Metropolitan Police area alone. However, this is at best a conservative figure because it only accounts for those who were known to the police (Acton 1857). In all likelihood there were many more regular prostitutes in London and even more irregular ones (those who were forced by financial circumstances to one or two desperate acts). This was certainly the picture painted by Henry Mayhew, a journalist, and Samuel Bracebridge, whose 1861 study estimated the total number of prostitutes in London at 80,000. Their figures were broadly supported by an article in the medical journal *The Lancet* in 1857, which declared that one in every 16 women was a prostitute and one in every 60 houses was a brothel. If true, then the number of brothels and prostitutes in poorer areas of the capital would have been especially large if, as seems likely, more affluent areas were under-represented because women there had little or no need to resort to prostitution for financial reasons alone. The 'Great Social Evil', as even progressive, liberal-minded commentators referred to it, did spark a huge swathe of social investigation (such as Mayhew, Bracebridge and the doctor William Acton) from which modern-day historians continue to benefit (see, for example, Greg 1850 and Acton 1857).

Who were the prostitutes? Most sources tend to suggest that they were the 'unskilled daughters of the unskilled classes' (Abraham Flexner, cited in Walkowitz 1980: 15). More accurately, they were overwhelmingly the offspring of unskilled and semi-skilled working men and with a background of low-status, low-paid jobs such as servants, laundry and charwomen, and street sellers (Walkowitz 1980: 15–16). Often local variations can be detected such as the preponderance of former mill workers among Glasgow's prostitutes and street sellers in Liverpool's. Most came from poor families that could not support them and, therefore, they were forced by circumstance to leave home and find their own way in the world. Many came from families with only one living parent – a factor that would often have resulted in poverty. This would then have triggered the need for extra income and pitched the young woman into prostitution – usually at around 18 years of age. Moreover, as a result of employment legislation, both women and children were progressively removed from the factories and other growing sectors of the economy. For some women, the lack of economic opportunities left but one option – prostitution. However, we should guard against overstating this as a causal factor. The majority of prostitutes were young and single with no children and most had given up 'the trade' after only a few years – perhaps when one or all of these factors no longer applied to them. These temporary, part-time

courts. Thus, in the early nineteenth century, immigrants to London from Africa and/or the Caribbean do not seem to have been discriminated against in the criminal justice system.

In the aftermath of the Second World War, however, more significant numbers of immigrants began to arrive from the Caribbean. The West Indies were, at the time, suffering high levels of unemployment and the British Nationality Act (1948) guaranteed West Indians entry into the United Kingdom. The famous ship *Windrush*, which bought the first immigrants from this region, docked in February 1949. In 1952 the USA imposed restrictive immigration legislation with the knock-on effect that the black population of Britain increase to approximately a million by 1964 (Whitfield 2004: 22). Hundreds of thousands of immigrants also arrived from India and Pakistan during the same period. Many settled in London but cities in the Midlands (such as Birmingham and Leicester) and Yorkshire (such as Leeds) also developed large immigrant communities. Compared to the African and African-Caribbean immigrants of previous centuries, these new arrivals entered a wider range of occupations. However, most were still focused on areas of the economy that lacked indigenous labour, and this largely meant low paid, semi-skilled work.

During the 1950s and 1960s there were concerns expressed (in the press, and by the public at large) about the effect of the arrival of the 'Windrush' generation on the availability of housing and other local services, but there was initially no particularly marked association made between immigration from former colonies and crime. In fact when the parliamentary Home Affairs Committee investigated race relations in the early 1970s, most of the witnesses who appeared in front of it were generally of the opinion that 'Afro-Caribbeans were less criminal that whites' (Smith 1992: 1053). This situation changed dramatically during the 1970s, however. Immigration from the Caribbean had declined following the Commonwealth Immigrants Act (1962) and entry controls were tightened still further with a new Commonwealth Immigrants Act in 1968 and passing of the Immigration Act of 1971. With hindsight, it would appear that public opinion in relation to immigration from the former colonies began to change from this point onwards.

During the 1970s there were a series of confrontations between the police and members of African-Caribbean communities. The most significant among these took place at the Notting Hill Carnival in the years 1976–78, and strained relations between the police and ethnic minority groups. During the same period, the press focused increasingly on disorderly behaviour in some predominantly African-Caribbean areas of major cities and disseminated claims that young black men were responsible for a large proportion of 'muggings' (a term newly coined in the decade). The line between media perception and reality is hard to discern here. It is true that there were violent struggles between the police and young men from African-Caribbean descent at many points, and Metropolitan Police statistics do appear to evidence a rise in muggings by black men. However, Hall *et al.* (1978) argued that the sudden appearance of mugging as a new 'crime' problem enabled the police both to further marginalize young black men and to lobby for the introduction of more authoritarian modes of policing. Equally, Gilroy (1987) has claimed that the Metropolitan Police sought actively to present their mugging data so as to define African-Caribbeans in particular as a problem, and thereby to bolster public support for the force.

Thus, while young men of African-Caribbean descent were perceived, by the 1970s, as a criminal 'other' by some sections of the British population, comparison with the nineteenth century (and even the first half of the twentieth century), shows that this was not always the case. While the size and population density of ethnic groups are doubtless significant factors, attitudes among the press and other opinion formers are also important vis-à-vis the visibility of minority groups. It seems likely that if public opinion and the press *perceive* a group as problematic, then that group may well become more closely policed, leading to higher arrest levels and more convictions. Parallels with other groups highlight the variability of the stereotypes applied to ethnic groups. For example, the Irish in Britain were often seen during the nineteenth century as a criminogenic, ethnic 'other', while the influx of Eastern European Jews at the end of the nineteenth century was not.

The Irish were easily the most numerous immigrant minority in Britain during the first half of the nineteenth century. Their treatment is explored in more detail in the 'Modern parallels' section below, but the numbers involved and the relative rapidity of their arrival ensured they were the focus of both debate and scrutiny. The phrase 'thieving like an Irishman' was common parlance in England and Wales in the first half of the century (O'Leary 2002: 162). By 1880 data published in the *Journal of the Statistical Society* (1880: 46) showed that the Irish formed approximately 14 per cent of the prison population, despite making up only approximately 2.5 per cent of the general population. A study by King (2013) confirms what other historians have found – that the Irish were massively over-represented in the criminal courts. However, King's work adds a further nuance. Although massively over-represented, the Irish were not proportionally more likely than any other group to be convicted at trial. This finding seems to indicate the possibility that the Irish may have been the victims (at least in the early part of the nineteenth century) of particular patterns of policing (or perhaps attitudes) on the part of the police, rather than other actors within the criminal justice system.

Towards the end of the nineteenth century immigration from Ireland was declining somewhat, but new arrivals were coming from Eastern Europe (particularly from Russian Poland). Most of these new immigrants were Jewish and it is possible that up to 50,000 Russian Poles arrived between 1875 and the end of the century. While far fewer than the Irish, these Eastern European immigrants tended again to settle in tightly defined geographic areas (such as the East End of London), which increased their visibility and impact. They also tended to cluster in professions such as the clothing trade, and 'within [. . .] a short period of time the immigrants and refugees introduced a new, distinctive, immigrant cultural life into their areas of settlement' with the result that 'the East End and Stepney in particular became an island of immigrant Jewish culture' (Holmes 1988: 46). There were certain social anxieties that became anchored on this group

190,000 Irish immigrants living in England and Wales (just under 2 per cent of the total population). By 1871 this figure had risen to over half a million, or 2.5 per cent of total population (Holmes 1988: 2). Although the Irish population in England and Wales declined at the end of the nineteenth century (with the 1911 census showing around 375,000 – 1 per cent of the total population) the numbers involved mid-century, and the relative rapidity of their arrival, ensured they were the focus of both debate and scrutiny.

Emigrating largely for economic reasons, the social conditions awaiting Irish immigrants were often not ideal. While large numbers of Irish served in the armed forces and in the police, too, towards the end of the nineteenth century, there is no doubt that living conditions for the majority were harsh. In northern England, the Irish worked primarily in agriculture, travelling around to take on short-term harvest work. Further south, many took up residence in towns and cities, often living in densely populated 'Irish quarters'. Many Irish men worked in semi-skilled and unskilled trades (such as dock work and general labouring), while Irish women often worked in textile factories or in domestic service.

By the time Irish immigration was reaching a peak in the mid-nineteenth century, 'crime' was a topic of social concern and the notion that Irish men and women were somehow predisposed to crime and disorder became widespread. Thomas Carlyle, for example, noted in 1839 that 'in his squalor and unreason, in his falsity and drunken violence', the Irishman was 'the ready-made nucleus of degradation and disorder' (Swift and Gilley 1989: 163). Similarly, the journalist and social investigator Henry Mayhew believed that, of the habitual criminals of London, 90 per cent of them were 'Irish Cockneys' – individuals born in London to Irish parents (Mayhew and Binney 1862: 402). A specific link was often made between the Irish, 'drink' and petty crime. The Select Committee on the Police of the Metropolis (1817), for example, was informed that 'the effects of liquor upon the Irish in every scene of depredation and murder, needs only to be adverted to'. Alcoholism was seen to be an Irish weakness, and such beliefs were widespread. In 1834, for example, a Manchester magistrate noted:

> if there be a company of English drinking in a beer-shop, they are very good friends if they get drunk together, and they can go home with each other and behave with the utmost kindness; but if it be a party of Irish drinking whiskey or spirits, they will quarrel or fight before they reach home.
>
> (Swift and Gilley 1989: 167)

The hostile reception the Irish received in Britain probably owed much to the timing of their arrival. Impoverished immigrants fleeing famine in Ireland in the 1840s came to a country where vagrancy, travelling labourers and poverty were already the focus of much public attention, with the 'Condition of England' Question (a term coined by Thomas Carlyle in 1839 to describe popular anxieties over the living conditions of the new industrial working class) the subject of much

activity. Much police endeavour, particularly in the period up to 1880, was directed towards 'policing the poor and the very poor' (Lawrence 2000: 64). As Robert Storch (1976) and others have shown, perceptions of crime as a 'class issue' may well have led to the development of patterns of policing, which were directed particularly towards the lower classes. As growing, geographically concentrated immigrant communities often tended to be clustered in the lower socio-economic groups also, it is likely that part of their over-representation in the criminal statistics can be explained by general traits shared with the working class (drinking, taking entertainment on the streets, and a tendency to settle arguments by violence, for example). Scapegoating and scare-mongering by the popular press must also have had a part to play.

Overall, as Wiener (1987) has argued, it seems important to approach criminal policy not from an *internalist* standpoint (looking at it primarily from a legal perspective) or from a *pragmatic* viewpoint (taking the view that policy was constructed by pragmatists merely responding to events as best they could), but rather to take *cultural* approach to the study of criminal policy. In other words, to investigate how society's broad views of the 'individual' and of the 'criminal type' frame the formation of criminal justice policy.

Key questions

When attempting to understand why rates and patterns of offending have changed over time, a key question must be – in what ways have perceptions of the *causes* of crime and the *nature* of criminals changed since 1750? At the start of the century, crime was viewed by many as primarily a 'moral' issue, an issue of 'character'. Criminals were those (primarily among the poor), who chose not to rein in their more primitive desires and who were unable to delay their gratification. Later, and particularly from the 1870s onwards, many came to believe that the harsh physical conditions prevalent in the large, new industrial cities were leading to a degradation of the mind and body of many (poorer) individuals. Exhausted both mentally and physically, criminals were thought to be those who could not cope with the demands of modern life. Rather than wilful and cunning, they came to be seen as sick and weak – often more in need more of medical help than harsh discipline. Clearly, changing perceptions of who criminals were, and their motivations, led to changes in both patterns of policing and prevalent court practices.

Another interesting question is whether Victorian (and later) fears of a 'criminal class' have a basis in reality? Vic Bailey's (1993) essay on the concepts of the 'dangerous' and 'criminal' classes is a useful starting point. McGowan's (1990) 'Getting to know the criminal class' is also helpful. For the later nineteenth century, Davis (1980) and Sindall (1987, 1990) should be consulted and for the twentieth century, Harris (1995) and Macnicol (1987) are worth a look. For an excellent overview of the development of the concept of an 'underclass' over time, see Welshman (2005).

When considering the treatment of women within the criminal justice system you should read D'Cruze (1999), Zedner (1991) and Godfrey *et al.* (2005), and then compare these historical works with more modern analyses from Carlen (1985) and Worrall (1990). If you are interested in finding out more about ethnicity and crime, you should first consult Godfrey *et al.* (2007b), Holmes (1988) and then compare these historical treatments with (for example) Philips and Bowling (2002).

responsible for their actions. This is known as *doli incapacitas* and during the eighteenth century was set at 7 years of age. Above the age of 7, children were granted the same status as adults: they could drink alcohol and gamble, but were often expected to work and were not spared the legal consequences of their actions. Indeed, in the eighteenth century, child offenders could be imprisoned, transported or executed – youth was not considered a defence in law although it could be used in *mitigation*. In the nineteenth century, changes in the conception of childhood forced a change to the law relating to criminal responsibility: the principle of *doli incapacitas* remained, but added to it was that of *doli incapax*, whereby children between the ages of 7 and 14 were presumed in law to be incapable of criminal intent unless it could be proved otherwise. At the same time as the law was adapting, a rise in juvenile offending was observed. Shore (1999: 17) shows that indictments in Middlesex of juveniles under 16 years of age rose from 3 per cent in 1797 to 15 per cent in 1847, with the sharpest rise occurring between 1807 and 1817. However, does this rise in the recorded number of prosecutions equate to a genuine rise in juvenile crime?

Concern about a supposed rise in young people and crime was most heightened in the period immediately following the Napoleonic Wars. In May 1816 a government report gave rise to the concept of juvenile delinquency. The report found that: 'Juvenile delinquency existed in the metropolis to a very alarming extent; that a system was in action, by which these unfortunate Lads were organized into gangs; that they regularly conspired together in public houses, where they planned their enterprises, and afterwards divided the produce of their plunder' (*1816 Report of the Committee for Investigating the Causes of the Alarming Increase of Juvenile Delinquency in the Metropolis*, cited in Shore 1999: 6). In the same period, a number of developments in the supervision of young people – especially outside the home – contributed to the notion of a moral crisis in early industrial Britain. In many ways these concerns reflected wider issues surrounding the process of industrialization and the changing position of young people both in the home and in the productive or industrial process. Traditionally, children had gone from the parental home directly into an apprenticeship. This cycle was less common by the end of the eighteenth century as new modes of production shifted the industrial emphasis from small-scale but highly skilled producers to larger mechanized factories where labour did not need the same high degree of training. Apprenticeships were in decline and by the early nineteenth century they ceased to form any part of the life-cycle for the majority of young people.

This in turn affected family composition as more young people remained at home or moved into cheap rented accommodation rather than 'living-in'. The altered dynamics of home life focused concerns about the ability of certain families to deal with their unruly youth and the 'unattached' young workers who lived in lodging houses. Apprenticeships did remain, but often in a very different form to the traditional one. A report of 1843 drew attention to the depravity and hardship suffered by children, often orphans, who were legally bound to their employer until the age of 21 even though many did not receive wages and the

that impacted on many aspects of society. For example, the Factory Act 1819 banned children under 9 years of age from working in cotton mills and introduced a restriction to 12 hours a day for children over 9 years old. (other acts restricting child labour followed 1833, 1844 and 1864). Why did children become the focus of reform? We have already mentioned the impact of industrialization and urbanization and we should bear in mind that these were revolutionary times. Revolution continued to plague much of Europe, and even Britain – whose relative stability many thought would make her immune from such chaos – faced widespread unrest for much of the nineteenth century. In this volatile climate the moral character of the next generation was regarded as an essential ingredient for the future well-being of the nation (and its growing empire). A very visible sign of morality was church attendance – and that appeared to be in decline.

The perceived decline in religion had been an on-going concern since at least the early-modern period. Once again children were not just the problem, they were also the solution. In 1788 'The Philanthropic Society for the Prevention of Crimes and the Reform of the Criminal Poor; by the Encouragement of Industry and the Culture of Good Morals, among those children who are now trained up to Vicious Courses, Public Plunder, Infamy and Ruin' was formed. Through a programme of religious and industrial instruction, the society sought to rescue delinquent and destitute children from 'the vices of the street'. The establishment of a separate place of safety for children was the key to reversing the moral decline. But the central tenets of the society – improvement through religious adherence *and* industry – were themselves characteristics of eighteenth-century ideas that linked poverty to idleness and immorality.

In 1817, just one year after the publication of the report into 'the alarming increase in juvenile delinquency in the metropolis', the Society for the Improvement of Prison Discipline and the Reformation of Juvenile Offenders was established. Its purpose was to establish a separate system for juvenile offenders where they could be reformed and reclaimed as useful members of a future society away from the pernicious influence of adult criminals. The argument was a simple one: that moral improvement was only possible if boys were isolated from the contaminating effects of men's prisons.

The establishment of the first juvenile penal institution at Parkhurst (which was solely for boys) did not happen until 1838, but pressure did lead to the separation of boys from adults within the existing prison system. This necessitated a new approach that led to the classification of prisoners into either juveniles or adults – a process that consolidated the conceptualization of juvenile delinquency.

Ideas about the nature of delinquency, and the possibility of reform if children could be directed in the right way, remained persistent in the minds of many during the nineteenth century. By 1849 the Philanthropic Society had established its own agricultural farm at Redhill in Surrey, where delinquents and young vagrants were 'rescued' with a diet of religion, exercise and self-denial. Reformist ideas were further developed by a number of Victorian philanthropists including Mary Carpenter. The daughter of a Unitarian minister, Carpenter was one of a new wave of mid-nineteenth-century 'humanitarian' reformers, who were highly critical of the penal system – including the Parkhurst establishment. However, Carpenter did not separate her wider concerns from the 'moral crisis' that she believed was the blight of many young people in working-class families. The primacy of the family was central to her argument – an argument that would exert considerable influence on government policy in the 1850s.

Carpenter regarded immoral boys as potential criminals, and immorality in girls, she believed, made them especially vulnerable to prostitution. She further identified two 'classes' among the immoral poor: the 'perishing' (or destitute) and the 'dangerous' (or delinquent). While she believed that those in the perishing class could be put to useful work in industrial schools, the dangerous class needed to be reformed. Carpenter's ideas, which echoed earlier Philanthropic Society practices of placing orphans in the Manufactory and delinquents in the Reform, were soon formalized in legislation: the Youthful Offenders Act 1854 and the Industrial Schools Act 1857. Approximately 4,000 young offenders were housed in 48 reformatories by 1860 and by 1900 over 30,000 young people were held in over 200 state reformatories or industrial schools. Where it was believed that the parents had failed to provide for the moral well-being of their children, therefore, the state had intervened. This amounted to one in every 230 juveniles (Radzinowicz and Hood 1990: 181). Britain, it seemed, had come a long way from the *laissez-faire* ideology of the eighteenth century. Despite the growth of state involvement it would be a mistake to view the nineteenth century as being characterized by progressive initiatives aimed at 'improving' working-class morals. Many opposed the ideas of reformers and the government could not afford to alienate this body of opinion. Accordingly, the new legislation did not supersede the existing more punitive measures and magistrates retained the *option* of prison or reformatory. In any case before entering a reformatory, juveniles were required to serve a 14-day prison sentence. Again, the importance of the legislation, from the historian's perspective at least, is that it further consolidated and formalized the *idea* of juvenile delinquency.

Whatever the cause, measures were deemed necessary to prevent the evolutionary problem from occurring. Increasingly the state, through both public (state initiatives) and private (philanthropic and charitable) means, sought to intervene where it saw the danger signs. These varied from perceived bad parenting, to the exposure of children to immorality, to insanitary living conditions, to cases of extreme poverty, to what might be interpreted as the first steps towards a career in crime and so on. In this way, ideas about children who were in danger (and therefore in need of care) or children who were a danger to society (and therefore in need of control) became conflated.

Twentieth-century care and control

As we have seen, many of the concerns of nineteenth-century reformers were driven by society's response to young offenders. This was equally true of youth

vagrant, associating with reputed thieves or even if the parents were deemed unworthy. In these circumstances the juvenile court was empowered to act in the name of welfare. As with earlier concerns about moral crises that we have already noted, ideas about how to deal with both the *troublesome* and the *troubled* were blurred, distinctions were confused and solutions, therefore, became merged with little or no differentiation in 'sentencing'.

One solution that emerged during the late nineteenth and early twentieth centuries was the Scouting movement and similar organizations such as the Sea Scouts and Girl Guides. The purpose of such organizations was to remove children from the unhealthy cities – albeit temporarily – and take them to the countryside where they could partake of healthy pursuits such as hiking, cycling and camping. This was not only motivated by fears about crime   there had also been grave concerns over the physical fitness of volunteers for the British army during the Boer War (1898–1902). But the two issues were linked because of the supposed degeneration or poor evolution of city dwellers. In fact, Baden-Powell expressed a preference for hooligans – 'the best sort of boy' – for his scouting movement (however, when the courts labelled a child a 'hooligan' he was likely to be incarcerated rather than carted off to the Boy Scouts).

There was renewed concern about delinquency during and after the First World War. This was caused by fears surrounding the effects of absent fathers who were serving in the armed forces and mothers who were working in munitions factories and driving buses and such like. The Board of Education noted a serious increase in delinquency during the war years, especially among children aged between 11 and 13 (*Report of the Board of Education 1916–17*, cited in Marwick 1991: 158). The disruption to family life and to education caused by the war was to blame, according to some, while the influence of the cinema was held responsible by others. A most notorious case concerned the appearance at court of nine boys who called themselves the Black Hand Gang of St Luke's. Concerns were sufficient to instigate an investigation of the cinema by the National Council of Public Morals, which rejected the suggestion of a pernicious influence and urged the problem of delinquency to be considered in the context of the prevailing social and economic conditions. Other factors also contributed to the rise in juvenile crime during the First World War, as one witness – a probation officer – informed the inquiry:

> There has been a tendency in recent years to increase the variety of offences with which children may be charged. For instance, children are now charged with wandering, with being without proper guardianship, with being 'beyond control'. Our streets are now more rigidly supervised than ever before. There is a large and increasing army of officials whose duty it is to watch over child life. In many cases it has seemed to me that the zeal of those officers was not always tempered by humanity and expediency.
>
> (National Council of Public Morals, *The Cinema*,
> 1917, cited in Marwick 1991: 158)

and we should regard the intervention of the State in matters concerning children's welfare in this context while recognizing also the continuity with pre-war developments.

Evidence of the effects of war and concerns about crime, often involving juveniles, can be found in a number of post-war British feature films (as well as elsewhere). *Brighton Rock* (1947), based on the 1938 Graham Greene novel, graphically portrays violence and youth crime through the character of Pinkie (played by Richard Attenborough), the juvenile leader of a vicious gang based in Brighton. But it is the explicit portrayal of violence rather than the plot that was (and remains) so shocking about this film. *Hue and Cry* (1947) – the first of the Ealing comedies – shows the devastation of the war on London and also featured a juvenile gang in a mischievous manner as they take on a criminal gang. In fact it is not unreasonable to speak of these films, together with others such as *Waterloo Road*, as an identifiable genre that emerged from the wartime experience and concerns. Interestingly, the censors (often reflecting government attitudes) were sympathetic to the graphic representation of violence and crime that occasionally characterized some of these films. Eventually, however, there would be a reaction to this permissiveness and it came in the form of the 1950 film *The Blue Lamp*, which also featured a delinquent juvenile. Not only did this film introduce to British audiences a new folk hero, PC George Dixon (played by Jack Warner), it also portrayed a far more sanitized version of crime and violence, and thereby advocated new standards of 'decency'. George Dixon was a visible moral counterpoint to the new images of youth that pervaded the television screens of the 1950s and 1960s: 'Teddy Boys' ripping up the seats of local cinemas; mods and rockers in pitched battles in seaside resorts; and young women screaming hysterically at the Beatles. Modern television programmes now concentrated on another great cause of concern: the gangs.

Modern parallels

An assassin sips tea in a south London cafe before stepping up behind two men and firing a handgun into the back of their heads [. . .] This is modern gangland Britain [. . .] Organised crime in the UK is [. . .] a 'substantial' and growing problem.

(*The Independent*, 21 August 1995)

This article describes a gang war between two local gangs - the Peckham Boys and the Ghetto Boys:

For more than 20 years the gangs have been warring with each other [. . .] 'It's all about whose [sic] got the best bottle of champagne, who's wearing the best trainers, who's pushing the biggest weights, who's got the biggest jewellery, who's driving the best car.'

(*The Guardian*, 11 February 2007)

How different are these gangs from the razor gangs and petty mobsters of the late nineteenth and early twentieth centuries? The type of gangs reported in today's newspapers are reminiscent of the operations of the racecourse gangs of the 1920s or 1930s (Shore 2011). Equally, they sound similar to the London-based organizations or the 1950s and 1960s The Krays, and their ilk, for example, ran successful extortion operations with the threat of violence. The gangs were semi-structured, with casual members bolstering the core membership of a few 'names' or 'faces'. In many ways, however, these gangs are and were unusual. The majority of gangs are locally embedded, formed of teenage, rather inexperienced offenders, who are desperate to prove their 'ownership' of a particular area – with violence offered to those who dispute their power – and although their activities may include acquisitive crime or drug dealing, they are mainly about display, belonging and identity than organized crime. Are today's gangs the legitimate inheritors of unease about unrestrained youth, a development or upgrading of youth-gang organization, or a completely new and different form of organization from those of the 1890s or 1920s?

In the 1880 to 1900 period there was internationally felt unease about the state of youth. Concerns centred on visible youth problems, such as teenage prostitution, and, particularly, the groups of youths that hung around the streets. Labelled as 'hooligans', they took names of their own choosing – Birmingham's 'Peaky Blinders' and Liverpool's 'corner-men' for example. Pearson (1983) has written on the nature of these gangs and the moral panics that accompanied them by reference to Victorian newspapers, for whom these gangs held particular fascination, and Davies has deepened our knowledge by detailed study of the Manchester Scuttlers (Davies 1999, 2000). This notorious fighting gang were responsible for a number of violent affrays in the late nineteenth-century, and they deserved their tough reputation (they committed numerous woundings and five homicides between 1870 and 1900). However, below this 'hooligan aristocracy', most urban centres had their own gangs, indeed neighbourhoods could hold 10 or 20 competing gangs of boys who fought over territory, prestige and reputation as the toughest of the local 'mobs'. As Godfrey *et al.* noted in *Criminal Lives*, youths collected together:

> whistled at girls, clogged up street corners, and smoked cigarettes. They got drunk, swore and were boisterous, gambled in the street or acted as look-out for pitch and toss games; played football, cricket, and snowballing in the street – all of those offences in themselves; and usually attracting adverse comment from more established members of society [. . .] Occasionally young men congregated together to commit more serious crimes of violence or property offending. Stores such as Woolworths and Marks and Spencer were favourite targets for shoplifting because of their 'open' layout. One of the main crimes was the 'jemmying' of gas meters from unattended or empty houses.
>
> (Godfrey *et al.* 2007: 66)

men and women who did not meet these 'standards'. Concerns about juvenile delinquency appear to have surfaced periodically at times of national crises: often immediately following wars (crises of youth, crime and authority followed the Napoleonic, First and Second World Wars). Other factors heightened concerns about delinquency: the fear of revolution that affected most of Europe (including Britain) after 1789; changes in the means of production and employment ranging from the ending of apprenticeships to larger-scale industrialization; and the decline in religiosity. Each represented a crisis or upheaval in society to contemporary observers. Underpinning all these concerns was the fear of a moral crisis, much of which was rooted in the process of urbanization and particularly the degradation associated with the city slums.

Moments of crisis within society, it appears, have a tendency to focus concerns on crime. Often it is in relation to juvenile crime that these fears are most heightened. As Pearson has argued, these fears are closely associated with more general concerns about the breakdown of order or the collapse of society (Pearson 1983; see also Alker 2014). Why this should be the case is clear: it is a lingering concern for the future, represented by the next generation. However, by the mid-twentieth century rather than representing different approaches to two different problems affecting young people (the offended or the offender), the two had become synonymous in youth justice.

As we have seen, the foundations of the reform process lay in medical, criminological and popular discourses that could not be described as benign since many children suffered informal and terribly abusive punishments and abuse at the hands of the very people who were supposed to look after them. Juveniles brought up in working families, with parents of poor education, poor employment, poor housing and low pay, were expected to conform to ideal images of childhood or else be subject to police scrutiny and public condemnation. It seems that ideas about the proper (or natural) behaviour and position of women and children at this time combined with ideas about respectability and social hierarchy to produce a penal-welfarist system that many found (and find) contentious, not least after the very many recent revelations about the scale of abuse (physical, emotional and sexual) that permeated 'care' institutions for children in the twentieth century.

Key questions

So what are the key questions that we need to bear in mind when exploring the topic of youth crime and youth justice? First, we should consider to what extent the whole notion of 'juvenile delinquency' was an invention of the early nineteenth century. In the eighteenth century and the centuries preceding it, young people committed crimes. Indeed, the disrespectful, troublesome and dishonest apprentice is a common figure in eighteenth-century literature. However, the combination of legislative acts, procedural changes in the administration of justice in the courts and the changes brought by urbanization/industrialization all appeared to contributed to create a new category in the public imagination – the juvenile

Chapter 9

Control and surveillance since 1750

Introduction

We seem to live in a world where we are closely watched over. At work and in the streets we are viewed by CCTV cameras and recent revelations about the large-scale surveillance of emails by various governments suggests that levels of social control in the UK are very high. This chapter explores the historical roots of this trend towards ever greater surveillance. It starts by examining surveillance at work – something that grew out of a concern with workplace theft. In particular it focuses on the possibilities that the factory system of production offered employers increased powers of surveillance over workers. It then explores how attempts to keep track on habitual criminals and ex-prisoners lead to the creation of a bureaucracy of surveillance, before moving on to explore how techniques of surveillance gradually extended over the whole population of the UK. In essence, we pose the question: are we now living in a 'Big Brother' society, and if so, how and when did it come about?

Workplace theft, 1750–1950

In the eighteenth century (and before) many workers considered it a customary right to keep for themselves some part of the materials used in their stage of production. The taking home of workplace materials by employees has various labels attached to it – some refer to the practice as workplace appropriation, pilfering, 'fiddling' or 'embezzlement'. The terms reflect that some considered the practice a customary right established by tradition, others as a form of theft (see Hobsbawm 1968; Godfrey and Cox 2013). The majority of workers viewed taking pieces of workplace material or waste goods produced in manufacturing as a traditional entitlement passed down through the ages. However, many traditional rights were gradually criminalized.

These included gleaning (collecting corn left after harvesting), firebote (gathering small amounts of wood from forests for the fireplace), the rights of grazing (on common land) and the poaching of small game, rabbits and pheasants. Although the taking of customary perquisites (and their subsequent criminalization) was common to most industries, this chapter concentrates on the textile industry because the factory/mill owners were most active in trying to eradicate customary rights in the workplace both by use of the law and also through the physical/ hierarchical organization of the workplace. The factory facilitated higher levels of surveillance over employees, and allowed employers to use both informal punishments and the law to 'police' the behaviour of their workers.

Perhaps the most discussed example of eighteenth-century workplace appropriation is the taking of 'chips' (pieces of wood) from the Royal Dockyards. However, Emsley (2005a: 143–73), Styles (1983) and Rule (1981: 124–46; 1986: 107–38) have catalogued a series of outworker appropriations – including 'bugging' by hatters and shoemakers (whereby cheap material was substituted for the more valuable material they were supposed to use). Indeed, most industries saw some form of appropriation of finished goods or raw materials. However, the taking of waste materials was also rife, particularly in the textile trades. The creation of waste was an inevitable consequence of most manufacturing processes. In some industries the waste could be valuable, although often it consisted merely of scraps. The property rights to the waste products often rested on unspoken customary agreements between employers and employed, with periodic redrawing of the boundaries. If the waste product itself acquired value, as it did in the textile trade with the growth of the recovered wool industry in the latter half of the nineteenth century, then the redrawing of the customary line usually became final, and in favour of the employers.

Textile manufacturers attempted to use various strategies, including the law, to combat workplace appropriation. Indeed, Linebaugh (1991) and Hobsbawm (1968) have both asserted that both the eighteenth and nineteenth centuries saw the employers attempt to criminalize customary rights within the workplace (see also Davis 1987, 1989a), just as other historians have argued that a parallel process was occurring in the countryside. Marxist historians like Peter Linebaugh place the large body of eighteenth-century legislation against workplace frauds within the context of what they believe was a defining character of eighteenth-century criminal law – the transformation of a large number of infractions that had previously been violations of trust or corporate obligation into criminal offences against property. This view is typified in the work of Hay (1983: 53) who said:

> The custom of [. . .] payment in perquisites, either part of the product or raw materials, became the subject of extensive penal legislation. Employers did not always want to eliminate perks: allowing such appropriation by employees could be a way of escaping employers' wage-fixing agreements in times of labour shortage, and also a way of avoiding monetary wage payment during downturns in the trade cycle. At such times both capital and labour tacitly agreed on the custom, within limits, of taking perks. But those limits were always contested, and in the long term, with expanding

informal, private sanctions. The criteria that decided whether an offending employee faced a fine, dismissal or the magistrate are:

1   The more serious the offence, the more likely the case was to go to court (i.e. cases of theft were often dealt with by formal prosecution).
2   If unemployment was high, then dismissal and blacklisting would often ensure that the offender went to the workhouse or left the district, and therefore provided a substantial penalty for the offending worker.
3   Higher status workers were prosecuted less often, though, again, if the theft involved cash rather than goods then even higher grades could be prosecuted. For example, Locker (2004) found that the railway companies prosecuted office clerks if they found proof of embezzlement.
4   Those who had already established a good relationship with their supervisor might escape punishment, and some women offered/were forced to give sexual favours in return for no action being taken.
5   Female workers and juveniles were more likely to be physically chastised than prosecuted. These physical punishments could be brutal, but after factories became largely unionized, both the ferocity and the frequency of the physical beatings reduced.

This last point warrants further consideration. Why is it that, whereas men received more formal punishments, foremen favoured more retributive, visible and physical forms of control and punishment for women and child workers, at least until the final quarter of the century when over-physical supervisors began to be prosecuted by their victims in significant numbers (probably as a result of unionization)? It may be that the factory reproduced gender inequalities and patriarchal controls similar to those exercised by husbands in domestic settings – the foremen physically disciplining women in the same way as many men physically (violently) controlled their wives in eighteenth- and nineteenth-century households. Some of the violent assaults on child workers and female employees were taken to court. When they were, some magistrates considered it their duty to protect female workers from physical abuse, others sympathized more with factory management, and even when assaults were proved, female workers could be cautioned on their behaviour. For example, when one foreman was convicted of assault he pleaded for mitigation on the grounds that the victim had provoked him by swearing. The magistrate fined him 2 shillings, but also chastised the woman for using such foul language to her overlooker (Godfrey 1999b). There may be other reasons why women were not prosecuted in the numbers that men were: they might have had less opportunity to commit thefts because they were subject to greater surveillance, or they might have been protected from prosecution by legal convention. In the end, the character and personal philosophy of individual foremen may still have been the most influential factor in the decision to prosecute workers. Prosecution remained more likely if the route from detection to prosecution did not involve the foreman, or if he decided that the offence was

Did the factory eradicate workplace theft?

The criminal law was clearly an important weapon in the employers' armoury, but some believe that it was changes in the organization of the workplace that had the greatest impact on levels of workplace appropriation. Indeed some have suggested that the factory can be ranked alongside the prison, the asylum and the barracks as a 'total institution' (see Ignatieff 1983). A number of commentators have debated the existence of 'total institutions' (which controlled most aspects of their inhabitants' lives) in the eighteenth and nineteenth centuries, and have drawn out the similarities between the factory and the prison. For Foucault (1991), Melossi and Pavarini (1981) and others, the differences between working conditions and prison conditions were minimal:

> For the worker the factory is like a prison (loss of liberty and subordination); for the inmate the prison is like a factory (work and discipline) [. . .] The ideological meaning of this complex reality can be summarized by the attempt to rationalize and conceptualize a dual analogy: *prisoners must be workers, workers must be prisoners.*
>
> (Melossi and Pavasini 1981: 188)

They believe that the factory did not consciously imitate the prison, nor the prison the factory, but both evolved from ideas concerning the control of time and space. Giddens (1995: 135–6) stated that: 'The commodification of time, and its differentiation from further processes of the commodification of space, hold the key to the deepest transformations of day-to-day social life that are brought about by the emergence of capitalism.' Clearly, the factory acted upon the will or the character of the worker in unknown ways, which may have been of benefit to capitalistic society by encouraging workers to be disciplined, compliant and 'civilized' with middle-class morality.

For these commentators, the employers' search for greater efficiency led both to mechanization and the establishment of centralized production areas in order to facilitate greater control over labour. For example, the development of the factory therefore accomplished four aims in Dickson's (1989) opinion: first, the suppression of 'embezzlement'; second, control over the pace of production; third, the centralization of labour that both facilitated machine technology and allowed the control of the workers' adverse reaction to new machinery; and lastly, it made capitalists indispensable to production because the factories needed large and frequent capital investments. Although the first two aims were explicitly concerned with labour control, Dickson, rightly, saw the other aims as also being primarily work discipline measures. The origins of the factory were therefore embedded in the desire to control labour, and this desire inevitably spawned supervisors and surveillance techniques in the workplace. Marglin (1976, 1984) asserts that this explains why factories were established with the kind of technology already in place in much of the cottage textile industry, and also why many factories did not mechanize until years after their establishment. After all, Gott's mill in Leeds, a huge and highly developed complex, was managed for 25 years without mechanization taking place in any key area of production.

The alternative theory that factories were developed to increase the pace of production, has been put forward by Landes (1987). He has attacked the 'workplace social control' thesis on a number of grounds. First, he argues that the specialization of labour and the introduction of machinery created a higher level of profits for their owners than any other system. In other words, factories were more profitable and so they made the cottage industry redundant. Second, mechanization became possible once factories had been established and that as soon as employers could raise the funds, they mechanized. Even Landes, however, believed that mechanization was only possible as long as workers were under the supervision of employers or their agents. Recently, Pollard (1965), Berg (1984) and Hudson (1992) have adopted a more measured response to the debate, arguing that both mechanization (combined with the specialization and division of labour) and social control, were motivating forces behind the move to factory production.

It seems that the debate, which has been presented by the protagonists as 'technology versus discipline', is actually a debate about the *relative* importance of the two main reasons for the growth of the factory system. For example, *all* of the theorists in this debate believe that workplace indiscipline, especially appropriation, was rife in the domestic system, and also that the factory engendered and increased managerial control over the workforce. If the employers had not seen the benefits of centralization in terms of labour control and/or as a way of controlling workplace theft, then the domestic system with its unspecialized and dispersed labour force could have continued as the primary form of work organization unhindered for many decades more than it did. However, the assumption that centralization, and the concomitant surveillance systems, were successful in controlling the workers and eradicating workplace theft must be questioned, particularly since the criminal law continued to be used until the mid-twentieth century, well beyond the point when the factory was supposed to have made the law redundant and workplace theft impossible. Indeed there is a mass of newspaper and oral evidence to suggest that workplace appropriation continued as an occasional or routine practice for many workers. For example, surviving Worsted Committee minute books suggest that, until at least 1951, employers still used the criminal law to punish workplace offenders. Moreover, modern studies by Ditton (1977), Mars (1983) and others show that appropriation continues in factories today. People who were seen, and who saw themselves, as normal committed the 'offence'. Linebaugh (1972: 9) said of the eighteenth century that, 'Crime – in the sense of being on the wrong side of the law – was, for vast numbers of undifferentiated people, normal.' Studies of workplace appropriation are similarly studies of ordinary people in everyday work situations, a history of, what many might consider, routine human activity.

for the Metropolis. This national register recorded everyone subject to the provisions of the Act (approximately 25,000 to 30,000 people).

When it became clear that the police could not possibly hope to achieve any real form of control or supervision over such a large number of people, a new Act passed in 1871. The 1871 Prevention of Crimes Act (34 and 35 Vict. *c.*112) reduced the number of people that the police were required to supervise, and granted additional powers to the police and penal authorities. For example the routine use of photography to capture the likeness of each individual offender, which could then by circulated around every police station when the offenders were released from prison. By 1873 a committee reported that within a little over 12 months of the Act being enforced, some 43,634 photographs had been received by the Metropolitan Police, and that during the same period, 373 cases of positive identification had been made following examination of these photographs in the Habitual Criminal Office.

As Godfrey *et al.* noted (2010), habitual offender legislation and other forms of legislation designed to incapacitate habitual and dangerous offenders (such as preventative detention laws) were largely ineffective. Surveillance did not aid reform, in fact it hindered it, since the supervised men and women on the registers found it hard to settle in one area – employers were tipped off by police that they were employing a known thief, and potential marriage partners were probably also 'warned off'. In government circles too, the Acts lost their savour after the First World War, and they were largely abandoned by the 1930s:

> the overwhelming impression is that the greatest contribution that habitual offender legislation made (despite the intention to identify, track, and incapacitate habitual offenders) was to create and sustain a huge bureaucracy which connected government bodies in a way which established the ideal of inter-agency partnership which still today remains an aspiration for modern policy makers, even if it remains outside of their grasp. As today, it may be that the amassing of such a huge amount of data meant that the 'system' itself was unusable in a 'systematic' way. The 1869 Habitual Offenders Act swamped the police with thousands of people to supervise, at least until the system was scaled down in the 1870s. Thereafter the numbers of offenders and ex-convicts to be supervised were smaller, although they were still considerable, and, as we have shown, too large for the authorities to cope with. There are parallels today. The sex offender register established by legislation in 1997 [. . .] had 8000 people on its books in 2000. By 2006 the number had grown to 30,000, with approximately 10–14 per cent growth each year. Each year over 1000 offenders breached the regulations imposed on them – and, in 2007, 322 offenders had simply disappeared from the system (*The Times*, 31st October, 2007). The 'No Fly List' which attempts to stop terrorists boarding aircraft now holds over 44,000 names, but failed to prevent an attempt to blow up Northwest Flight 253 to Detroit on December 25th 2009

The National Register was being used to generate the National Health Service Central Register after the War, but the Act that created the register was repealed in 1951 following disquiet by the judiciary that an Act brought in for the administration of rationing was carrying on after rationing had ended. It was a Conservative administration that ended the ID card scheme in 1951, and a Conservative government that tried to re-introduce it approximately 40 years later.

In the wake of the Hillsborough tragedy, Conservative politicians associated football fans with disorder, lawlessness and violence, and Prime Minister Margaret Thatcher intended to bring in a compulsory identity card scheme for football supporters. She may even have wanted to extend the scheme to all members of the public, but, in any case, the scheme to have football fans register on a compulsory basis was abandoned. The idea was still not dead though. Within a few weeks of 11 September 2001 and the attacks on the World Trade Center, the Labour government proposed compulsory ID cards. In addition to preventing terrorism, however, the government also alleged that the ID cards would also protect Britain against organized crime and prevent identity theft, illegal immigration and illegal working until April 2004. The bill itself was published in November 2004. Despite protests from civil libertarians, lawyers, human rights experts, and many others, the Home Secretary alleged that the ID scheme was 'profoundly civil libertarian measure because it promotes the most fundamental civil liberty in our society, which is the right to live free from crime and fear'. The Identity Cards Act was enacted in 2006. It provided National Identity Cards, a personal identification document and European Union travel document, linked to a database known as the National Identity Register (NIR). It also specified 50 categories of information that the National Identity Register could hold on each registered person, including fingerprints, digitized facial scans and iris scans, past addresses and places of residence – and, in keeping with the intentions of previous schemes, which linked the ID cards to other forms of government-kept data – details of a person's National Insurance number. Rather chillingly, the Act made provision for additional undefined information to be demanded once the scheme was up and running. Perhaps fortunately, the libertarian-leaning Conservative/ Liberal Democrat Coalition formed after the 2010 general election announced that the ID card scheme would be scrapped.

Modern parallels

Has the Victorian bureaucratic impulse to collect ever more information, and quietly but consistently survey a greater and greater proportion of population now evolved from the surveillance of criminals to the survey of everyone? For Coleman and McCahill (2010: 7–8) the surveillance society 'invades privacy and lacks democratic oversight or constraint, and leaves little or no room for political debate as to the consequences'. Quite rightly then, citizens and academics have been concerned about surveillance expansion and intensification into hitherto unobserved areas of social life (including the home, telephonic and web communications, education, health and travel). Given the recent revelations about the electronic mass observation of emails by governments across the world, it seems that Coleman and McCahill have underestimated, if anything, the expansion of government surveillance into social lives of its citizens. Previously we have been discussing the private surveillance carried out by employers within property over which they had a legal right and some control, so how did the conditions of the factory come to be experienced by those in normal society? Orwell's concept of 'Big Brother' was first used over 70 years ago, just after the Second World War, in his dystopian novel *1984*. It was describing a state that Orwell foresaw rather than one he was experiencing at the time (Orwell 1948). Orwell prophesied a system that exerted omnipotent power over the general population:

> At the apex of the pyramid comes Big Brother. Big Brother is infallible and all-powerful [. . .] Nobody has ever seen Big Brother. He is a face on the hoardings, a voice on the telescreen. We may be reasonably sure that he will never die, and there is already considerable uncertainty as to when he was born [. . .] in the past no government had the power to keep its citizens under constant surveillance. [Now] every citizen, or at least every citizen important enough to be worth watching, could be kept for twenty-four hours a day under the eyes of the police and in the sound of official propaganda, with all other channels of communication closed. The possibility of enforcing not only complete obedience to the will of the state, but complete uniformity of opinion on all subjects, now existed for the first time.
>
> (Orwell 1948: 148)

Since Orwell wrote those words, some allege that the introduction of credit, cashpoint and identity cards, and the myriad number of forms that need to be filled in with personal biographical information on a weekly basis, all point to a growing control by the State over the lives of ordinary people. In Britain over 250 million pounds per year is now spent on a surveillance industry and there are more than four million CCTV cameras silently watching over public areas, housing estates, car parks and shopping complexes: public: one camera for every fourteen people. This is an amazing growth in automated electronic surveillance, given the quite modest beginnings of CCTV in the UK.

The surveillant state has had the tables turned on it on occasion. In 2006 Wikileaks (https://wikileaks.org) started 'to bring important news and information to the public [. . .] One of our most important activities is to publish original source material alongside our news stories so readers and historians alike can see evidence of the truth'. The website published details of previously unseen documents – thousands and thousands of documents – relating to the cost of the war in Iraq and Afghanistan; the killing of civilians in 'collateral damage' bombings by US aircraft; the site mapping 109,032 deaths in 'significant' attacks by insurgents in Iraq, including about 15,000 that had not been previously revealed; and secret files

Western world now feel able to claim more and more information about the daily activities of ordinary people. Preventing terrorism is certainly something that the state uses to justify surveillance over those it deems 'suspect': 'The use of covert techniques by law enforcement agencies are a vital part of protecting the public both from terrorism and crime' (Rt. Hon. Damian Green MP, Minister of State for policing, criminal justice and victims, 2013). The government's strategies for combating and controlling those that should be watched over (CONTEST and PROTECT for example; see www.gov.uk/government/policies/protecting-the-uk-against-terrorism) use many of the techniques criticized by the creators of Wikileaks, Edward Snowden and others. They include phone-tapping, electronic surveillance, 'tailing' suspects, infiltrating faith communities, social clubs and political pressure groups. It involves plain-clothes police officers pretending, lying and, in some cases, committing criminal acts, in order to become trusted and therefore learn more information about people or groups, and their intentions, criminal or otherwise. For many, this kind of behaviour will be unacceptable, for others, they will justify it as a necessary evil: something that is distasteful but essential for democratic society to protect itself. The problems arise, however, not only when innocent people face unwarranted, and overweening intrusion into their lives, or when the state over-steps its powers and carries out illegal surveillance, but also when the state uses these measures against those it is there to protect (the population of the country) in a routine process that resembles something along the lines of Orwell's Big Brother. In any case, as this chapter has demonstrated, the demand for information on the powerless by the powerful is not new, but many will feel that the historical road from the factory foreman in private businesses to the anonymous controller of CCTV cameras on public streets and the electronic surveillance of emails and private correspondence is a long and uncomfortable one.

Key questions

First of all, how was the criminal law used in the workplace, and did the rise of the factory end workplace appropriation? The 1777 Worsted Acts were used before the factory system began, and long after it was established. The legislation was most effective, however, when the workers were collected and supervised centrally. This allowed the internal supervisory hierarchy of foremen/overseers to detect workplace appropriations and summon a Worsted Inspector. The approximately 3,000 prosecutions over a 40-year period and the length of time the Worsted Inspectorate continued to prosecute offending workers, shows that the law played an important role, but research shows that informal discipline was also very evident. The foremen could decide who and which acts of appropriation were worthy of prosecution rather than a fine, dismissal from employment or physical punishment. In practice, the gender and age of the 'offender' was critical, as was the employment situation at the time – times of high unemployment made dismissal as harsh a penalty as formal prosecution (without all the expense for

By selecting particular topics for discussion in this book – the development of policing and punishment; how criminality, victims of crime and offenders have been conceived; violence; and the rise of surveillance – we have added to the literature that has helped to define a body of knowledge that can be described as 'crime history' (together with, for example, Taylor 2010; Rawlings 1999; Emsley 2005a). While it is true that a comprehensive study of crime history would be incomplete without most if not all of these topics, the broad boundaries that have been constructed around this sub-discipline will surely expand over time. Crime history (if we can use that term for the large and somewhat sprawling collection of historical studies of criminal justice agencies, offences, legislation and individual offenders that has developed over the last 30 or 40 years) is now taught on both history and criminology degree courses. The methods used, the approaches taken and the intellectual preoccupations of those who have written on crime history, are recognizable to social historians, sociologists and criminologists alike. Although, as Lawrence (2012) has outlined, there are still differences of intent between historians and social scientists (or perhaps we should say other social scientists?) there is little practical difference in the way crime history is taught and researched in history or sociology/criminology departments.. We hope and anticipate that the conversations and interplay between the two disciplines will continue to deepen over the next decade.

Glossary

Assize courts – The highest form of regional court between medieval times and the twentieth century. Assize judges, based in London, went round the country on various circuits trying serious crimes in front of a trial jury. Most offences tried at the assize had at one time carried the death penalty. Most counties held assizes twice a year.

Bentham, Jeremy – As one of the most influential exponents of Utilitarianism, Jeremy Bentham (1748–1832) had maintained that social organization had to be adjusted in such a way as to maximize human happiness and that the best way to effect this was via a series of specialized government departments controlling public administration from Whitehall.

Bloody Code – A long series of statutes (over 200 in 1820) under which the death penalty could be applied. Many applied to relatively minor offences and the existence of the 'Bloody Code' led early historians of crime to conclude that justice in the late eighteenth century was excessively harsh. However, more recent research indicates that judges used their discretion a great deal and the practical operation of the code was less harsh than might at first be imagined.

Borstal – An institution for the detention and training of young offenders. First introduced in 1908 and replaced in 1982 by Young Custody Centres.

Bow Street Runners – Formed by the magistrate Henry Fielding in London in 1749, the Bow Street Runners consisted originally of eight constables. Initially nicknamed Robin Redbreasts because of their scarlet waistcoats, their functions included serving writs, detective work and arresting offenders. The Bow Street Runners could, on occasion, travel around the country and were engaged by magistrates and private individuals.

Capital crimes – Any crime carrying the death penalty as punishment. While most crimes of theft were capital before the 1820s, more than 90 per cent of death sentences for property crime were never carried out but replaced by transportation for life. These kinds of crimes were originally termed 'felonies'.

Force majeure – A legal term referring to the settlement of an issue by the application of irresistible force or overwhelming power.

Justice of the Peace – The name Justice of the Peace is the official title of a magistrate. JPs were (and still are) unpaid volunteers from the local community. These officials preside over the lowest courts in the UK's criminal system. Before the twentieth century, magistrates were invariably prominent local people, usually landowners or industrialists, heavily involved in local government. Since 1750 there has been an increase in the number of paid or stipendiary magistrates, usually appointed to the larger urban areas.

Laissez-faire – Meaning allowing people to do as they think best, it usually describes a philosophy where government does little to interfere or regulate (depending on your point of view) industry or trade.

Luddite disturbances – The Luddite disturbances took place in the counties of Nottinghamshire, Lancashire, Cheshire, Derbyshire, Leicestershire and Yorkshire during the period 1811–13. Led by a fictional leader called 'Ned Ludd', the Luddites attacked new machinery and mills in an attempt to maintain the price (money) paid to them as textile workers and control over their work practices.

Magistrate – See Justice of the Peace.

Misdemeanour – A less serious crime than a felony, for which the law has fewer powers than it does in a case of felony. These crimes were usually tried in the lower (magistrates') courts. The distinction no longer has force in UK law, but to an extent it survives in the form of 'non-arrestable offences'.

Open prison – A minimum security facility (often with only a wire fence and unlocked gates) designed to enable low-risk prisoners or those coming to the end of long sentences to become acclimatized to a living situation more akin to life on the outside. The first open prison was built near Wakefield in 1933.

Petty sessions – A court operated by between one and three Justices of the Peace, sitting between once a week and daily. Petty sessions began as informal but were formalized in the nineteenth century. Felonies (i.e. serious crimes of violence and most crimes of theft) could not be tried at these sessions. By the early twentieth century petty sessions were normally referred to as magistrates' courts.

Police courts – London's Metropolitan Police Courts assumed their final form in 1839. Staffed by stipendiary (salaried) magistrates, these summary courts dealt with a wide range of minor offences such as drunk and disorderly charges, vagrancy offences and petty theft. While handling mostly cases brought by the police, they were also an arena wherein the working class could seek justice.

Bibliography

Acton, W. (1857) *Prostitution Considered in its Moral, Social and Sanitary Aspects in London and Other Large Cities; with Proposals for the Mitigation and Prevention of its Attendant Evils.* London: Frank Cass.

Agar, J. (2005) 'Identity cards in Britain: past experience and policy implications', *History and Policy*, paper 33. Available at: www.historyandpolicy.org/archive/policy-paper-33.html.

Alker, Z. (2014) 'Street violence in mid-Victorian Liverpool'. Unpublished Ph.D. thesis, Liverpool John Moores University.

Alker, Z. and Godfrey, B. (forthcoming) 'War as an opportunity for divergence and desistence from crime, 1750–1945', in S. Walklate and R. McGarry (eds), *Criminology and War: Transgressing the Borders.* London: Routledge.

Anderson, J. (1929) 'The police', *Public Administration*, VII: 192–202.

Archer, D. and Gartner, R. (1984) *Violence and Crime in Cross-national Perspective.* New Haven, CT: Yale University Press.

Archer, J. (1999) 'The violence we have lost? Body counts, historians and interpersonal violence in England', *Memoria y Civilización*, 2: 171–90.

Archer, J. and Jones, J. (2003) 'Headlines from history: violence in the press, 1850–1914', in E. Stanko (ed.), *The Meanings of Violence.* London: Routledge, pp. 17–31.

Bailey, V. (1993) 'The fabrication of deviance: "dangerous classes" and "criminal classes" in Victorian England', in J. Rule and R. Malcomson (eds), *Protest and Survival: The Historical Experience. Essays for E. P. Thompson.* London: Merlin, pp. 221–56.

Baldwin, S. (1926) *On England and Other Addresses.* London: Philip Allen.

Ballinger, A. (2000) *Dead Woman Walking.* Chippenham: Ashgate.

Barrie, D. (2008) *Police in the Age of Improvement: Police Development and the Civic Tradition in Scotland, 1775–1865.* Cullompton: Willan.

Barton, A. (2005) *Fragile Moralities and Dangerous Sexualities: Two Centuries of Semi-Penal Institutionalisation for Women.* Aldershot: Ashgate.

Beattie, J. M. (1986) *Crime and the Courts in England 1660–1800.* Oxford: Clarendon Press.

Beattie, J. M. (2001) *Policing and Punishment in London, 1660–1750.* Oxford: Oxford University Press.

Beattie, J. M. (2012) *The First English Detectives: The Bow Street Runners and the Police of London, 1750–1840.* Oxford: Oxford University Press.

Beccaria, C. (1986) *On Crimes and Punishments*, trans. with introduction and notes by D. Young. Indianapolis, IN: Hackett.

Becker, P. (1999) 'Weak bodies? Prostitutes and the role of gender in the criminological writings of nineteenth-century German detectives and magistrates', *Crime, History and Societies*, 3(1): 45–70.

Benewick, R. (1969) *Political Violence and Public Order*. London: Allen Lane.

Berg, M. (1984) 'The power of knowledge: comments on Marglin's "Knowledge and Power"', in F. Stephen (ed.), *Firms, Organization and Labour: Approaches to the Economics of Work Organization*. London: Routledge, pp. 165–75.

Blackstone, W. [1765] (1982) *Commentaries on the Laws of England: In Four Books*. London: Professional Books.

Bourke, J. (1994) *Working Class Cultures in Britain, 1890–1960*. London: Routledge.

Brewer, J. and Styles, J. (eds) (1980) *An Ungovernable People: The English and Their Law in the Seventeenth and Eighteenth Centuries*. London: Hutchinson.

Brooks, P. (1984) *Reading for the Plot: Design and Intention in Narrative*. Oxford: Clarendon Press.

Brown, A. (2003) *English Society and the Prison: Time, Culture and Politics in the Development of the Modern Prison, 1850–1920*. London: Boydell Press.

Brown, A. (2013) *Inter-War Penal Policy and Crime in England: The Dartmoor Convict Prison Riot, 1932*. Basingstoke: Palgrave Macmillan.

Burt, C. (1925) *The Young Delinquent*. London: University Press.

Butterfield, H. (1931) *The Whig Interpretation of History*. London: Bell.

Cain, M. (1990) *Growing up Good*. London: Sage.

Carlen, P. (1983) *Women's Imprisonment*. London: Routledge.

Carlen, P. (1985) *Criminal Women*. Cambridge: Polity Press.

Chadwick, W. (1900) *Reminiscences of a Chief Constable*. Manchester: J. Heywood.

Chan, J. (1997) *Changing Police Culture: Policing in a Multicultural Society*. Cambridge: Cambridge University Press.

Churchill, D. (2012) 'Crime, policing and control in Leeds, *c.*1830–*c.*1890'. Unpublished Ph.D. thesis, Open University.

Churchill, D. (2014) 'Rethinking the state monopolisation thesis: the historiography of policing and criminal justice in nineteenth-century England', *Crime, History and Societies*, 18(1): 131–52.

Clark, J. (2012) *The National Council for Civil Liberties and the Policing of Interwar Politics: At Liberty to Protest*. Manchester: Manchester University Press.

Clay, Revd J. (1853) *Chaplain's Report on the Preston House of Correction*. Preston.

Cohen, S. [1973] (2002) *Folk Devils and Moral Panics: The Creation of Mods and Rockers*. Routledge: London.

Coleman, R. and McCahill, M. (2010) *Surveillance and Crime*. London: Sage.

Colquhoun, P. (1800) *A Treatise on the Police of the Metropolis*. London: C. Dilly.

Conley, C. (1991) *The Unwritten Law: Criminal Justice in Victorian Kent*. New York: Oxford University Press.

Cox, D. (2010) *A Certain Share of Low Cunning: A History of the Bow Street Runners, 1792–1839*. Cullompton: Willan.

Cox, D. (2014) *Crime in England, 1688–1815*. London: Routledge.

Cox, D., Godfrey, B. and Johnston, J. (2014) *100 Convicts*. Barnsley: Wharncliffe.

Cox, P. (2012) *Bad Girls in Britain: Gender, Justice and Welfare, 1900–1950*. London: Palgrave Macmillan.

Dodsworth, F. (2008) 'The idea of police in eighteenth-century England: discipline, reform-ation, superintendence, c.1780–c.1800', *Journal of the History of Ideas*, 69(4): 583–605.

Dodsworth, F. (2014) *The 'Idea' of Policing*. London: Pickering & Chatto.

Duffield, I. and Bradley, J. (1997) *Representing Convicts: New Perspectives on Convict Forced Labour Migration*. Leicester: Leicester University Press.

Dunstall, G. (1999) *A Policeman's Paradise? Policing a Stable Society 1918–1945*. Wellington: Dunmore Press in association with the New Zealand Police.

Durkheim, É. (1961) *Moral Education: A Study in the Theory and Application of the Sociology of Education*. New York: The Free Press.

Eisner, M. (2001) 'Modernization, self-control and lethal violence: the long-term dynamics of European homicide rates in theoretical perspective', *British Journal of Criminology*, 41: 618–38.

Eisner, M. (2003) 'Long-term historical trends in violent crime', in M. Tonry (ed.), *Crime and Justice: A Review of Research*, vol. 30. Chicago, IL: University of Chicago Press, pp. 83–142.

Eisner, M. (2008) 'Modernity strikes back? A historical perspective on the latest increase in interpersonal violence', *International Journal of Conflict and Violence*, 2(2): 288–316.

Eisner, M. (2011) 'Killing kings: patterns of regicide in Europe, AD 600–1800', *British Journal of Criminology*, 51(3): 479–98.

Elias, N. (1978/2000) *The Civilizing Process: Sociogenetic and Psychogenetic Investiga-tions*. Oxford: Blackwell.

Emsley, C. (1985) ' "The thump of wood on a swede turnip": police violence in nineteenth-century England', *Criminal Justice History*, 6: 125–49.

Emsley, C. (1993) ' "Mother, what did policemen do when there weren't any motors?" The law, the police and the regulation of motor traffic in England 1900–1939', *Historical Journal*, XXXVII: 357–81.

Emsley, C. (1996) *The English Police: A Political and Social History*. Harlow: Longman.

Emsley, C. (2002) 'The history of crime and crime control institutions', in M. Maguire, R. Morgan and R. Reiner (eds), *The Oxford Handbook of Criminology* (3rd edn). Oxford: Oxford University Press, pp. 57–76.

Emsley, C. (2005a) *Crime and Society in England, 1750–1900* (3rd edn). Harlow: Longman.

Emsley, C. (2005b) *Hard Men: Violence in England since 1750*. London: Hambledon & London.

Emsley, C. (ed.) (2005c) *The Persistent Prison: Problems, Images and Alternatives*. London: Francis Boutle.

Emsley, C. (2009) *The Great British Bobby: A History of British Policing from the 19th Century to the Present*. London: Quercus.

Emsley, C. (2010a) *Crime and Society in England, 1750–1900* (4th edn). Harlow: Pearson.

Emsley, C. (2010b) 'A legacy of conflict? The "brutalized veteran" and violence in Europe after the Great War', in E. Avdela, S. D'Cruze and J. Rowbotham (eds), *Problems of Crime and Violence in Europe, 1780–2000: Essays in Criminal Justice*. Lampeter: Edwin Mellen Press, pp. 43–64.

Emsley, C. (2011) *Crime and Society in Twentieth-Century England*. Harlow: Pearson.

Emsley, C. (2013) *Soldier, Sailor, Beggarman, Thief: Crime and the British Armed Forces since 1914*. Oxford: Oxford University Press.

Emsley, C. and Clapson, M. (1994) 'Recruiting the English policeman, c.1840–c.1940', *Policing and Society*, 3: 269–86.

Godfrey, B. and Cox, D. (2013) *Policing the Factory: Theft, Private Policing and the Law*. London: Bloomsbury Press.

Godfrey, B., Farrall, S. and Karstedt, S. (2005) 'Explaining gendered sentencing patterns for violent men and women in the late Victorian and Edwardian period', *British Journal of Criminology*, 45(5): 696–720.

Godfrey, B. Cox, D. and Farrall, S. (2007a) *Criminal Lives: Family, Employment and Offending*. Oxford: Oxford University Press.

Godfrey, B., Lawrence, P. and Williams, C. (2007b) *History and Crime*. London: Sage.

Godfrey, B., Cox, D. and Farrall, S. (2010) *Serious Offenders*. Oxford: Oxford University Press.

Goldson, B. (2011) *Youth in Crisis? 'Gangs', Territoriality and Violence*. London: Routledge.

Gray, D. (2009) *Crime, Prosecution and Social Relations: The Summary Courts of the City of London in the Late Eighteenth Century*. Basingstoke: Palgrave Macmillan.

Greg, W. R. (1850) 'Prostitution', *Westminster Review*, no. 53.

Gregory, D. (1982) *Regional Transformation and Industrial Revolution: A Geography of the Yorkshire Woollen Industry*. Basingstoke: Macmillan.

Griffiths, P. (1996) *Youth and Authority: Formative Experience in England 1560–1640*. Oxford: Oxford University Press.

Gurr, E. (1981) 'Historical trends in violent crime: a critical review of the evidence', *Crime and Justice*, 3: 295–353.

Hall, S., Critcher, C., Jefferson, T., Clarke, J. and Roberts, B. (1978) *Policing the Crisis: Mugging, the State and Law and Order*. Basingstoke: Palgrave Macmillan.

Hansard (1856) Third series, vol. 140, cols 229–45. London: HMSO.

Hanway, J. (1772) *Observations on the Causes of Dissoluteness Which Reigns Among the Low Classes of the People*. London.

Harris, A. (2003) 'Policing and public order in the City of London, 1784–1815', *London Journal*, 28(2): 1–20.

Harris, J. (1995) 'Between civic virtue and Social Darwinism: the concept of the residuum', in D. Englander and R. O'Day (eds), *Retrieved Riches*. Aldershot: Scolar Press, pp. 67–88.

Hart, J. (1955) 'Reform of the borough police, 1835–1856', *English Historical Review*, LXX: 411–27.

Hassett, M. (2007) 'The British government's response to mainland Irish terrorism, *c*.1867–*c*.1979'. Unpublished Ph.D. thesis, Open University.

Hay, D. (1975) 'Property, authority and the criminal law', in D. Hay, P. Linebaugh, J. Rule, E. P. Thompson and C. Winslow, *Albion's Fatal Tree: Crime and Society in Eighteenth-Century England*. London: Allen Lane, pp. 17–63.

Hay, D. (1983) 'Manufacturers and the criminal law in the later eighteenth-century', *Past and Present Colloquium on Police and Policing*, conference proceedings, Birmingham University.

Hay, D. (1989) 'Using the criminal law, 1750–1850: policing, private prosecution, and the state', in D. Hay and F. Snyder (eds), *Policing and Prosecution in Britain, 1750–1850*. Oxford: Clarendon Press, pp. 3–52.

Hay, D. and Snyder, F. (eds) (1989) *Policing and Prosecution in Britain 1750–1850*. Oxford: Clarendon Press.

Hay, D., Linebaugh, P., Rule, J., Thompson, E. P. and Winslow, C. (1975) *Albion's Fatal Tree: Crime and Society in Eighteenth-Century England*. London: Allen Lane.

Heidensohn, F. (1981) 'Women and the penal system', in A. Morris and L. Gelsthorpe (eds), *Women and Crime*. Cambridge: Cropwood Conference Series 13.

Heidensohn, F. (1989) *Crime and Society*. Basingstoke: Palgrave Macmillan.

Heidensohn, F. (1996) 'Feminist perspectives and their impact on criminology and criminal justice in Britain', in N. Rafter and F. Heidensohn (eds), *International Feminist Perspectives in Criminology*. Buckingham: Open University Press, pp. 27–37.

Heidensohn, F. (2002) 'Gender and crime', in M. Maguire, R. Morgan and R. Reiner (eds), *The Oxford Handbook of Criminology* (3rd edn). Oxford: Oxford University Press, pp. 491–535.

Himmelfarb, G. (1984) *The Idea of Poverty: England in the Early Industrial Age*. New York: Alfred Knopf.

Hitchcock, T. and Shoemaker, R. (2014) *London Lives: Poverty, Crime and the Making of a Modern City, 1690–1800*. Cambridge: Cambridge University Press.

Hobsbawm, E. (1968) 'Customs, wages and workload', in E. Hobsbawm (ed.), *Labouring Men: Studies in the History of Labour*. London: Weidenfeld & Nicolson, pp. 75–105.

Hoggart, R. (1955) *The Uses of Literacy: Aspects of Working Class Life*. London: Penguin.

Hohenberg, P. and Lees, L. (1985) *The Making of Urban Europe, 1000–1994*. Cambridge, MA: Harvard University Press.

Holmes, C. (1988) *John Bull's Island. Immigration and British Society, 1871–1971*. London: Macmillan.

Howard, J. (1929) *The State of the Prisons*. London: Dent & Sons.

Hudson, P. (1992) *The Industrial Revolution*. London: Edward Arnold.

Hughes, R. (1987) *The Fatal Shore: A History of the Transportation of Convicts to Australia 1787–1868*. London: Collins Harvill.

Iggers, G. (1997) *Historiography in the Twentieth Century*. Hanover, NH: Wesleyan University Press.

Ignatieff, M. (1978) *A Just Measure of Pain: The Penitentiary in the Industrial Revolution, 1750–1850*. New York: Columbia University Press.

Ignatieff, M. (1983) 'State, civil society and total institutions: a critique of recent social histories of punishment', in D. Sugarman (ed.), *Legality, Ideology and the State*. London: Academic Press, pp. 75–105.

Innes, J. and Styles, J. (1986) 'The crime wave: recent writing on crime and criminal justice in eighteenth-century England', *Journal of British Studies*, 25(4): 380–435.

Jackson, L. (2003) 'Care or control? The Metropolitan women police and child welfare, 1919–1969', *Historical Journal*, 46(3): 623–48.

Jackson, L. (2006) *Women Police: Gender, Welfare and Surveillance in the Twentieth Century*. Manchester: Manchester University Press.

Jackson, L. (2008) '"The coffee club menace": policing youth, leisure and sexuality in post-war Manchester', *Cultural and Social History*, 5(3): 289–308.

Jewkes, Y. (2004) *Media and Crime*. London: Sage.

Johansen, A. (2011) 'Keeping up appearances: police rhetoric, public trust and "police scandal" in London and Berlin, 1880–1914', *Crime, History and Societies*, 15(1): 59–83.

Johnston, H. (ed.) (2008) *Punishment and Control in Historical Perspective*. Basingstoke: Palgrave Macmillan.

Joyce, P. (1980) *Work, Society and Politics the Culture of the Factory in Later Victorian England*. New Brunswick, NJ: Rutgers University Press.

Lawrence, P. (2004) 'Policing the poor in England and France, 1850–1900', in C. Emsley, E. Johnson and P. Spierenburg (eds), *Social Control in Europe 1800–2000*. Columbus, OH: Ohio State University Press, pp. 210–25.

Lawrence, P. (2011) *The New Police in the Nineteenth Century*. Farnham: Ashgate.

Lawrence, P. (2012) 'History, criminology and the use of the past', *Theoretical Criminology*, 16(3): 313–28.

Lawrence, P. (2014) *Policing the Poor*. London: Pickering & Chatto.

Leps, M. C. (1992) *Apprehending the Criminal: The Production of Deviance in Nineteenth-Century Discourse*. Durham, NC: Duke University Press.

Levi, M. and Maguire, M. (2002) 'Violent crime', in M. Maguire, R. Morgan and R. Reiner (eds), *The Oxford Handbook of Criminology* (3rd edn). Oxford: Oxford University Press, pp. 795–844.

Linebaugh, P. (1972) 'Eighteenth-century crime, popular movements and social controls', *Bulletin for the Society for the Study of Social History*, 7: 9.

Linebaugh, P. (1991) *The London Hanged: Crime and Civil Society in the Eighteenth-Century*. Cambridge: Cambridge University Press.

Lloyd, A. (1995) *Doubly Deviant, Doubly Damned*. London: Penguin.

Loader, I. (2006) 'Fall of the platonic guardians: liberalism, criminology and political responses to crime in England and Wales', *British Journal of Criminology*, 46(4): 561–86.

Locker, J. (2004) '"This most pernicious species of crime": embezzlement in its public and private dimensions, *c*.1850– *c*.1930'. Unpublished Ph.D. thesis, Keele University.

Locker, J. (2005) 'Quiet thieves, quiet punishment: private response to the "respectable" offender, *c*.1850–*c*.1930', *Crime, History and Societies*, 9(1): 2–20.

Locker, J. and Godfrey, B. (2006) 'Ontological boundaries and temporal watersheds in the development of white collar crime' in S. Karstedt, M. Levi and B. Godfrey (eds), *Markets, Risk and 'White-collar' Crimes, Special Edition of The British Journal of Criminology*, 46(6): 976–92.

Lombroso, C. and Ferrero, W. (1895) *The Female Offender*. London: T. Fisher Unwin.

Lyon, D. (1994) *The Electronic Eye: The Rise of Surveillance Society*. Cambridge: Polity Press.

McGowan, R. (1983) 'The image of justice and reform of the criminal law in early nineteenth-century England', *Buffalo Law Review*, 23: 89–125.

McGowan, R. (1987) 'The body and punishment in eighteenth-century England', *Journal of Modern History*, 59: 651–79.

McGowan, R. (1990) 'Getting to know the criminal class in nineteenth-century England', *Nineteenth Century Contexts*, 14(1): 33–54.

McGowan, R. (1999) 'From pillory to gallows: the punishment of forgery in the age of the financial revolution', *Past and Present*, 165: 107–40.

McGowan, R. (2005) 'The Bank of England and the policing of forgery 1797–1821', *Past and Present*, 186: 81–116.

McKenzie, A. (2005) '"Saving our unfortunate sisters"? Establishing the first separate prison for women in New Zealand', in B. Godfrey and G. Dunstall (eds), *Crime and Empire 1840–1940*. Cullompton: Willan, pp. 159–74.

McLevy, J. (1975) *The Casebook of a Victorian Detective*. Edinburgh: Canongate.

Macnicol, J. (1987) 'In pursuit of the underclass', *Journal of Social Policy*, 16(3): 293–318.

Major, J. (1994) Speech given to the Social Market Foundation [9 September]. Available at: www.johnmajor.co.uk/page1384.html.

Radzinowicz, L. and Hood, A. (1990) *A History of the English Criminal Law and its Administration from 1750, Vol. V: The Emergence of Penal Policy*. Oxford: Clarendon Press.

Rawlings, P. (1999) *Crime and Power: A History of Criminal Justice 1688–1998*. Harlow: Longman.

Rawlings, P. (2002) *Policing: A Short History*. Cullompton: Willan.

Reiner, R. (2010) *The Politics of the Police*. Oxford: Oxford University Press.

Reith, C. (1943) *British Police and the Democratic Ideal*. London: Oxford University Press.

Report of the Select Committee on the Police of the Metropolis (1822). London: HMSO.

Reynolds, E. (1998) *Before the Bobbies: The Night Watch and Police Reform in Metropolitan London, 1720–1830*. Basingstoke: Macmillan.

Robb, G. (2002) *White-Collar Crime in Modern England: Financial Fraud and Business Morality 1845–1929*. Cambridge: Cambridge University Press.

Rock, P. (1990) *Helping Victims of Crime: The Home Office and the Rise of Victim Support in England and Wales*. Oxford: Clarendon Press.

Rock, P. (2004) 'Victims, prosecutors and the state in nineteenth-century England and Wales', *Criminal Justice*, 4(4): 331–54.

Rogers, N. (1992) 'Confronting the crime wave: the debate over social reform and regulation, 1749–1753', in L. Davison, T. Hitchcock, T. Keirn and R. Brink Shoemaker (eds), *Stilling the Grumbling Hive: The Response to Social and Economic Problems in England, 1689–1750*. Stroud: Sutton, pp. 77–98.

Roodhouse, M. (2013) *Black Market Britain: 1939–1955*. Oxford: Oxford University Press.

Roth, R. (2009) *American Homicide*. Cambridge, MA: Harvard University Press.

Rule, J. (1981) *The Experiences of Labour in Eighteenth-Century Industry*. London: Croom Helm.

Rule, J. (1986) *The Labouring Classes in Early Industrial England, 1750–1850*. Harlow: Longman.

Rusche, G. and Kirchheimer, O. [1939] (1968) *Punishment and Social Structure*. New York: Russell & Russell.

Rylands, G. (1889) *Crime: Its Causes and Remedy*. London: T. Fisher Unwin.

Sanders, W. B. (1974) *The Sociologist as Detective: An Introduction to Research Methods*. New York: Praeger.

Sayers, A. (1997) 'Michael Evans, village constable, tailor and smuggler', *Devon Historian*, 54: 24–6.

Schubert, A. (1981) 'Private initiative in law enforcement: associations for the prosecution of felons, 1744–1856', in V. Bailey (ed.), *Policing and Punishment in Nineteenth Century Britain*. London: Croom Helm, pp. 25–41.

Sharpe, J. A. (1999) *Crime in Early Modern England, 1550–1750* (2nd edn). London: Longman.

Sharrock, D., O'Kane, M. and Pilkington, E. (1993) 'Two youngsters who found a new rule to break', *The Guardian*, 25 November, p. 1.

Shaw, A. G. L. (1966) *Convicts and the Colonies*. London: Faber & Faber.

Shore, H. (1999) *Artful Dodgers: Youth and Crime in Early Nineteenth Century London*. Woodbridge: Boydell Press.

Shore, H. (2008) 'Punishment, reformation, or welfare: responses to "the problem" of juvenile crime in Victorian and Edwardian Britain', in H. Johnston (ed.), *Punishment and Control in Historical Perspective*. London: Palgrave Macmillan, pp. 158–76.

Shore, H. (2011) 'Criminality and Englishness in the aftermath: The racecourse wars of the 1920s', *Twentieth Century British History*, 22(4): 474–97.

Shore, H. (2013) '"Constable dances with instructress": the police and the queen of night clubs in inter-war London', *Social History*, 38(2): 183–202.

Shpayer-Makov, H. (2002) *The Making of a Policeman*. Aldershot: Ashgate.

Shpayer-Makov, H. (2011) *The Ascent of the Detective: Police Sleuths in Victorian and Edwardian England*. Oxford: Oxford University Press.

Sindall, R. (1983) 'Middle-class crime in nineteenth-century England', *Criminal Justice History: An International Annual*, IV: 23–40.

Sindall, R. (1987) 'The London garrotting panics of 1856 and 1862', *Social History*, 12(3): 351–9.

Sindall, R. (1990) *Street Violence in the Nineteenth Century: Media Panic or Real Danger?* Leicester: Leicester University Press.

Skidelsky, R. (1990) *Oswald Mosley*. Basingstoke: Macmillan.

Smith, D. (1992) 'Race, crime and criminal Justice', in M. Maguire, R. Morgan and R., Reiner, *The Oxford Handbook of Criminology* (1st edn). Oxford: Oxford University Press, pp. 75–87.

Smith, D. and Gray, J. (1983) *Police and People in London: The Police in Action, Vol. 4*. London: Policy Studies Institute.

Smith, R. (1981) *Trial by Medicine*. New York: St Martin's Press.

Smith, V. (1990) *All Muck and Nettles: The Early Life of Burler and Mender No. 57*. Huddersfield: Amadeus Press.

Soothill, K. and Walby, S. (1991) *Sex Crime in the News*. London: Routledge.

Spierenburg, P. (1991) *The Prison Experience*. New Brunswick, NJ: Rutgers University Press.

Spierenburg, P. (1996) 'Long-term trends in homicide: theoretical reflections and Dutch evidence, fifteenth to twentieth centuries', in E. Johnson and E. Monkkonen (eds), *The Civilization of Crime: Violence in Town and Country since the Middle Ages*. Chicago, IL: University of Illinois Press, pp. 63–108.

Spierenburg, P. (1998) *Men and Violence: Gender, Honor, and Rituals in Modern Europe and America*. Columbus, OH: Ohio State University Press.

Spierenburg, P. (2001) 'Violence and the civilizing process: does it work?', *Crime History and Societies*, 5(2): 87–105.

Spierenburg, P. (2005) 'The origins of the prison', in C. Emsley (ed.), *The Persistent Prison: Problems, Images and Alternatives*. London: Francis Boutle, pp. 27–49.

Spierenburg, P. (2008) *A History of Murder: Personal Violence in Europe from the Middle Ages to the Present*. Cambridge: Polity Press.

Stedman Jones, G. (1971) *Outcast London: A Study in the Relationship Between Classes in Victorian Society*. London: Verso Books.

Steedman, C. (1984) *Policing the Victorian Community: The Formation of English Provincial Police Forces, 1856–80*. London: Routledge & Kegan Paul.

Stone, D. (2001) 'Race in British eugenics', *European History Quarterly*, 31(3): 397–425.

Storch, R. (1975) 'The plague of blue locusts: police reform and popular resistance in northern England 1840–57', *International Review of Social History*, 20: 61–90.

Storch, R. (1976) 'The policeman as domestic missionary: urban discipline and popular culture in Northern England, 1850–1880', *Journal of Social History*, IX: 481–511.

Storch, R. and Philips, D. (1999) *Policing Provincial England, 1829–1856: The Politics of Reform*. London: Leicester University Press.

Weinberger, B. (1995) *The Best Police in the World: An Oral History of English Policing*. Aldershot: Scolar Press.

Welshman, J. (2005) *Underclass: A History of the Excluded, 1880–2000*. London: Hambledon.

Whitfield, J. (2004) *Unhappy Dialogue: The Metropolitan Police and Black Londoners in Post-War Britain*. Cullompton: Willan.

Wiener, M. (1987) 'The march of penal progress?', *Journal of British Studies*, 26(1): 83–96.

Wiener, M. (1990) *Reconstructing the Criminal: Culture, Law and Policy in England, 1830–1914*. Cambridge: Cambridge University Press.

Wiener, M. (1998) 'The Victorian criminalization of men', in P. Spierenburg (ed.), *Men and Violence: Gender, Honor, and Rituals in Modern Europe and America*. Columbus, OH: Ohio State University Press, pp. 197–212.

Wiener, M. (1999a) 'Judges v. jurors: courtroom tensions in murder trials and the law of criminal responsibility in nineteenth-century England', *Law and History Review*, Fall: 467–506.

Wiener, M. (1999b) 'The sad story of George Hall: adultery, murder and the politics of mercy in mid-Victorian England', *Social History*, 24(2): 174–95.

Wiener, M. (2004) *Men of Blood: Violence, Manliness and Criminal Justice in Victorian England*. Cambridge: Cambridge University Press.

Williams, C. A. (1998) 'Police and crime in Sheffield, 1818–1873'. Unpublished Ph.D. thesis, Sheffield University.

Williams, C. A. (2004) 'Review of guns and violence, the British experience by Joyce Lee Malcolm', *Journal of Modern History*, March: 168–9.

Williams, C. A. (2014) *Police Control Systems in Britain, 1775–1975: From Parish Constable to National Computer*. Manchester: Manchester University Press.

Williams, C., Patterson, J. and Taylor, J. (2009) 'Police filming English streets in 1935: the limits of mediated identification', *Surveillance and Society*, 6(1): 3–9.

Williams, L. (2014) '"At large": women's lives and offending in Victorian Liverpool and London'. Unpublished Ph.D. thesis, University of Liverpool.

Williams, L. and Godfrey, B. (2014) 'Familial and intergenerational offending in Liverpool and the north west of England, 1850–1914', *History of the Family*.

Wood, J. C. (2003) 'Self-policing and the policing of the self: violence, protection and the civilising bargain in Britain', *Crime, History and Societies*, 7(1): 109–28.

Wood, J. C. (2004) *The Shadow of Our Refinement: Violence and Crime in Nineteenth-Century England*. New York: Routledge.

Wood, J. C. (2007) 'The limits of culture? Society, evolutionary psychology and the history of violence', *Cultural and Social History*, 4(1): 95–114.

Wood, J. C. (2008) '"Mrs. Pace" and the ambiguous language of victimization', in L. Dresdner and L. Peterson (eds), *(Re)interpretations: The Shapes of Justice in Women's Experience*, Newcastle: Cambridge Scholars Publishing, pp. 79–94.

Wood, J. C. (2010) '"The third degree": press reporting, crime fiction and police powers in 1920s Britain', *Twentieth Century British History*, 21(4): 464–85.

Wood, J. C. (2011) 'A change of perspective: integrating evolutionary psychology into the historiography of violence', *British Journal of Criminology*, 51: 479–98.

Wood, J. C. (2012a) *The Most Remarkable Woman in England: Poison, Celebrity and the Trials of Beatrice Pace*. Manchester: Manchester University Press.

Wood, J. C. (2012b) 'Press, politics and the "police and public" debates in late 1920s Britain', *Crime, History and Societies*, 16(1): 75–98.

ID cards 161–2
Identity Cards Act (2006) 162
Ignatieff, M. 79, 83
immigration 125–30
Immigration Act (1971) 126
Independent Police Complaints Authority
    29
India 126
industrial disputes 25
industrialization 79, 99, 106
industrial production 152, 156
Industrial Schools Act (1857) 139
inequalities 60, 61
infanticide 98–9, 121
Infanticide Act (1938) 121
Infant Life Protection Act (1872) 122
institutions, controlling 80, 156
insurance 48, 85
'internalism' (Wiener) 81, 132
interwar period (1919–38) 25, 28, 142
investigations 62, 97
IRA 110, 160
Ireland 22
Irish immigrants 127, 128–9
Irish Nationalism 110, 130

Jack the Ripper 102–3
Jackson, L. 27
Jemmison, S. 89
Jervis Acts (1848) 57
Jewish immigrants 127
Johnston, J. 89
judiciary 50, 54, 64, 67, 155; see also
    magistrates
juries 54, 60, 121, 122
justice (Hay) 60
Justice of the Peace 171; see also
    magistrates
juvenile courts 56, 140–1
juvenile crime 135, 136, 140, 141, 144;
    see also children
juvenile delinquency 118, 134–9, 141–2
Juvenile Offenders Act (1847) 136
juvenile prisons 138, 140; see also
    Borstals

Karstedt, S. 120
Kenny, C. 154

King, P. 53, 54, 55, 61, 106, 125, 127
Kirchheimer, O. 79

labour 79, 156–7
laissez-faire policies 33, 139, 171
Lancet, The 123
Landes, D. 157
Langbein, J. 60
larceny 63
Lawrence, P. 161
Ledbetter, G. 45
Legal Aid 54
legal capacity 134–5
legal profession 53, 56, 67
legal representation 54, 56–7, 101, 140
Leps, M. C. 102
liberal democracies 111
Liberty (National Council for Civil
    Liberties) 26, 160
licence system 88–90, 158; see also ticket
    of leave
Life and Labour of the People 85
Linebaugh, P.151, 157
Lister, E. 155
Little, D. L. 120, 121
Liverpool 123, 145
Liverpool Metropolitan Police 160
living standards 50, 117
local controls 12, 23–4
Lombroso, C. 117
London 56, 62, 103, 123; see also
    Metropolitan Police
London Underground 160
lower classes 61, 63
Luddite disturbances (1811–12) 18,
    171
Ludovici, A. 87
Lyon, D. 164

McCahill, M. 162–3
McGowan, R. 33, 78
McKay, A. 46
McLevy, J. 35
Madan, M. 53, 60
magistrates: female 56, 67; matrimonial
    disputes 66; petty sessions 55; police
    courts 56; and public dissent 65;
    quarter sessions 12; self-interest 155;

prosecution societies 45
prosecutions: 'compounding' of a felony
    47; costs 55; employers 152–3, 155;
    lower classes 61, 63; numbers of 62;
    police 34, 40, 49; propaganda tools
    100; and the state 33, 34; women 153;
    see also private prosecutions
prostitution 123–4
protests *see* demonstrations; public order
public executions 74, 78–80, 81–2, 91;
    see also Bloody Code; death sentences
public galleries 68–9
public opinion 26, 34, 126–7
public order 27–8, 42, 44, 48, 63, 64–5,
    160; *see also* demonstrations
Public Order Act (1936) 25, 44
public prosecutions 33, 34, 55–6
public space 120
Punishment and Welfare 83
punishments 71–91, 152, 153–4, 155
putative underclasses 91

quarter sessions 12, 55, 56, 62, 75, **172**

racecourse gangs 145
race (ethnicity) 125, 128
Radzinowicz, Sir L. 7, 59, 78
rationing 161–2
'reductionist' theories 79
reformative punishments 72, 76; *see also*
    prisons
reformatories 85, 139; *see also* Borstals
registers of offenders 158
rehabilitation 88; *see also* penal
    welfarism
Reiner, R. 111
Reith, C. 19
religion 138
remand prisoners 55
re-offending 89–90
residuum 63, 119, **172**
Restoration of Order in Ireland Act
    (ROIA) (1920) 110
retribution 41, 72, 84; *see also*
    self-defence
revisionist historians 20–1
rewards 16, 45–7
Reynolds, E. 15, 21

Riot Act (1715) 64
riots 28, 42, 64; *see also* demonstrations;
    public order
Romanian gangs 128
Romilly, Sir S. 78
Roth, R. 107
Royal Commission on a Constabulary
    Force (1839) 18, 19, 115
Royal Dockyards 151
Royal Scots Regiment 33
Rule, J. 151
rule of law 54, 64
ruling classes 60
Runners *see* Bow Street Runners
Rural Constabulary Act (1839) 18
rural policing 13, 18, 54
Rusche, G. 79
Russell, Lord J. 18
Rylands, G. 117

Scotland 22
Scouting movement 141
Second World War 26, 44, 109, 126, 161
segregative sector policies 85
Select Committees **172**; on Criminal
    Laws (1819) 55; on Metropolitan
    Police Offices (1837) 63; on the Police
    (1822) 12; on the Police (1853) 18;
    on the Police of the Metropolis (1817)
    129; on Transportation (1837–1838)
    75
self-defence 40–3, 44–5; *see also*
    retribution
sentencing 66, 75, 120; *see also* prison
    sentences
Sex Discrimination Act (1975) 27
Sex Disqualification (Removal) Act (1919)
    56
sexual behaviour 123–5
shaming 34, 103
Sheffield 14, 15, 36, 37–8, 41–2, 46, 47
shoplifting 35, 73
Shore, H. 135
'sin' 81, 114; *see also* morality
Sinn Feiners 110
Smith, A. 52
Smith, V. 154
Snowden, E. 164, 165

social alienation 99, 116
social control 63, 120, 137, 160
'social crimes' 13
social discontent 107
social elites 86, 101
social purity movement 124
social trends: and punishment 81
societal norms 104
Society for the Improvement of Prison
    Discipline and the Reformation of
    Juvenile Offenders 138
soldiers 33, 48, 109; see also courts
    martial
solicitors 48, 54, 56
solitary confinement 76, 83
South Africa 67
Special Branch 24, 110
special constables (specials) 24, **172**
spending cuts 27, 69
Spierenburg, P. 81, 96, 106–7
state intervention 62, 85, 106, 140–1, 142
*State of the Prisons in England and Wales,
    The* 71, 75–6
state power 79–80, 90, 103
Stead, W. 124
Steedman, C. 18, 46
Stephen, J. F. 62
sterilizations 87
stipendiary magistrates 56, 62; see also
    magistrates
stolen property 46, 47
Storch, R. 20, 132
strikes 25
Styles, J. 47
suffragette movement 27
suicides 83, 97
Summary Jurisdiction (Married Women)
    Act (1895) 66
summary prosecutions 40, 55, 57, 62, 121;
    see also magistrates
Supreme Court of the United Kingdom
    56
surveillance 150–68
Swift, R. 129

Taylor, H. 96–7, 99
'technology versus discipline' debate
    157

terrorism 109–11, 160–1, 164–5
Terrorism Prevention and Investigation
    Measures Act (2011) 110–11
Thatcher, M. 162
theft 63, 109
thief-taking 14, 45
Thompson, E. P. 7, 60
Thompson, R. 105
ticket of leave 75, 88, 158, **172**; see also
    licence system
time, controlling 152, 156
tolerance 34, 105
Tomes, N 66–7
Tomlinson, I. 27, 29
Tonypandy strike (1910) 65
total institutions 80, 156
Townsend, J. 45
Toxteth Riots (1981) 28
training 85, 143
transportation 75, 88, 90–1
Transportation Act (1718) 75
treason 33
Treatise on the Police of the Metropolis
    16, 115
trials 54, 55, 68–9, 100
Trower, M. 44
trust 151

unions 25
Union with Ireland Act (1800) 128
urban decay 117
urbanization 99, 106
urban-metropolitan policing model 18
USA 107

Vagrancy Act (1824) 136
vagrancy/vagrants 13, 48, 62, **172**
Vanstone, M. 86
Venables, J. 105
venereal diseases 124
vice 115
victims 32–51, 54, 60, 100–1
Victorian reformers 58
violence 95–113; attitudes to 35; levels of
    2, 34, 95–108; moral panics 134; police
    28–9, 111–12; prosecutions 60, 63;
    tolerance 57, 104; against women 63,
    65–6, 122–3; see also murders